THE NEW AUSTRALIA

1883

Frontispiece : Edmond Marin La Meslée

THE NEW AUSTRALIA

EDMOND MARIN LA MESLEE

1883

*Translated and edited
with a critical introduction
by Russel Ward*

HEINEMANN
LONDON AND MELBOURNE

Heinemann Educational Books
LONDON EDINBURGH MELBOURNE TORONTO
AUCKLAND JOHANNESBURG SINGAPORE
IBADAN NAIROBI HONG KONG NEW DELHI
KUALA LUMPUR

ISBN 0 435 32895 6
Translation © Russel Ward 1973
First published 1973

Published by Heinemann Educational Books Ltd
48 Charles Street, London W1X 8AH

and

Heinemann Educational Australia Pty Ltd
24 River St, South Yarra, Victoria 3141

Printed in Great Britain by
Butler & Tanner Ltd, Frome and London

Contents

Part One

From Melbourne to Brisbane

Chapter I

Chapter II

Chapter III

Chapter IV

Chapter V

CONTENTS

CONTENTS

List of Illustrations

Acknowledgements

I am very grateful to Mr Donald H. Simpson, Librarian of the Royal Commonwealth Society, London, for lending me a copy of *L'Australie Nouvelle* to work on at home for some months in 1970 while I was on study leave in England; to Mrs Jillian Oppenheimer, research assistant in the University of New England's History Department, for finding out so much about Marin La Meslée's life in Australia while I was away; to Dr Lionel Gilbert of the Armidale Teachers' College, for checking some of the author's references to native plants; to Mrs M. Pittendrigh, the departmental secretary; and to my wife, Barbara, for her patient encouragement and help with typing.

The author and publishers would also like to thank the following for their kind permission to reproduce the photographs: The Royal Commonwealth Society (frontispiece); Associated Rediffusion Picture Library (Plates 9, 11 and 12); Mary Evans Picture Library (Plates 1–8, 10).

Russel Ward
University of New England
Armidale
New South Wales
September 1972

Introduction
by Russel Ward

The author of this book merits a minor place in any cultural history of Australia.

Edmond Marin La Meslée, son of Colonel Edmond La Meslée, was born in France in 1852. As a lad he joined the navy, but fought on land during the Franco-Prussian War at the disastrous Battle of Sedan in September 1870. After the military *débâcle* he retired from the navy and went to Mauritius, where for some years he taught French in the Jesuit College. On 16 January 1876 he sailed thence for Melbourne as a passenger on the three-masted British ship *Alphington*. His movements during the next four years are graphically described in the pages that follow.

In Melbourne he obtained a position as private secretary to the French Consul-General, Monsieur Le Comte de Castelnau. With the Count, his Brazilian mistress and her twelve-year-old son, he travelled by train to Wodonga and then by coach to Gundagai along the bush track that is now known as the Hume Highway. Shaken by this experience of travel in the Royal Mail Coach, the Count hired a private conveyance to take the party on to the railhead at Yass, whence they continued to Sydney by train. Thence they took ship for Queensland, sailed up the Brisbane River to Ipswich and made a brief tour of the Darling Downs.

When the Consul returned to Melbourne, Marin La Meslée remained in Sydney, possibly because he fell in love. At any rate he obtained work in the government Surveyor General's office and on 17 January 1880, at St Michael's Church, Cumberland Street, he married Clara Louisa Cooper, daughter of Alexander Cooper. Marin La Meslée was twenty-eight and his bride twenty-three. She had been born at Wattle Flat near Bathurst. Perhaps we see her through her young husband's eyes in his description of a beautiful young girl at the Melbourne

Cup, born in New South Wales, 'for all I know . . . on the gold-fields at Bathurst, at Ophir or at Wattle Flat'.

Only seven or eight months after the wedding, in the spring of the same year, the bridegroom set out on an extended tour of the western division of New South Wales. With Mr Russell Barton, grazier, businessman and chairman of directors of the Great Cobar Copper Mining Company, he visited Cobar, Bourke and several stations in the north west. In Cobar he was present when Barton made his 'maiden speech' to the electors on a Saturday night when the miners had finished with work for the week. Not to be confused with Edmund Barton, the future Commonwealth prime minister, but like him a strong federalist, Russell Barton was successful in his first attempt at parliament. He represented Bourke in the colonial legislature from 1880 till his retirement in 1886. Marin La Meslée could hardly have found a better man to show him the country. Landing in Adelaide at the age of nine and orphaned at twenty, Barton was a self-made man and a first-class bushman. He had been, among other things, a 'shepherd, stockman, horsebreaker, farmer, miner, butcher, fellmonger, soapboiler, woolsorter, carpenter, wheelwright, blacksmith, stonemason, builder and squatter'. The two men obviously got on well together and the major part of the book describes their western tour.

In 1882 Marin La Meslée returned to France for a visit. While there he gave a paper to the Geographical Society of Paris and arranged for the printing of his book with E. Plon & Cie., the leading French firm which recently published General De Gaulle's memoirs. It seems that he returned to Sydney before the proofs were ready for checking. The French compositor produced a good clean text from the manuscript in most respects, but he was clearly baffled by many English – and Australian – proper names. A deserted goldfield known as *Ironbark* is printed, for example, as *Pronbartes*. Throughout the following English text my editorial emendations or notes are indicated by asterisks (*), while the author's explanatory footnotes are numbered, as in the original French edition, 1, 2, etc. . . .

When *L'Australie Nouvelle* was published in 1883 Marin La Meslée was already back in Sydney. It is clear that the young French draftsman in the Survey Department was primarily responsible for the foundation of the *Geographical Society of Australasia* in that year. A geographical section of the Royal Society of New South Wales had existed for some time, but 'the Chairman and Secretary [became] ultimately the only attendants at meetings'. So a preliminary meeting of 'gentlemen interested in geographical science' took place at Dr Belgrave's house on 2 April 1883. Mr Du Faur, chairman of the defunct body, took the chair and after a few opening remarks called on 'Mr La Meslée – who had doubtless thought over the subject carefully – to explain his views with reference to the direction the movement should take'.

He had indeed. He read to the gathering an admirably pertinent and succinct paper which showed, among other things, how deeply he had already identified himself with the interests of his adopted country. Six years before Henry Parkes in 1889 issued his 'clarion call' for federation at Tenterfield, Marin La Meslée declared, 'We propose to name this Society the Federal Geographical Society of Australasia, because the work to be done is in every sense a national one, for the information and the benefit of the people of Australasia in general'. His paper was received 'with evident marks of warm appreciation'. After further discussion the meeting 'resolved itself into a Committee to carry into effect the idea of an Australian Geographical Society'. Marin La Meslée was unanimously elected honorary secretary and those present each contributed a guinea to a fund for meeting preliminary expenses. A sub-committee consisting of Marin La Meslée, Dr Belgrave, Mr Gerard and 'another gentleman', was then charged with the task of preparing a draft constitution.

A few weeks later the enthusiastic secretary called the first meeting of the provisional committee. Among the seventeen men who attended were Du Faur and another fellow of the Royal Geographical Society, Hon. W. A. Brodribb, M.L.C., P. F. Adams, the Surveyor General of New South Wales, and Professor Stephens from the University of Sydney. This meeting considered the draft constitution, which seems to have been substantially the work of the secretary, and then made arrangements for the 'first general meeting of the founders of the Geographical Society of Australasia'.

Interestingly the most contentious matter discussed seems to have been whether to include the word 'Federal' in the society's title. Marin La Meslée clearly wanted it but seems to have dropped it from the draft in order to gain the widest possible support for the substance – if not the name – of an Australia-wide body. At the founding meeting, the third in the series held on Tuesday 31 May, there were no fewer than seventy present including that staunch Sydney-sider and anti-federalist, Sir John Robertson. The draft constitution was read out by the secretary and adopted after only one division. Dr Belgrave moved an amendment to the first clause, that the word 'Federal' should be restored to the name of the society which should be 'The Federal Geographical Society of Australasia'. The minutes record that 'Sir John Robertson objected to the word "Federal" in regard to the Society, and he thought that if it were employed many of the gentlemen who were now the best friends of the Society would become greatly opposed to it'. Professor D. B. Sladen of Sydney University, the early anthologist of Australian verse, seconded the amendment. Despite this weighty backing it was lost and the Geographical Society of Australasia was launched. Officers, including Marin La Meslée as secretary, were then elected by ballot.

The inaugural meeting was held on 22 June 1883 at the Protestant Hall in Castlereagh Street, Sydney. The huge attendance of between 700 and 800 people is some measure of Marin La Meslée's zeal and organizing ability. Perhaps too it was due partly to the topicality of the subject: *Past Explorations of New Guinea, and a Scheme for the Scientific Exploration of the Great Island*. Queensland had annexed the eastern part of the country only a few weeks before, but then Marin La Meslée, the founder and honorary secretary of the society, was also the first speaker to address it, and he chose to speak on this currently burning issue. It is an excellent paper,* cogent and learned but lively, and it was 'warmly applauded' by the great audience. Sir Edward Strickland moved the vote of thanks to the speaker.

Although his book was never translated into English, Marin La Meslée became widely known in Sydney cultural and intellectual circles during the 'eighties, and as widely respected. In

---

* *Proceedings of the Geographical Society of Australasia, New South Wales and Victorian Branches*, Vol. I, Sydney 1885, ed. E. Marin La Meslée and A. C. Macdonald, pp. 5–23.

1884, as one of the joint honorary secretaries, he organized the first Australian Geographical Conference in Melbourne and at it represented the Sydney branch of the Society: but his interests were far from being narrowly geographical. He contributed regularly to the *Nouvelle Revue, Le Temps, Le Courier Australien* and other journals. Perhaps because he was a foreigner, he became more deeply interested than most native or British-born Australians in the growth of Australian nationality and the federal movement. He was on visiting terms with Sir Henry Parkes and did a good deal of 'devilling' for the old political warrior.

On 15 May 1892 he had a long article published in the *Revue des Deux Mondes*, as he joyfully wrote to Parkes, 'the most critical and exclusive, as well as the most universally read, of all European reviews'.* It was entitled (in French) *The Social and Political Condition of British Australasia: An Australian Statesman: Sir Henry Parkes and the Federation of the Australian Colonies*. On 9 October he wrote Parkes a long letter about 'German Labor Colonies'. Sir Henry had asked him to find information on these institutions and he referred him to 'a very excellent article' in the *Nineteenth Century* for January 1891 by the Earl of Meath, to Herbert Mills' *Poverty and the State*, to General Booth of the Salvation Army's *Darkest England* and to other articles and papers. There is also a P.S. 'N.B. I forgot to mention that I shall send you in a day or two a specially selected French novel for Miss Parkes.'†

There are other letters about personal matters, projected visits and Parkes' 'great work for federation'. All were written from Marin La Meslée's home at 171, Glenmore Road, Paddington, or from the office of the Chief Statistician, the famous T. A. Coghlan, to which branch of the public service Marin La Meslée had been transferred some years previously. Not long before his death, he seems to have moved to McMahon's Point.

On the afternoon of Sunday 17 December 1893 he and his wife were picnicking on Sydney Harbour with nine friends in the yacht *Ripple*, sailed by Mr J. Phizackerley. About 150 yards to the north west of South Head the ladies wanted to sail

---

* Parkes, Sir Henry – Correspondence. Vol. 23, A893, CY Reel 45, 119; Mitchell Library.
† *Loc. cit.*, Vol. 47, A917, CY Reel 69, 84.

out into the open sea. Marin La Meslée thought this would be too dangerous and so the yacht put about. In doing so she gibed, capsized and sank, dragging the dinghy down with her. The steamers *Reliance* and *Mermaid* and the yacht *Era* quickly came to the rescue. Six people were saved but Mr and Mrs La Meslée and five others were drowned. Their three surviving children, Athol (13), Raymond (11) and Rennie (8) were only a hundred yards or so further up the harbour in another boat, which fortunately turned and sailed for home a few minutes before the accident. One other boy and a girl, Yvonne, had died in infancy. Next day the *Sydney Morning Herald* devoted its third editorial to the tragedy. After an inquest the bodies were buried at Rookwood Cemetery on 19 December 1893. T. A. Coghlan was among the mourners.

Like every other worthwhile writer, Marin La Meslée reveals as much about himself as he does about his subject. Between the lines in the pages that follow we see an intelligent and civilized man, urbane and tactful, yet with a tremendous zest for living and a deep interest in other people and the conditions of their lives. He has dry wit and a keen sense of humour – or farce: his description, for instance, of the miseries of a coach journey by night between Albury and Gundagai, is hilarious.

Despite all this he was occasionally gulled, like almost every other visitor, by some tall story, probably told by an Irish-Australian. He retails in good faith, for example, the old Ipswich pioneer's fantasy (or leg-pull?) about an early battle with man-eating aboriginals. In a day-long struggle many whites were killed and a 'very fat settler' captured. In the evening,

> . . . the blacks took their prisoner to the top of the hill where Ipswich Grammar School now stands. They killed, roasted and ate him, in full view of the horrified colonists who could do nothing to save him.
>
> 'We saw them dancing round their victim,' the old Irishman told us. 'We heard them chanting their savage yells, as they argued with each other over the tit-bits. But what could we do? There were four hundred of them, and only ten of us were left.'

He was also, inevitably, a man of his time. Like most other educated Europeans of the period he harboured the most vicious racist and anti-Semitic illusions: which is not to suggest that contemporary Australians were any more enlightened. If

anything, they were less so. Marin La Meslée never mentions
the Chinese without a sneer, usually to the effect that they look
as though they are suffering from chronic jaundice. Aboriginals
are presented as repulsively filthy and degraded people doomed,
like other 'dusky races', to inevitable extinction in the face of
'competition' from the 'superior' whites. Yet he is too intelligent
and open-minded to think the aboriginals congenitally stupid:
he gives interesting and perceptive accounts of aboriginal life
which demonstrate the contrary.

Naturally he was struck by many of the same features of
colonial life as impressed Trollope, Froude, Percy Clarke and
other overseas visitors at the time. In Australia, he wrote, even
gentlemen must quickly learn to wait on themselves – 'unless
they are as rich as Croesus'. Australians were mad about sport,
particularly horse-racing: Marin La Meslée's description of Cup
Day in Melbourne has probably never been bettered since.
Materialism, vulgarity and poor taste were more blatantly
evident than in older societies. The bigger and more costly a
picture in the Melbourne Art Gallery, the better it must be.
Australian drunkenness had to be seen to be believed. His
description of a drunken spree, and a fight, in a Yass hotel is as
vivid as any written in the period. Bustling, brash, 'yankee-fied'
Melbourne is contrasted with staid and conservative Sydney,
often then referred to derisively as 'Sleepy Hollow' by Victorians. Now, of course, the images are reversed.

In all these and other ways the book is among the best accounts
of Australian society written by visitors in the second half of
the last century: but what makes it peculiarly valuable is its
author's foreign birth and nurture. His French eyes fix upon a
whole range of phenomena which were barely noticed, or
simply taken for granted, by native-born observers or British
visitors: and the fact that comparisons are usually made with
France, rather than with England, often throws a refreshingly
new light on the subject under discussion – the relationship
between larrikins and police for instance.

Similarly, English visitors rarely have much to say about
Australian meals or cooking; simply because they were inured to
our essentially British 'home'-like practices. Marin La Meslée, to
say nothing of the Count of Castelnau, was appalled by both:
yet he stresses that the uncooked food, the raw material of a

cuisine, was probably better than that to be found anywhere else in the world, and he praises from the heart the rare cook – even a Chinese one at Gundagai – who proved an exception to the rule.

English writers were just as impressed by Australian drunkenness but few at the time noticed the fanatical strain of 'wowser' reaction to it which triumphed for so long in the twentieth century with the imposition of six o'clock closing. The Frenchman records this scene at dinner in the Mittagong Railway refreshment room in the late 1870s:

> Whilst we were attacking a fowl, we hit on the idea of tasting the wine of the country.
>
> 'Waiter! a bottle of Albury wine.'
>
> 'Sir, we are not licensed to sell any kind of alcoholic drink whatever.'
>
> 'What!' cried Monsieur de Castelnau, 'what can people drink here then when they are thirsty?'
>
> 'We have coffee, tea, lemonade, seltzer water, . . .'
>
> 'That stuff! Do you want to make yourselves a laughing-stock to the whole world?'
>
> 'No, sir, it is the same in every railway refreshment room in New South Wales: they are all run on strict temperance principles. It's a government rule.'
>
> 'But, heavens, if it is warm, people can't drink coffee or boiling hot tea. That would not be very refreshing?'
>
> 'There is lemonade, *gingerbeer*, . . .'
>
> 'Never mind: how much is it? . . .'

Most British and Australian writers naturally took for granted the democratic, self-governing institutions enjoyed by the colonies. The Frenchman, on the contrary, is fascinated by them. He contrasts the freedom and prosperity of these colonial societies with what he sees as the torpor of French colonies, burdened with a highly centralized, distant and bureaucratic administration.

He also sees developing, a full decade before the nationalist and federal movements of the 'nineties, the growth of an Australian national ethos and he became one of its most skilful advocates. He writes, for instance, of some agitation, then strongest in New Zealand, to replace English governors with local citizens selected by the colonial parliaments themselves. It has, of course taken nearly a hundred years for this practice to become the rule rather than the exception, but it is some measure of Marin La Meslée's insight into the developing trends in Australasian society that he should have foreshadowed it in 1883.

It is currently fashionable to suggest that the upsurge of Australian national sentiment in the 1890s was created by, rather than reflected in, the works of Lawson, Furphy, Paterson and other writers and artists of the time; and consequently that the national ethos was a product of the cities, rather than the bush. English visitors to the colonies often endorsed, or at least by their silence about the matter, failed to contradict the view that local nationalism sprang fully armed from the *Bulletin's* pages. When British or native-born writers on Australian life in the 'seventies or 'eighties did discuss the growth of a local patriotism, they tended inevitably to do so in a manner biassed in one way or the other, by the circumstances of their birth and nurture. The Frenchman suffered from no such disability. At the end of his thirty-six-day bush journey with Russell Barton in 1880, on their return to comparative civilization at the Royal Hotel in Dubbo, he remarked on the toughness of the handyman who had ridden the whole way alongside their dog-cart without seeming

to have suffered at all by so doing. 'I am not an *English new chum'*, he said. There was an ironic overtone to his voice, and it was not the first time that I had noticed among the Australians this disdainful attitude towards the young English dandies who come to live among them.

This perceptive and acute piece of empirical observation led Marin La Meslée to continue with some general remarks on the nature of the distinctively Australian ethos and on the reasons for its divergence from contemporary English *mores*.

The passage shows the writer at his wisest and best:

It is a curious but remarkable fact that everywhere in the Australian colonies the *colonials* waste very little love on Englishmen, even though they are their first cousins. It is only fair to add that, if this sentiment is widespread, it is clearly the fault of the latter. Englishmen think of the colonials as an inferior race. They know that they are for the most part the descendants of emigrants by no means chosen from among the fine flower of the British aristocracy. They regard them therefore as their inferiors in birth and often in education; and unfortunately, with the stupidity and self-assurance characteristic of youth, they neglect no opportunity of impressing on the *colonials* the sense of superiority on which they plume themselves.

Strongly independent by nature and with a pride that yields nothing to that of their English cousins, the Australians believe themselves every bit as good as they are. Being simple and forthright in manner themselves, they cordially detest the affected fops who, lispingly and inordinately accentuating their vowel sounds, strut the Sydney streets with yellow gloves, cane and monocle and who – ultimate horror – even allow themselves to court pretty Australian girls, who sometimes prefer them to their own inarticulate compatriots. For it must be admitted that Australian men often desert their girls for the superior attractions of athletic games, horses, races and *cricket*. It is only fair to add that they are among the best horsemen in the world, and that they have often proved their athletic prowess on the rivers and *cricket-fields* of both England and Australia.

All in all the Australians are good fellows. They have excellent qualities; and who is without faults?

Mr Anthony Trollope reproaches them with being great *blowers*, with boasting about their country, the beauty of their cities, the grandeur of their public monuments and institutions and the incomparable wealth of their agricultural, pastoral and mineral resources etc.

Ah, dear Mr Trollope! Let them have their say. They are not so far wrong after all; for no country in the world, not even America in proportion to its population, can show such astonishing progress and that, for most practical purposes, in the last quarter of a century. And then, they are a young people with the faults of youth. Let them shout, therefore, 'We have done this! We have done that!' What harm is there in it?

L'AUSTRALIE
NOUVELLE

PAR

E. MARIN LA MESLÉE

MEMBRE DE LA SOCIÉTÉ ROYALE DE SYDNEY
ET DE LA SOCIÉTÉ DE GÉOGRAPHIE COMMERCIALE DE PARIS

—

PRÉFACE DE L. SIMONIN

—

Ouvrage enrichi de gravures et d'une carte

PARIS
E. PLON et Cᵢₑ, IMPRIMEURS-ÉDITEURS
10, RUE GARANCIÈRE

—

1883
Tous droits réservés

P. F. ADAMS, Esqre,
Surveyor general of New South Wales.

Sir,
It is mostly owing to the fact that I found in your department a great assistance that I have been enabled to compile this work. Had it not been for the spirit of liberality towards foreigners that animates you, and my being admitted to participate in the work of the department you so ably manage, I would have found it difficult, if not impossible, to thoroughly understand the system of colonisation of New South Wales, and place before the eyes of the French public the extraordinary results which have been attained.

My aim has been to open the eyes of my countrymen to the numerous advantages they might derive from a direct intercourse with the colonies, and to impress upon them the fact, that in New South Wales as well as in the neighbouring provinces, those who might be tempted to emigrate thither with a view to help in developing their resources, shall meet with the same goodwill and the same liberal treatment which has been granted to me and my countrymen in your department.

As a tribute of gratitude to the country of my adoption, I have strived to make its wealth and its resources known to those I left in the land of my birth.

As a tribute of the same gratitude to you who greatly helped in making the task easy to me, I dedicate you this work, hoping you will accept it as the homage of
    Your obedient servant
        Marin La Meslée.

Preface

In Paris one day in 1882 I had a visit from a compatriot, Marin La Meslée, who had come back from Australia.

He told me that after various turns of fortune down there he had taken a job in the colonial government service as a surveyor in the Lands Department at Sydney.

M. la Meslée had come to address the Geographical Society of Paris on his impressions of Australia and at the same time to publish an account of his travels in the antipodes.

He asked me to write a few lines to introduce the material in this book.

After some natural hesitation – for I have never seen Australia – I accepted. What made up my mind in the end was that I have always had a sort of partiality for that country, whether from being interested in the Australian sections of the universal exhibitions at Paris and Philadelphia, or from my friendship with some who have spent years in Australia and told me of the wonderful developments in that far-away and curious land, of its fertile soil, its rich mines and the toughness of its indomitable colonists.

Nearly three years ago, when the French government decided to subsidise a mail service to Australia, I had the honour of being nominated by the Minister of Posts and Telegraphs as a member of the extra-parliamentary commission appointed to study the matter and even of being chosen as its chairman. There again I learnt more about Australia, the manly and enterprising spirit of its people, and its varied and innumerable resources.

The work just mentioned began towards the end of last November and already, as I write this, a magnificent brand-new steamer, the *Natal*, built expressly for this line in the Ciotat dockyards, has completed its maiden return voyage. Every Australian hailed its landfall. In the absence of her husband, Lady Loftus, wife of the Governor of New South Wales, herself came aboard to salute this, in some sense unexpected, guest and to bid her, as the English say, *welcome*. On her return voyage the *Natal* carried Australian products in exchange for her French merchandise. A cargo of tallow, which had to be trans-shipped at Marseilles, was received by our merchants and quickly resold on the spot. All this augurs well for the future.

French-Australia line ships leave Marseilles every twenty-eight days, thus making thirteen voyages per year. They sail via the Suez Canal, touch at the Seychelles, at our beautiful island colony of Reunion, at Mauritius – our ancient Ile de France, now British – and thence to Adelaide, Melbourne and Sydney whence the postal service continues on to Noumea, the capital of New Caledonia.

From now on this regular steamship service will export directly to Australia French products which hitherto went through London and sometimes lost their trade-marks *en route*. We shall be sending chiefly silks, fine textiles, millinery, and novelties; oil, wines, spirits, liqueurs and jams; jewellery, clocks, perfumes and *objéts d'art*. In return we shall take from Australia for our northern spinning-mills fine merino wool, of which we are the largest buyers, to the tune of more than a hundred million francs a year, and also wheat, tallow, hides, leather, frozen meat, copper, lead, tin and gold.

Good quality coal, of which Australia has a surplus, will be sent to Mauritius and Reunion which have none, and in return the islands will send to Australia more and more of their surplus sugar. It is true that Australia is now beginning to grow its own sugar cane, at least in the colony of Queensland.

Our luxury liners will carry English travellers to and from Australia. *En route* they will visit Marseilles and Paris and thus French and Australian people will learn to know each other better, to esteem each other and to be bound together more and more by common interests.

This country is in fact a continent. With its dependencies of Tasmania, New Zealand and Fiji it makes up what the English call Australasia – that is to say a new, a southern, an Austral-Asia. It is rich in minerals, especially gold, tin, iron, zinc, antimony, lead and copper. The discovery of the gold-fields in 1851 gave new life to the country. Prior to that year England kept it as a receptacle for her convicts. Yet the pastoral industry had already taken root and merino sheep were acclimatized from the beginning of the century. Then came grain-growing and for some time Australia has been, like California its rival in gold-production, like Chile and the Argentine republic, indeed like India and the United States, one of the granaries of Europe; but it is above all in the raising of stock – cattle, sheep and horses – that Australia has taken a leading position. It has more sheep, sixty-five million head, than any other country in the world and it is among the leading cattle-producers. Wool, hides, leather, tallow and meat are and will always be the mainstay of Australia, especially meat, if a successful freezing process is invented to ensure its regular shipment to Europe.

A whole race of sturdy pioneers, of tireless *squatters*, people this extraordinary continent. The women willingly accompany their fathers, husbands or brothers on exploring expeditions which are not always without danger. While the wilderness is being populated and cleared, the coastal and inland towns grow and ports open their docks to the whole world's ships. The continent itself is already divided into several different states or colonies, each of which has its own autonomous government, legislative chambers and even its own particular economy. England superintends this colonial development from far away, and says herself that perhaps when the fruit is quite ripe it will fall naturally from the tree and begin another life even more independent than its first. No matter – the real bonds, at least the economic and commercial ones, will endure and relations with the mother-country will always increase.

I have tried to salute in my fashion this country which I know only by hearsay, but which I appreciate and love deeply, not less than those who live and work in it. I hope that France, who till now has held herself somewhat aloof from these distant shores, will visit and understand them in her turn, and that fortune-seekers among my countrymen may also go, like our English cousins, to build their homes there.

I thank the author of these interesting pages, Marin La Meslée, for his part in revealing to me some Australian horizons and I wish him all the success which his book deserves.

L. Simonin
Paris, April 1883

PART ONE

From Melbourne to Brisbane

Chapter One

On 16 January 1876, after living for some years in its fascinating society, I left the island of Mauritius for Melbourne aboard the three-masted English ship *Alphington*.
Love of novelty and travel drew me towards the great Australian continent. My somewhat confused ideas of that country were so intriguing as to make me want to know more. Thus, when the chance came, I did not hesitate to make for its distant shores.

Towards the end of February the Australian coast appeared on the horizon and on 1 March, the *Alphington*, doubling Cape Otway, replied to signals from the shore: our landfall was signalled to Melbourne.

It was about six o'clock in the morning when we came in sight of the lighthouse and telegraph station which the Victorian colonial government has erected on this headland. The coast looks well-wooded, and this part of the country is indeed covered with forests in which the trees grow to a tremendous height, comparable with that of the great firs in California.

The Cape Otway lighthouse soon disappeared from view and, favoured by a strong breeze, the *Alphington* made rapid sail towards the entrance of the magnificent Port Phillip Bay. For the whole sixty-odd miles we could see the distant coastline with tall columns of smoke from huge bush-fires[1] rising above the land. We reached the *Heads* – Port Phillip Heads – only quite late in the afternoon; but one could still make out the narrow entrance to this veritable inland lake, nearly a dozen leagues in both length and breadth. At the far side on

[1] Literally, *la brousse*. The Australian countryside in general is called the *bush*.

3

Hobson's Bay stand the two ports of Melbourne, Williamstown and Sandridge, between which debouches the river running through the great capital of the colony of Victoria. We had to drop anchor and wait for the tide, as it would have been dangerous to risk entering the Heads at low water in the dark.

At about half past eight a magnificent steamer passed some distance from the spot where we were anchored. All her lights were ablaze and it was a truly beautiful spectacle to see this giant of 4,000 tons majestically cleaving the waves. The pilot told us she was the Peninsula and Oriental Company's *China*, carrying the mails between Melbourne and Galle Face [in Ceylon], where they are trans-shipped to another vessel of the same company for forwarding to Europe.

Many other ships, steamers for the most part, passed us during the eight hours we stayed off Point Lonsdale. One sensed the proximity of a great maritime city.

At last, at four o'clock in the morning, we weighed anchor and at five entered Port Phillip Bay, forty-five days after sailing from Port Louis. I was on the bridge from the first glimmerings of a brilliant dawn.

The sight was magnificent. Behind, the Heads separated us from the vast ocean that had just released us: on our left stood the village of Queenscliff with its two lighthouses marking the entrance to the bay and the two batteries that protect it. The distance between Queenscliff and Sandridge, the main port of Melbourne, is about 32 miles. This gives some idea of the extent of Port Phillip Bay, whose entrance between Point Lonsdale and Point Nepean is scarcely more than a league wide. In front the sun shone on the calm surface of the water and gilded the low, sandy shores, generally arid looking, which enclose the bay, whilst on our starboard bow projected the bold and rocky foreland of Schnapper Point. Beyond the cape, on the distant horizon, one could distinguish the dark blue line of mountains which serves as a back-drop to the rather monotonous countryside round Melbourne.

The wind had fallen and the *Alphington* dawdled along, too slowly for my taste, on the calm waters of Port Phillip. Happily, at about three in the afternoon, we met a little tug which took us in tow and at six we anchored finally in Hobson's Bay at a place equally distant from the Williamstown and Sandridge wharves.

At last I was about to tread this soil, where scarcely half a century ago none but the lonely savage walked. but on which the colonizing genius of Great Britain has laid the foundations of an empire! As a child I had been fascinated by stories of Australian discovery. I had admired the superhuman courage of the first explorers of this continent where the white man had scarcely set foot, and later I had followed as far as possible, with an ever increasing interest, the development of these colonies, born only yesterday, whose names began to resound in Europe and appeared from time to time in the pages of our reviews. However I had hardly any very well-informed knowledge of these lands, and the thought of actually walking on Australian soil filled me with joy.

Stepping onto the jetty, I was struck first by the practical genius of our neighbours. The shores of Hobson's Bay are everywhere low-lying and sandy and the River Yarra, which runs through the centre of the city of Melbourne, is neither wide nor deep enough to allow ships of any considerable draught to reach its wharves. It was therefore necessary to build, at the spot most accessible to the town, a port for the largest ships and to build piers alongside which they could lie safely and load and unload quickly. At Sandridge, then, was built a wooden jetty a quarter of a mile long and wide enough to carry four railway tracks which were immediately connected to the centre of the city by the Sandridge–Melbourne line, opened to traffic in 1856 – that is to say, at most, twenty-five years after the first settlement. Later this jetty, long as it was, proved insufficient. So the municipality of Sandridge built at some distance another jetty, less wide, but which went far enough out into the bay for the biggest ships. To-day the two piers are not enough. The volume of trade in the port of Melbourne has grown so large that ships' captains complain bitterly of the difficulty of getting a berth alongside the piers. To avoid interminable delays in waiting their turn, many are reduced to the primitive expedient of using lighters to land their cargo. To-day the immense steamships of the two great British companies which contend for supremacy in the Australian trade, the Orient Line and the Peninsula and Oriental

Company, cannot, because of their length and draught, approach the piers either at Sandridge or at its rival, Williamstown. They are forced to anchor in Hobson's Bay and there to take on coal, loading and unloading their cargo in the old-fashioned way which often causes considerable delays, for the waters of the bay are not always calm and are sometimes dangerous for lighters.

Thus on the one hand Sandridge, situated scarcely two miles from Melbourne, offers in addition to its jetties great advantages to maritime commerce in the form of rapid transport. On the other hand Williamstown, founded by the government, has more, even if smaller jetties, connected like those of Sandridge by about nine miles of railway to the central station at Spencer Street in Melbourne, thus giving direct communication with the interior of the country and allowing the *squatters* (stock-breeders) to send their wool and other products, without re-loading, directly aboard the ships berthed at the wharves.

Moreover in Williamstown the government has built docks which can accommodate the largest ships for repairs. The Alfred Graving Dock, 450 feet long, proportionally wide and capable of taking the largest vessels afloat, was opened in 1874 and has already given immense help to navigation. Private enterprise has also provided dry-docks, patent-slips, etc., etc., and the Williamstown dockyards have produced very fine examples of naval architecture.

However, in spite of all these facilities, Sandridge has kept the first place. Passengers appreciate keenly its closeness to Melbourne. In a few minutes they can reach the centre of the city by the line to Flinders Street Station, the centre of traffic to the suburbs, which can thus be reached without their having to cross half the town.

Still other factors tend to increase the commercial advantages of Sandridge. Recently the suburban line from that port to Melbourne was connected with the great railway from Flinders Street to the eastern part of the colony of Victoria, without a doubt one of the richest agricultural districts in Australia. This line extends for 125 miles into Gippsland, a district clothed with magnificent forests and containing, in addition to its rich farms, all sorts of minerals which will one day be exploited and exported. Before long the two central stations whence the railway systems spread to the interior will be joined to each other. An iron road will span the distance between Flinders and Spencer Street, thus unifying communications between the west, north and east of the colony. This new line will necessarily tend to increase the importance of Sandridge which will become the true port of the great city of Melbourne and consequently the principal commercial outlet of the whole southeast of Australia.

Sandridge is far from responding to its destiny as one could wish. The streets are wide indeed and they cut each other at right angles, but their cleanliness leaves much to be desired and the ground is so flat that it can be drained only with difficulty. There are no underground drains. Thus the stenches that rise from the open gutters, cleansed only when heaven pours veritable torrents of rain on the suburb, produce a most disagreeable impression on one's sense of smell.

It was night when the locomotive deposited me on the platform at Flinders Street station. Many trains came in from different directions or set out for the southern or eastern suburbs. The scene, although very animated, was not noisy. There was not a single shout and the most perfect order seemed to rule this great station despite the considerable comings and goings. Contrary to the French custom, movement over all the platforms is free and people are not penned up like sheep in waiting-rooms until their trains leave. There were neither more nor fewer mishaps for that. The checking of tickets takes no less and no more time, and from the point of view of economy this system allows a number of employees to be dispensed with.

I also noticed that each traveller looks after his own luggage, without having to run to a certain room and there wait his turn to obtain his trunks. Besides, the English know how to travel and do not encumber themselves with a great load of packages. One suitcase is enough for them, and, in case these should clutter up the compartment, they put them under the seats, a habit which simplifies matters considerably when the train arrives. The custom has the further advantage that the traveller may carry his own baggage from the platform to the waiting omnibus or carriage, without having to use a porter who would fleece him mercilessly, demanding a whole shilling (1 franc, 25 centimes) for carrying a trunk thirty yards. One of the first

7

things that struck me on my arrival in Australia was the utter
necessity of learning to wait upon oneself, unless one is as
rich as Croesus. If one does not, one is likely very quickly to
lose a good deal of change.

A few minutes after getting out at the station I took a cab to
the United Services Club Hotel in Collins Street. I was given
quite a small room looking onto an equally small courtyard
which, however, was filled with tree-ferns, orchids and other
exotic plants that gave the air a pleasant freshness. After a
quick wash and brush-up, I went out of the hotel to walk around
the streets of this great Australian city.

It was about six: the evening air was beautifully light, clear
and balmy. As a stranger I scarcely knew which way to turn
and so I decided simply to walk straight ahead. The United
Services Club Hotel stands on a corner where two main streets,
as wide as boulevards, cross at right-angles like all other streets
in the city. Opposite it in Collins Street stands another large
hotel, the *Oriental*, which has a very good name but where
travellers are fleeced by all hands. Perhaps it was because of the
clarity of the night air, perhaps because of the width of the
streets – a hundred feet from one footpath to the other; but for
such an important city Melbourne by night struck me as
wretchedly lit and rather deserted. Hardly a soul passed me as I
walked down Collins Street. I soon realized that at night the
busiest part of the town was a little removed from the quiet
quarter where I had chosen to put up. I turned then to the
right and, walking along Swanson Street for two minutes,
found myself in another street parallel to mine, very brightly
lit and packed with not very noisy crowds of pedestrians coming and going on the wide pavements, while omnibuses, cabs
and vehicles of all kinds passed each other in the street. On the
right a little further on a crowd was pouring out of a large
theatre, the *Opera House*, at the entrance of which two great
posters showed that an English translation of the *Fille de
Madame Angot* had been charming the inhabitants of the
Antipodes for the past four weeks. On the opposite side of the
street the *Theatre Royal* was staging a different kind of French
drama, *Froufrou*.

In the middle of this crowd there was comparatively little
noise, though from time to time the piercing shriek of a news-

boy yelled the name of some evening paper whose second edition had just come out. This is Bourke Street, a great thoroughfare which at one end confronts Spencer Street Central Railway Station and at the other a monumental building, still unfinished, but which already houses the two representative-chambers of the colony, the Legislative Assembly and the Legislative Council. Bourke Street is in some sense to Melbourne what the Rue de Rivoli is to Paris. Situated in the middle of the town, lined with magnificent shops, theatres and public monuments, it forms the centre of Melbourne's retail trading. By night it is very attractive and would be absolutely enchanting, if only the architecture of the buildings were a little more harmonious and if they were tall enough to correspond to the length and breadth of the street. Straight as an arrow and a mile in length, traversed by innumerable vehicles with multi-coloured glass lamps, with its brilliantly lit theatres and cafés with real American-type *bars* as bright as day, Bourke Street has *panache*. The crowd is orderly. There is hardly a sign that the public peace needs guardians, save for an occasional policeman near a theatre, promenading in frockcoat with silver buttons and black helmet embossed with the interlaced V and R of Queen Victoria's monogram. It was not always thus in the old days, when gold-fever had infected the population and when Melbourne had become the rendezvous for adventurers from the four corners of the earth, the infant Bourke Street often witnessed scenes a little more noisy and anything but peaceful. Nowadays things have changed: gold and quarrels are both harder to find.

Chapter Two

The city of Melbourne, monuments, public gardens, suburbs – The universal Exhibition of 1880 – Flemington race-course and horse-racing – The Melbourne Cup – Some Australian types, male and female.

After a little time I came to know Melbourne, its suburbs and surroundings, like the palm of my hand, and my astonishment grew daily as I learnt more about the size and wealth of this magnificent city which had been in existence for only forty years.

It was in September 1836 that Captain Lonsdale chose the site of to-day's city for the head-quarters of the Port Phillip settlement. Sir Richard Bourke, then governor of New South Wales, later gave his name to the county in which it is situated. Originally the town comprised an area of about one square mile, divided into numerous *blocks* which the government put up to public auction at an upset price of £8, that is about 200 francs, per acre. Times have changed somewhat since then. In certain parts of the city to-day, in Collins Street for example, an acre of land with say three hundred feet fronting the street and 133 feet deep, could not be bought for less than £700 per foot. That would bring to £210,000, say, 5,250,000 francs, the value of one of those acre-blocks which the government willingly sold scarcely forty years ago for 200 francs apiece. This fact alone demonstrates, more clearly than volumes of print could do, the prosperity of these lucky colonies.

Melbourne and its suburbs now extend over a radius of ten miles: it has a population of about 256,000 people and its annual revenue exceeds 25 million francs.

The city proper stands on the right bank of the little River Yarra-Yarra, navigable only up to the rapids just below Princes Bridge. It occupies the site originally chosen by Captain Lonsdale, and is laid out in wide parallel streets running north and south, crossed by others of the same width (99 feet) running east and west. Between each pair of the latter, long narrow lanes divide the blocks in halves. These lanes bear the same names, but preceded by the adjective *little*, as those of the great arteries which they parallel. Thus Flinders Street is flanked by Little Flinders Street, Collins Street by Little Collins Street, and so on. Each of these streets is a mile long and each has a main railway station at one end and a great public building at the other. At the eastern end of Collins Street stands the Treasury, a magnificent edifice in the Italian style, which houses certain of the Governor's offices and those of the Finance and *Audit* departments. Behind the Treasury and surrounded by beautiful gardens there rise enormous buildings housing different public ministries and the government printery. Higher up at the eastern extremity of Bourke Street, a huge palace to accommodate both houses of the colonial legislature is in course of construction. The plans are reminiscent of the Capitol in Washington but the building will not be completed for many years.

At two main city corners, and almost in the centre of the city proper, there are two more fine public buildings, the General Post Office and the Town Hall. The last-named, particularly, does great credit to the architect who conceived its proportions. The main hall is used frequently for concerts at which dilettante Melbournians hear celebrated European artists render the masterpieces of music. The City Council has installed in this hall what Victorians consider one of the wonders of their capital, a superb organ worth 125,000 francs. Melbourne people have a great love for music: no self-respecting house is without its piano and even artisans' cottages have their spinets. Rich and poor, fashionable ladies and their chambermaids, everyone believes in the necessity of pounding, with more or less talent, or rather force, the keys of these unhappy instruments. There is not a working-girl who does not 'strum', and every *barmaid* would consider herself insulted if any uncouth person should permit himself to question her talent as a pianist. But in spite of their love for the art, the Australians are no more musically gifted than the English, and they will willingly pay high prices to hear it played quite badly. Whoever needs to be convinced of this has only to help in the production of some opera,

11

especially a comic opera: the orchestra will be pitiful, the voices more than mediocre and frequent false notes will not appear to trouble the audience. As long as the scenery is well done, the dancers pretty and attractive and their costumes diaphanous, the performance will be a success. They have a much better appreciation of comedy, but a great many Australians rate classic Shakespearian tragedy as the lowest form of dramatic art. As to grand opera in general, the companies come directly from Italy. As it often happens that the choice of actors is confined to singers of a certain standard, this kind of production is better classed under the heading of music. But since the entrepreneurs who have introduced Italian opera to the Australian stage have usually lost money, opera seasons are becoming more and more rare. Melbourne has many theatres, and in recent years many French comic operas have been presented. Lecoq's and Offenbach's music are very popular and wherever you go you are almost certain to hear some urchin whistling through his teeth tunes from *Fille de Madame Angot* or from the *Grande-Duchesse*.

On a hill to the east of the city stands the 1880 Exhibition Palace in the middle of a public garden of which it occupies fully a third. Its cupola dominates the city and, no matter from what direction the traveller approaches Melbourne, he cannot avoid seeing this landmark. Certainly its proportions are far from being harmonious, but on the other hand it can boast of having cost the colony almost £300,000 sterling (7,500,000 francs).

But if the Victorians have no cause for satisfaction in their *Exhibition Building*, they have the right to glory in plenty in other institutions among which the Public Library, with its attached art gallery and technological museum, should be mentioned first. After going through the gate of a fine wrought-iron fence and across a lawn, one climbs a flight of granite steps between two great bronze lions and walks first into the sculpture museum which contains little more than reproductions of statuary of all the ages. Further on one finds another museum housing a host of Australian and New Zealand exhibits – native arms and clothing of New Zealand flax, objects from the South Sea islands, etc., etc. In a large room nearby are hung many paintings, some of them very good, and nearly all belonging to the modern school. The gallery has some French works, among them many of Gerome's charming little *genre* pictures: one is of an Arab interior, admirable down to the smallest detail. A huge canvas by Layraud, depicting English travellers in the hands of a band of Calabrian brigands, by itself takes up a good part of the gallery. To judge by the number of people almost always staring at it, this painting must have great merit.

They say – but I only repeat what I was told – that the dominating personage in this painting was none other than the Marquis of Lorne, and that it portrays an episode in the life of this young man before he had the supreme honour of becoming the son-in-law of Her Majesty, Queen Victoria, by marrying Princess Louise. The young lord is squiring a charming damsel whose beauty the painting suggests and whose seductive figure, well set-off in the costume of an Amazon, it shows. It would certainly have had an astonishing effect on a gang of Italian brigands in some pass of the Calabrian mountains or perhaps of the Abruzzi. The bandits let the travellers continue their journey only after they had received a heavy ransom, and the painting shows the young man just about to sign some important document.

It seems (still according to the story as I heard it) that this picture penetrated to England only some time after the Marquis of Lorne had been approved as the son-in-law of his gracious sovereign. It created a fuss for the painter had, people said, given to his hero the features of the lucky marquis without, however, committing the indiscretion of letting the public identify those of the blonde and bewitching *miss* who was sharing his unhappy fate. One felt only that she must have been beautiful. It is said that the scandal reached the ears of the Queen, and there was no lack of tittle-tattle to embellish the episode that the French artist had seen fit to represent. It would have been barbarous to destroy a fine work of art because of malicious gossip, but how was this offensive and embarrassing picture to be got rid of? Happily a benevolent providence provided a timely solution to the problem. The city of Melbourne had begun to build an art gallery and it had commissioned buyers to hunt for celebrated canvasses. The existence of Layraud's masterpiece was easily brought to their attention. They examined it and were delighted. Were they ignorant of the gossip? Who knows? In any case that is how the brigands came to adorn the Melbourne Art Gallery and to engross the attention of visitors every day. The scandal, if committed to the antipodes, does not reach so close to the Throne, and the Australians will be able to admire at their leisure a French work of art for which they have paid in hard cash.

For the rest, the brigands have good company in their new home which shelters also royal portraits, among others one of the German Kaiser William I who himself presented it to the gallery. The technological museum contains models of all sorts of machines, mainly those for treating gold-bearing quartz and other mineral ores which contribute to the wealth of the province. But strangers are interested most by the replicas, in gilded plaster, of the famous *nuggets* found by the gold-seekers in the early days of the great 'Rush'. Among them is the *welcome nugget*, grubbed up at a depth of 180 feet in the soil of Bakery Hill near Ballarat. It weighed 1,217 ounces, that is to say nearly 100,000 francs for a single stroke of the pick. The most splendid of all is a nugget of 2,280 ounces, worth nearly 200,000 francs, and found within an inch of the surface. The sight of these masses of pure gold gives one vertigo. It explains in some fashion the madness that seized on the whole population when the gold-fields of Ballarat, Mount Alexander, Ophir and Bathurst gave up their immense treasures to the lucky Australian miners. Besides the specimens of the colony's mineral wealth, the visitor may study at his leisure examples of its industrial products. Wool of every grade, hanks of silk, raw hides and leather, woods for cabinet-making etc., etc.: here in a word, is gathered everything to give the visitor a complete picture of the primary and secondary products of the colony of Victoria. At the entrance to the museum, two great columns of rails and other iron-work inform the European traveller that, as regards the smelting and manufacture of iron, the Victorians from now on can surpass the mother country by making on the spot whatever things they need.

The public library on the first floor occupies almost the whole length of the building and it already contains more than a hundred thousand volumes and manuscripts. The reading-room is very beautiful. It is divided into compartments by

14

fluted columns, topped with capitals, which give a very pleasing effect.

The University, situated on the outskirts of the city, has a natural-history museum rivalling those of the greatest cities in Europe. The University of Melbourne was founded in 1855. It has the right to confer degrees, equal in all respects to those granted by English universities. Further, it has the only chair of Medicine so far in Australia. This institution, though completely independent, receives from the colonial government an annual grant of about 300,000 francs. The rest of its income, more than 500,000 francs, comes from students' fees and private donations. These latter sometimes amount to considerable sums. For example in 1878 a colonial millionaire, Sir Samuel Wilson, gave the university £30,000 sterling (750,000 francs) for the express purpose of building a great assembly hall to perpetuate his name. To-day this Wilson Hall is completed. Moreover Sir Samuel Wilson has not got out of this admirable habit, and there is hardly a literary or artistic undertaking in the colony which this Australian Maecenas has not patronized.

Many of the churches have quite pleasing exteriors though some are architecturally odd, notably that of the *Congregational* sect in Collins Street, which looks more like a theatre than a religious building. The Catholic cathedral is still being built – in dark granite with window embrasures and facings in a different, lacklustre, friable stone. Although it may be quite impressive, the sombre and melancholy tone of the building materials makes it an unattractive sight. Architecturally the façade is a complete failure, the tiny main door being overshadowed by a huge rose-window out of all proportion to the rest of the building. The finest of all the Melbourne churches is still that of the Presbyterian Scots which faces the Congregational theatre at the intersection of two splendid streets, Collins and Russell.

The city is surrounded by suburbs and separated from them by noble parks, like the Botanical and Fitzroy Gardens, which remind a European of his own more temperate climes. Under these great avenues of oaks, poplars, alders and weeping-willows a foreigner might imagine himself in France or England – if he were not suddenly reminded by magnificent tree-ferns

15

growing beside a stream, or by an undisturbed corner here and there where eucalyptus have been left in their natural state, that he is in the antipodes. The Fitzroy Gardens are the most beautiful and the least cultivated in Melbourne.

Not far from them on the top of a hill stands Government House with the Observatory nearby. The Governor's residence is a large building in brick covered over with cement, as indeed are the majority of buildings in Melbourne and its suburbs. From a distance it could easily be mistaken for a large candle factory.

It is situated more or less in the centre of Melbourne's fashionable suburbs – South Yarra, Toorak,* Prahran, Windsor, Saint Kilda and Emerald Hill. In all of them some of the houses are prettier than others but all are surrounded by gardens and green lawns.

In Toorak* along the left bank of the River Yarra, and at Saint Kilda beside the sea, stand the princely homes of squatters and great merchants who constitute the colonial aristocracy. Because of its proximity to the sea Saint Kilda is an especially exclusive area and its baths, with separate sections for the two sexes, are very well patronized. Trouville or Saratoga fashions have not yet reached Australia. Melbourne beauties never promenade on the beach in those costumes, as fetching as they are flimsy, which are all the rage at sea-bathing resorts in France and America. So far no-one has complained.

These Saint Kilda baths, enclosed by a massive fence to protect the bathers from the sharks that swarm in Port Phillip Bay, are situated at the end of a fine walk known as the Esplanade. Here on Saturday and Sunday afternoons people from every quarter of the city and the other suburbs come to stroll, some to breathe the pure air of the bay, others – pretty Australian girls, and there are plenty of them – to be admired, and we to admire them.

Brighton is just as fashionable during the bathing season. It is a pretty and populous suburb some miles from the town.

All these suburbs are served by an excellent system of railways, omnibuses and vehicles of all sorts, and in spite of the vast extent of this great city, one can travel easily from one side to the other for quite a reasonable sum.

The village of Flemington is scattered round a great race-

* A printer's error in the original – 'Foorak'.

course where meetings take place throughout the year, but the most popular are held in the spring. Then it is that the Derby, and the greatest race in the country, the Melbourne Cup, are run.

The Australians, like the English, are great horse-lovers: among them racing has been raised to the status of a national institution. The Victoria Racing Club Spring Meeting lasts for a week, during a good part of which the whole country celebrates. They begin on Saturday with the Derby. The following Tuesday is concentrated to the great race: Cup Day is Melbourne's *Mardi Gras*. The city is deserted and the whole world flocks to the race-course. Shops, banks, government offices, establishments of every kind, shut their doors. The hotels, crammed from basement to attic with visitors from the neighbouring colonies and every part of Australia, disgorge their torrent of humanity onto the Flemington race-course. In short, no-one is left in the city but the blind, the senile, the halt and infants still too young to walk. To see the Melbourne Cup run the one-eyed beg, borrow or steal telescopes, and the lame new crutches. In fact there is no extravagance which Australians of every class and condition do not permit themselves on the great day.

At Flemington itself the spectacle is truly magnificent.

To carry the vast crowds converging thither from all points of the compass, the Victorian railways perform miracles. A specially-constructed branch-line runs right onto the field behind the grand-stand and to the foot of a mound from which race-goers have a better view of the track than from anywhere else. On Cup Day this line carries about fifty thousand passengers, not to mention the thousands who come by omnibus and every other kind of vehicle that can be pressed into service for the occasion.

Alongside the superb four-horse carriage bearing some ravishing Australian girls with their correct escorts, fathers or brothers perhaps, wallows a humble buggy bulging with its load of common humanity. There go half a dozen workers, adorned with multi-coloured neckties and accompanied by their sweethearts in three-shillings-a-yard silk dresses, topped off with gaudy hats on which feathers and ribbons battle for position. Gaiety shines on every face: jokes ricochet from one

17

vehicle to another, and races start on the dusty road in anti-
cipation of the great event which all are going to watch a
little later.

People have been crowding onto the hill since early in the
morning, and below on the flat surrounding the actual course a
compact mass of humanity swells in number right up to the
moment when the horses appear. Long before the first race, the
crowd of visitors promenading on the magnificent lawn between
the track and the grandstand, take their seats in the latter.
There you will find gathered the fine flower of Australian
aristocracy: rich squatters down from the bush with their wives
and daughters for the Melbourne Cup, to win or lose perhaps
two or three hundred pounds on the favourite; princes of
finance, miners whom a lucky stroke of the pick has made
millionaires, businessmen whose signature is worth a hundred
thousand pounds sterling in no matter what bank, and judges
with a salary of £3,000 a year who have abandoned their
magisterial gravity for the day to mix with the Cup crowd. All
Australia is there to see and be seen while some thirty superb
horses, ridden by jockeys in brilliantly-coloured silk vests and
caps, compete for the much-coveted prize: the cup and the two
thousand guineas given by the City of Melbourne, loss of which
may make a rich man to-day into a beggar tomorrow.

In the midst of this multitude of men, every one of them
engrossed with the chances of some horse or other, beautiful
girls of this golden land move along almost unnoticed on the
arms of their cavaliers.

Look, dear reader, at that tall young woman with the willowy
figure, a bit too slender perhaps, whose complexion has the
velvety look of a ripe peach and makes you want to bite it. The
little you can see of her golden hair under the big picture hat
dazzles you, and one glance from her great blue eyes forces you
to lower yours. If you go on looking at her in that way, you
will commit some outrageous indiscretion. This charming
apparition is a Tasmanian. She was probably born on the
picturesque banks of the River Derwent in the shade of blue-
gums and huge tree-ferns.

Let us look the other way.

The grandstand is filled from top to bottom: it is a forest of
beauties decked out in laces and silks of every colour, a superb

bank of living flowers, Australian roses, on this day without thorns.

There is a continuous movement up and down the aisles of the grand-stands, a rustling of silks, which sometimes become a little crushed in spite of the space. Some are climbing to their seats, more are coming down to walk back and forth in front of the stands. Flocks of pretty women draw admiring glances from the young men, generally tall and slim but carrying themselves rather stiffly, as they circulate on the lawn. In the crowd can be seen a good number of the sons and the attractive daughters of Israel, generally dressed very expensively if not in very good taste.

Look at those two ladies surrounded by a veritable court of eager young men. One, evidently the mother, is wearing a marvellous white satin dress, Paris-made they say, and sent out from the salon of a world-famous couturier – I have said 'Worth'. Her daughter, who has the figure of a goddess, wears pale blue satin from the same house. Quite plain except for some beautiful pearls and a little touch of lace, which one would imagine to be very costly, the gown fits perfectly with never a crease or wrinkle. These two must be the wife and daughter of one of those squatters who count their cattle in thousands and their sheep in hundreds of thousands.

This tall, beautiful creature coming towards us whose costume, close-fitting in the latest fashion, emphasizes the perfection of her figure, has a flawless complexion, and every limpid glance from her great brown eyes bestows on its recipients, if only for a moment, a vague sensation of happiness. Her mouth is a little big perhaps; but if you see her laugh – and she has the free, pealing laugh of a child – she shows a superb set of dazzling white teeth. It is true that her hands, gloved in silk, are long, even very long; but they are exquisitely shaped and in proportion to her figure. Everything about this beautiful being, from her royal bearing to the proud way she holds her head and seems happy to be alive, suggests candour and gaiety. She has known even bluer skies and hotter suns: she was born, perhaps, in the days when gold drew to the interior of the mother colony, New South Wales, people of every class and kind. For all I know she came into the world on the goldfields at Bathurst, at Ophir or at Wattle Flat.

Beside her a pleasant young person with a less vivid complexion and a less striking figure, whose coiffure reminds one of a Creole, stands chatting with a large, carefree, laughing young man six feet tall. She is a Queenslander whose cradle was shaded by the great Moreton Bay fig-trees. Her father, a rich planter, has presented her with this trip to Melbourne to show her southern sisters that tropical beauties, though they may lack the highly-prized roses-and-cream complexion of others, yet have an elusive loveliness of their own. The young man with her seems to think so, and perhaps she is destined never again to see a great sugar plantation. Who knows? Perhaps she is fated to cross the seas with her knight-errant for he has pitched his tent, as his tall and sturdy build and fair hair suggest, in the colder climate of New Zealand.

A stir in the crowd marks the arrival of His Excellency the Governor with a brilliant retinue. Hardly a uniform however: only two mounted policemen accompany his carriage. The crowd makes way for him instinctively and the band strikes up *God Save the Queen*: every head is uncovered as one during the strains of the national anthem. The Governor is a little late, for within half an hour of his arrival frantic cheers herald the appearance of the thirty magnificent horses which are going to race for the Cup and the two thousand guineas offered by the City of Melbourne.

There they are, prancing impatiently and reined in by jockeys rigged out in parti-coloured satin liveries which indicate the stables of the various owners. At last the signal is given! The splendid animals, free from all restraint and urged on by their riders, shoot forward with the speed of an arrow. For a few moments they remain bunched together: not one loses his place. But as they reach the first turn the order changes suddenly.

In the grandstand, on the lawn, on the hill and on the flat every face is drawn with anxiety, and conflicting emotions succeed each other as this or that horse takes the lead. In these moments the attention of this human sea is concentrated entirely on the result of the race. Nothing else in the world exists. The judge forgets his dignity, the young man his sweetheart, the girls themselves have eyes only for the galloping mass of horseflesh thundering now along the straight in front of the grandstand. Leading by a short head is a beautiful black beast ridden by a little jockey, almost a boy, whose vest of white satin crossed by a crimson band distinguishes him from all the others. The tense crowd raises only a feeble cheer, for the black horse, now leading the headlong group between two hedges which border the track, is by no means the favourite. But in another moment the black is outdistanced! The cheering rises to a mighty roar as the favourite takes the lead. Suddenly it is clear that none of the other horses has a chance and the crowd's whole attention focuses on the two leaders now locked in final struggle.

'Hurrah for the favourite!' roar a thousand throats as the crowd's darling appears from behind a tall rise, two necks ahead of the black horse now under the spur of its diminutive rider. But even as the cheering becomes deafening, there is another change. His flanks raked by the spurs, the black flashes past the favourite only ten yards from the judges' box – to carry off the prize of two thousand guineas and the golden Melbourne Cup itself.

Now one is struck by the despair in the faces of the losers, and there are many of these for the winner was an outsider whose name scarcely even appeared in the betting at Tattersalls or the leading Melbourne clubs. Among the gloomiest are the bookmakers, the plague of race-courses in every part of the world, for the black horse had been quoted as a hundred to one in their books. It is ruin for some of them, but few racegoers feel much sorrow on that account.

There are two more races, but once the Melbourne Cup has been run and won, interest falls away considerably. If you feel like it reader, we shall glance once more at the great bank of living flowers we admired together earlier and then return quietly to the city, without waiting for the last race, so as to avoid the clouds of dust that will inevitably choke the air later. The loneliness of the utterly empty city streets makes a striking contrast with the lively scenes we were moving in only a few moments ago. We know where all the people are, and we shall not be surprised if tomorrow's *Argus* reports that there were more than a hundred thousand at Flemington this afternoon. How many, alas, will return with empty pockets? Don't be surprised if the Bankruptcy Court figures show three times as many insolvencies in the weeks following the Melbourne Cup as at any other period of the year.

Gradually the city comes to life again. The returning omnibuses are so packed that ladies are to be seen perched among the outside passengers on the roof. Vehicles of every description drop their loads at every street corner. In a few more minutes crowds pouring out of the railway station fill the streets and every hotel, café and bar is soon humming with customers, for the day must be finished off in a fitting way.

After dinner this evening the city will be every bit as lively as the race-course was this afternoon. The theatres will be so crammed that movement, except on the stage, will be impossible. A free-for-all carnival atmosphere will pervade the seething streets. Revelry will continue till dawn extinguishes the last gas-lamps, and happy are those who will wake tomorrow without any kind of unpleasant feeling at the mere thought of horses.

Chapter Three

For some months I had been working as private secretary to the Count de Castelnau, whose health had deteriorated recently and who feared the approach of the Melbourne winter. One fine morning he announced that he had decided to take a trip to the north. He was planning to go by land to Sydney and thence by an *Australian Steam Navigation Company's* ship to Brisbane for the greater part of its mild and pleasant winter. With him was to travel Madame —— and her son, Édouard.

'Would you like to come with us?' he asked. 'You could learn a little of the other colonies in eastern Australia: we shall be going by land some of the way as I hate sea journeys.'

It goes without saying that I accepted without even stopping to think. The chance of such a trip does not turn up every day and I would not have been such a fool as to refuse M. de Castelnau's company.

Monsieur the Count de Castelnau, French Consul-General in Melbourne, is a man of about sixty-five whose tall frame stoops a little under the weight of his years, but whose step is still steady and grip firm. A distinguished scholar and traveller, science is indebted to him for extremely interesting accounts of his explorations of the South American continent. In Melbourne the Count lived very quietly, extending his friendship to only two or three other men, scholars like himself; and consequently he was generally thought to be rather eccentric. A man of simple tastes who perhaps neglected his appearance a little, M. de Castelnau was the warmest of friends to those who knew him intimately. He was a gifted *raconteur* who had seen much in his time and carried out many important missions. As for me, I must put it on record that many a night has slipped away in no time as I listened to his conversation, always enlivened as it was by some original ideas. However, he was a man whom one had to know well to appreciate, and he had not the knack of making a good first impression on people. He was said to be mean, but unknown to the world at large he did much good by stealth.

Madame de X***, mother of the boy whom I was to look after, was a pure-blooded Brazilian woman, for long accustomed to the implicit obedience of slaves* and so somewhat at sea with Australian servants. As for my little charge, he was a youngster of about twelve, small for his age, thin, even emaciated, thoroughly spoilt by the Count but not at all by Nature, and placed in this world for the sole purpose of making me do penance for my sins.

At five o'clock in the morning of 13 June 1876 we caught the train from Spencer Street station, festooned with such loads of superfluous luggage as women, especially Creoles, have such a genius for gathering. In a few minutes the train carried us through thickly populated suburbs and past the factories in Footscray, those seeds of a colonial manufacturing industry which it is said will one day supply the needs of the whole country. As you may well imagine, from the outset I had my eye glued to the window and a map in my hand; but I must admit that at first I was greatly disappointed at the general appearance of the countryside.

What! These endless plains without a single clump of trees, this featureless, flat land: is this that picturesque Australia Jules Verne describes so alluringly?

The fact is that this part of Victoria presents nothing very attractive to the visitor's gaze. After leaving the suburbs of the great southern city, the solitude is so palpable that one would think the train already entering the desert, if the wire fences dividing the huge squares of land they call *paddocks* did not suggest that the hand of man had passed that way.

The train carried us rapidly across a monotonous landscape which, they say, makes excellent pasture, and I noticed there was hardly any cultivated ground. The vast bulk of the land

* Slavery was not abolished in Brazil until 1888.

seems to be given over to the pastoral industry. But just here the properties seemed to be quite sufficiently sub-divided, to judge by the many fences, almost always made of wire, which criss-crossed the land. We passed in turn Essendon, Pentridge, the site of the colony's principal gaol, Woodstock, Donnybrook, Beveridge; and–further on between Wallan-Wallan and Kilmore– the landscape began to change and become less monotonous. We had crossed the mountains, or rather the hills, which form the watershed between the streams flowing north-west into the Murray and its tributaries and those flowing down the other slope towards the south.

At Seymour we crossed the River Goulburn, a tributary of the Murray. The soil looked rich, and one asked oneself how it was that so little of it was cultivated. Now and then, however, on one or the other side of the line we saw the shanties of *free-selectors*, literally 'free-choosers'. These farmers are the peasants of Australia. The word comes from the great inducements offered by the government to those who wish to make a living by cultivating the soil of the colony. Anyone undertaking this work may choose, wherever he likes on Crown land, an area big enough to support himself and his family: hence the name *free selector*. Little by little they are tending to replace the big graziers, squatters as they are called, on most of the land in Victoria. The squatter, naturally, looks with a very jaundiced eye on the intruders who select their land and pitch their tents on the very richest parts of his run. There is war to the death to-day between the squatter and the *free selector*, who is utterly scorned by his powerful enemy and given in his turn a derogatory nick-name. Just as the English, under the impression that we Frenchmen consume quantities of frogs at table, refer to us generically as *Jack Frog*; so the squatter pretends that his neighbours, the small selectors, are too poverty-stricken to eat anything but the meat of the white cockatoos which swarm in the country, and he never refers to these despised beings except as *cockatoo-farmers*.

We had now moved into country occupied mainly by squatters and their *stations*, each made up of one or more *runs* – vast stretches of land used solely for grazing their huge flocks of sheep. These *runs*, varying in area from about twenty-five to a hundred square miles, are sub-divided into smaller areas by all sorts of barriers. The commonest kind is formed by four or five strands of galvanized iron wire, about ten inches apart and stretched one above the other between sturdy posts planted at intervals in the ground. This system of sub-division, apart from the advantage of being cheap, prevents sheep of different ages or breeds, which have been carefully culled and separated, from becoming mixed up with each other in adjoining *paddocks*. To-day most big stations no longer employ *shepherds* as they used to do: they have been replaced by *boundary-riders*, whose main work is to maintain and repair these barriers between paddocks which people in Australia call *fences*. Whenever a break in a fence allows sheep to stray into a neighbouring flock, they must be picked out and driven back at once to their own *paddock*. Otherwise there could be inter-breeding that might affect the next season's lambs and cause a serious drop in the value of the staple station product, wool. Summer and winter alike, the flocks graze untended in their own *paddocks*.

From time to time we passed long trains of twenty or thirty trucks loaded with sheep from the inland, bound for Melbourne the great market of the south. It was a strange new sight for us to see these animals crammed together on two floors, one above the other, in these barred railway-wagons.

On both sides of the line at every stopping-place we saw big scaffoldings leading from yards enclosed by wooden railings. The sheep are first penned in these enclosures, then driven along a kind of narrow passage directly into the wagons which carry them to their destination.

The train stopped at one little village of four or five houses called Glenrowan. The place has since become famous as the site of a siege in which four determined *bushrangers* held at bay a detachment of Victorian police.

For eighteen months during the years 1879 and 1880 three bandits, of the type of Jules Verne's lifelike character, Ben Joyce, roamed over the whole countryside we were about to traverse, and set at defiance the fine flower of the colonial police forces. The band was made up by two brothers named Kelly and another young man of the district.

They began their career by murdering a police sergeant who, it seems, had seduced the Kellys' sister. This man with one or two subordinates, hunting the eldest of these young men,

Edward Kelly, for horse-stealing or some such misdemeanour, met them in the depths of a little valley in the mountains near the township of Mansfield. There took place the first battle between the police and the bandits. The sergeant was killed whilst his men were forced to surrender their arms, ammunition, horses, and even their uniforms to the enemy.

After this assassination, which they later pretended had been committed to avenge the honour of their family, the Kellys and their mate took to the bush – which becomes more and more rugged in proportion to distance from the railway. Living from day to day, hunted continuously by the police but helped by their numerous supporters, they continued the campaign for eighteen months. During this time their sister, a beautiful twenty-year-old and expert horsewoman, played an extremely romantic role. She it was who undertook to keep her brothers supplied, wherever they were, with the provisions they needed; and she did it with incomparable audacity. Everyone knew she continuously ranged the whole countryside, dressed in the most flamboyant of riding-habits – a long scarlet dress and a large, broad-brimmed hat set off with an ostrich feather. In spite of her provocative behaviour, and although everyone realized that she knew the bushrangers' hiding-place, the police remained powerless to capture her.

Mounted on a magnificent grey horse, she would suddenly appear a hundred yards from a camp of *troopers* (horse-police) who would knock up their mounts chasing her for hours through impossible country. Then she would give spur to her horse and disappear in a few minutes without the hapless men-at-arms ever being able to follow her tracks.

For all this time the *Kelly gang*, as they were called, held the country under a veritable reign of terror. One afternoon, in broad daylight the three friends rode into a township of some hundred inhabitants, situated on the railway line. There they unceremoniously entered a hotel full of people, and, while one of them, revolver in hand, had drinks served, the other two presented themselves at the neighbouring bank, the branch of a great Melbourne firm. In the banking chamber one of them kept the manager covered while his comrade forced the unhappy cashier, under pain of death, to hand over in gold and other forms of cash, a considerable sum – 50,000 or 60,000 francs. The job done, they rejoined their mate in the hotel, had drinks served all round, jumped on their horses and disappeared at the gallop in the direction of the mountains. The whole affair had taken twenty minutes. The police arrived among the stunned populace a few minutes later. They were again too late – as usual! The same day's evening papers, in both Sydney and Melbourne, carried the telegraphed story of the daring Euroa bank robbery and published as many as three editions which sold out at once. The Victorian government borrowed a squad of aboriginal police 'trackers' from the government of Queensland.

Much was hoped from these human bloodhounds for whom mountain and desert had no secrets but, in spite of all the skill they brought to the chase during these months, the Kellys were always warned in time and continued to escape. One fine morning people heard that the bandits had crossed the Murray and rumour said they had repeated in a township of the neighbouring colony the incredible Euroa exploit. When the news was published in Sydney the banks, by agreement with the governments of the two colonies, offered a reward of £8,000 sterling (200,000 francs) for the capture of the *Kelly gang* dead or alive.

The lure of this enormous sum redoubled efforts to catch them but, always kept in touch by their sister with what was going on, the Kelly's redoubled their daring. They joined in at dances in bush hamlets and, having had their fill of entertainment, would gallop off on their excellent horses to re-appear a few days later at a hotel a hundred miles away. The police, who had spies everywhere, arrested a few people and accused them of sympathizing with the outlaws – to no purpose. Months passed : people had begun to forget the Kellys and their deeds of derring-do when a frightful crime brought them back to the minds of the whole Australian population.

One of their old friends named Aaron Sherritt had been won over by promises to play the part of a police informer. For some time he had been sheltering troopers of the horse police in his lonely hut in the midst of a gum-tree forest.

One night, when the shack was lit up by a great log fire burning in the huge hearth typical of Australian farm houses, Sherritt was smoking his pipe and chatting with two of these troopers. It was pitch dark and absolutely still outside.

Suddenly a voice shouted: 'Sherritt! Sherritt!' The man thus called rose and opened the door of the hut, standing silhouetted clearly against the light of the fire. 'Ah! there you are, you scum!' continued the voice. 'Well it's Byrne of the *Kelly gang* come to show you how we treat spies. . . .'

A shot cut short any reply, and the wretched Sherritt fell dead on his own doorstep with a bullet through his heart.

Some days after this horrible assassination, the police at last learnt that the bandits were at a dance in a little hotel in the village of Glenrowan. For the first time in eighteen months they succeeded in surrounding the gang. The Kellys had enough warning to take defensive measures and they obtained a few moments' truce to allow the customers in the hotel to leave safely. Then began, between the bushrangers and police, a veritable battle that lasted for several hours. Bullets flew back and forth and many policemen were rendered *hors de combat*.

From hour to hour the citizens of Melbourne, Sydney and the entire country were kept in touch by telegraph with the events in Glenrowan.

At one stage the position of the forces of law and order seemed critical, and it was a question of despatching the commander-in-chief of the Victorian army, Colonel Anderson, with an artillery battery to bombard this shanty under regular siege by the police.

Suddenly shots were heard in the bush behind the police lines. Could the gang be more numerous than had been thought? Could it be that the police were themselves encircled?

Nothing of the sort, luckily. A single man dominated the situation. His body was enveloped by a grey overcoat and his head encased by a sort of helmet against which the troopers' bullets flattened themselves in vain. This lone man, who seemed invulnerable, exchanged revolver shots with several policemen. At last a bullet struck him in the knee and forced him to surrender.

The man was Edward, otherwise known as Ned, Kelly, the leader of the gang.

He was immediately carried on a stretcher to the railway station. Meanwhile a terrible scene had been enacted at the Glenrowan Hotel.

Under the eyes of Miss Kelly who had just appeared in her legendary costume, a policeman braver than his fellows and carrying an enormous bundle of straw as a shield, had crossed the open space around the hotel and set it alight, in the teeth of fire from the two besieged men.

In a moment the shanty was a sheet of flame. The shooting quickly ceased and, half an hour later when the avenging element had completed its task, a passing priest was the first to enter the gutted building and come upon the charred bodies of the two bushrangers. Beside them lay the extraordinary suits of armour, made from ploughshares, of the same pattern as that which for some time had rendered their leader immune to police bullets.

The Kelly story ended later in the criminal court. Many people warmly espoused the hardy gang-leader's cause. After he had been sentenced to hang, his lawyer, Gaunson, a member of the Victorian parliament, personally led a deputation to Government House to ask for commutation of the death sentence. There was widespread popular agitation in his favour. In Sydney people laid bets on his fate. Will he hang or not? Three to one he escapes! some were even ready to bet. But the walls of Melbourne Gaol are high, and Australian governors have not the power to reverse decisions of the Supreme Court. Ned Kelly was hanged. . . .

Having passed through a landscape haunted by a touch of profound melancholy, we were now approaching the Murray Valley.

One feels depressed by the sameness of this countryside, covered with eucalyptus forests scattered haphazardly over the immensity of the plains. But there are parts of the bush – the name people give to the entire interior of Australia – which are really terrifying.

There are areas, miles and miles in extent, where not a leaf or a piece of living bark is to be seen on the trees. Over immense tracts of land the forest has been killed.

Nothing can give any idea of the infinitely sad and desolate air of these dead forests. One might suggest a page, torn from a portfolio by Gustave Doré, showing a part of Dante's *Inferno*. It is the vision of Ezekiel: and the forest resembles a multitude of skeletons raising their long, fleshless arms to the sky.

The effect of a wind in these dead forests adds greatly to the feeling of melancholy. No rustling of leaves, but at long intervals the dry sound of a huge branch, breaking and crashing to the ground.

And all this is caused by the squatter's axe. Every tree had a ring cut through its bark one or two feet above the ground. This prevents the life-giving sap from coursing upwards to nourish the great body. The only purpose of this vandalism is to let the grass spring up more thickly so that a few more sheep can be fed per acre of land. It is a sight a poet would scarcely appreciate but one on the other hand which the squatter, with his characteristic love of gain, calculates will profit him a little for a few years, without caring that he is prejudicing his own future. The legislature of the neighbouring colony, where it is practised on an equally large scale, has just passed severe laws against this system of *ring-barking*. They have recognized in effect that this system of de-forestation was helping to make the climate, already too arid, drier than it has ever been.

After travelling seventy leagues and spending eight hours in the train, we got out at last on the platform at Wodonga, the last station on the line on the border of the colony of Victoria. There we waited for an omnibus which was to take us across the Murray to Albury in the colony of New South Wales. The distance is about a league. The banks of the Murray are covered with eucalyptus, true giants of the vegetable kingdom, a hundred feet high, sturdy in proportion and crowned with leaves to their summits. Their smooth white trunks are dotted with great bosses of rough bark, where the aborigines once carefully stripped off a piece to make a sort of basin for carrying water.* This utensil had other important uses in the domestic arrangements of the savages. The *gin* (woman, in the native language) used it as a bath for bathing her *picaninis* (little children) and the dogs, inseparable from the master of the *guniah* (hut), lapped water from it on returning from a kangaroo hunt. To-day the great gum-trees along the Murray retain their bark, the native race has almost totally disappeared, and the noise of the European colonist's axe knocking down some great eucalypt alone awakes the echoes which once rang to the savages' oo-eec![1]†

* Actually this operation left smooth, 'bald' scars on tree trunks. La Mesleé was wrongly informed.

[1] A long drawn-out hail and rallying cry common to almost all Australian tribes.

† Obviously a misprint for *coo-ee*.

31

We walked past the Victorian customs-house on our right without being challenged. The official raised his hat to us without worrying over the possibility of our carrying contraband, for the Victorian government imposes no duties on goods leaving the colony. It would have been different, however, if we had been travelling in the opposite direction: our baggage would have undergone a tiresome examination, for on every commodity entering Victoria is levied a customs duty of twenty per cent of its intrinsic value. The essentially protectionist policy of the Victorian government differs from that of their New South Wales neighbours who follow the opposite principle of free-trade and impose levies on only a very few imported articles, mainly luxury goods.

This circumstance shows that the Australian colonies are completely independent of each other in every respect. They are, in actual fact, little republics recognizing in principle the suzerainty of the mother-country, but completely self-governing. They have their own local laws and parliaments and as for English officials, they receive and pay for only one, the Governor. They have, like all free, independent states, their own ministers who are responsible, not to the Governor who represents only the Queen, but to Parliament which represents the country. The various ministers are responsible to the members of parliament and their subordinates are employed by the colonial *civil service*, which is in no way dependent upon the general colonial service in England. There is, necessarily, neither a ministry of war nor a ministry of marine, for these lands are too far away to be attacked by any other state and too weak to attack any other nation whatever. However, each colony maintains two or three batteries of regular artillery and some volunteer regiments which have absolutely nothing to do with the British army. These troops, recruited from the young men of the country, are commanded by colonial officers, generally drawn from reserve cadres of the British army, who must resign their commission before entering the service of the Australian colonies just as they would have to do if enlisting in a foreign service. Naval affairs are conducted in exactly the same way. Australians in all the colonies exhibit a certain pleasure in letting foreigners understand that they are free men and that not a single British soldier is to be found on their territory. In addition they will readily straighten their usually tall frames to assure visitors that they would not allow any Englishman to come and make their laws.

Going from one colony to another, one senses a quite different atmosphere. They are the same men but they do not hold the same ideas. Thus Victoria is dominated by a democracy whose principles approach those which the radicals of the extreme left want to see adopted in France. Its territory is divided into numerous municipalities and *shires* (kinds of rural districts), which run their own affairs and raise the taxes to maintain their streets and roads quite independently of the central colonial government. They form thus a collection of free communes in a free colony. As a rule these local authorities manage the matters confided to them sensibly. That is not to say that there have never been ridiculous debates in these assemblies where men of erudition are scarce – witness a piece of buffoonery that took up a whole meeting of the council of the city of Ballarat.

The town was surrounded by swamps. The municipal council, mindful of the health of its constituents, resolved to convert these muddy flats into lakes of limpid water. As there were considerable funds the work proceeded quickly. When the lake was finished there was discussion about its beautification. A meeting of the city fathers was re-convened and one of the councillors – he was a travelled man who had been to Venice – proposed that some thirty gondolas should be launched on the lake. The proposal was about to be put to the vote and carried when an old alderman, grown grey in the service and renowned for his great sagacity, took the floor: 'Gentlemen,' said he, 'I suggest that my honourable colleague's motion has not been considered carefully enough. God forbid that I should be a foe of the arts. I love those things which delight the eye and elevate the soul, but I oppose the motion before us on these very principles. What need have we of thirty gondolas? The expense of so many would be too great. We have no right to pillage the sacred funds of our ratepayers. In all seriousness I give you my advice. If it is held essential to have gondolas, it would be quite sufficient to import two of these animals from Italy and leave to nature and our bountiful climate the responsibility for creating the rest.'

Chapter Four

Albury, the first New South Wales town on our route, presents a striking contrast to Wodonga on the other side of the Murray. Well laid out with fine, wide streets and architecturally passable large shops, banks and public buildings, it lies at the foot of verdant hills where the vine grows in profusion.

The vineyards of Albury and the Murray valley are renowned not only throughout Australia. The prizes won by these wines at the Paris Universal Exhibition of 1878 extended their fame even into Europe. However Albury wines in general are far below the standard of those of Messrs Fallon and of the two or three other vineyards which were awarded prizes. The quantity grown, although increasing each year, is still not very impressive and the quality, though fair, still leaves considerable room for improvement.

Generally speaking most of these wines, not to say all Australian wine, fail in two important respects: they lack bouquet and their alcoholic content is much too high.

Australians give much thought to the future of this industry and would make any sacrifices necessary to introduce their best vintages to the English and Indian markets. So far they have had only moderate success: at best, their finest vintages have, sometimes, reached the United Kingdom market among the wines of France and Spain.

Australian consumption of wine is far from keeping pace with production. People still like colonial beer much better than their own wine: first because it is cheaper, and second because men and women of British antecedents do not suddenly lose their natural taste for their traditional national beverage. The problem will have to be met, perhaps by compulsory restriction of production, or perhaps by increasing it to such a peak that the surplus can be exported to France where these wines of very high alcoholic content would make the fortune of our vignerons, if they could be obtained at a reasonable price. If this could be done, Australia could very quickly produce enough wine to meet the demand, however great it might be.

But let us return to Albury. However attractive this pretty little town may be, we cannot stay in it too long for we have still to cover nearly two hundred miles of country before reaching the terminus of the New South Wales railway system. At this time the line extended only to Gunning beyond which point passengers had to travel by stage-coach, unless they could afford to travel in style in a private carriage. Count Castelnau, who knew what it was to commit himself to an Australian coach, leant towards this second alternative. But ill fortune had decreed that the landlord of the hotel had remembered that he and the count were 'old acquaintances': at any rate that was what he maintained. So we had to stay to be conscientiously fleeced.

On the subject of old acquaintances, Monsieur de Castelnau told me the following anecdote. It illustrates vividly the ways of these democratic Australians among whom Jack believes he is as good as his master, and class-distinctions as they exist in Europe are absolutely unknown.

For some months the mail had been delivered every morning to the consulate by an intelligent looking young man about thirty years old.

It often happened that the Count de Castelnau was impatiently waiting in his office when the postman arrived. With the self-confidence typical of Australians generally, and without waiting to be asked, the postman used to deliver little homilies on the political news of the country; and as he was far from being stupid, his remarks intrigued Monsieur de Castelnau who ended by accommodating himself to the free-and-easy demeanour of the postman-politician.

Returning from two or three months in the country, the Count saw his letter-carrier no more and, as he wished him well, thought no more about it.

One afternoon Monsieur de Castelnau was walking down

Bourke Street for his customary promenade when a *gentleman*, dressed in the latest fashion and crowned with a gleaming new top hat, came towards him with outstretched hand, slapped him on the shoulder, and cried:

'Hullo, Count! How are you?'

'But, monsieur,' replied the astonished Count, grimacing involuntarily from having his hand half crushed in the stranger's, 'but, monsieur, you have the advantage of me. I cannot for the moment remember with whom I have the honour of speaking.'

'Don't you remember me? . . . Ben, the postman,' the other replied with an astonished air.

'Ah!' said the Count, suddenly remembering the features of his old acquaintance, but still unable to account for his changed appearance, 'I am happy to see that your circumstances have improved. A legacy perhaps?'

'Oh! Gawd no! the fact is that carrying letters round Melbourne streets wore out an immense quantity of shoe-leather and did not pay me.'

'Ah!' resumed Monsieur de Castelnau, still floundering in the dark; 'and what has happened to you then, if it is not indiscreet of me to ask!'

'You remember I had a taste for politics. Well, as the other job did not pay, I threw myself into politics and I am now a member of Parliament.'

With these words the postman-become-politician again wrung the hand of his stunned questioner, and walked off.

Torn between the pain of his bruised hand and confusion at this meeting, the consul, fearful that he might meet another old acquaintance if he continued his stroll, went straight home and left next day for Mordialloc.

But such a thing could happen only in Victoria where the members of the Legislative Assembly receive a salary of £300 sterling a year: the other colonies have not yet adopted this system.

The landlord of the Exchange Hotel at Albury happened to belong to that cursed race condemned by the Almighty to wander over the face of the earth. He was a son of Israel and he had added to this title that of 'old acquaintance'. The count was bound to have been imposed upon, and he was. His intention was, as I said above, to cover the 200 miles separating us from

1. Hobson's Bay Railway Pier, Sandridge, Victoria, 1880

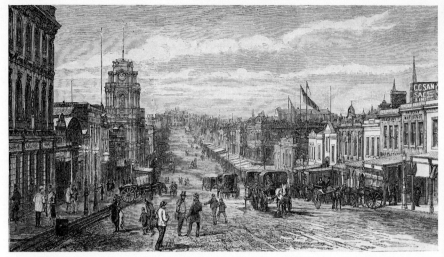

2

3

2. Bourke Street, Melbourne, looking East, 1880
3. Bourke Street, Melbourne, Saturday night, 1880

Gunning in a private carriage. He had therefore telegraphed from Melbourne before our departure, as arrangements for a conveyance could be made at Albury for a reasonable price. Fate had decreed that the only person in Albury able to provide this service was none other than our landlord, who, scenting a profitable deal, demanded an exorbitant price. Probably he thought that the poor lady who was with us would be so frightened at the idea of such a journey, and especially of spending the night in a roadless countryside, that she would beguile the Count into accepting any terms.

The cost of the coach journey was 375 francs and he demanded a thousand. We ransacked the town in search of a carriage. Impossible: the wretch had monopolized the traffic, and for one reason or another no one would risk conveying us across the 200 miles that lay between us and our destination.

But the price was so inflated that the Count held his ground and steadily refused. He preferred to undergo no matter what miseries than to have people say that he had, in effect, been made a fool of. To frighten Madame de X*** people came to tell us about *bushrangers* like the Kellys who were said to be infesting the country. At last the Count decided to do what everyone else does and spend a night in the diligence. I say diligence because we were expecting well-appointed and well-sprung vehicles for such a journey. Little did we yet know the Australian mail service.

The *coach* was due to leave in the morning and, after walking round the town for the rest of the afternoon, we had a good sleep to replenish our strength for the trials of the following day and night. We had been warned that the roads were atrocious.

Next morning we were in front of the hotel when a mis-shapen, covered cart, perched on high wheels, enclosed simply by more or less tattered raw-hide curtains and drawn by four strong horses, drew up in the middle of the street. We were informed that this was the diligence in the postal service of Her Britannic Majesty, and invited to take our seats. We could not believe our eyes. We committed ourselves for good or ill to the interior of this strange box suspended on raw-hide 'springs'. There was room for four reasonably built persons, but it had been thought fit to decree that there was room for eight, and it was not long before we enjoyed the company of two other passengers. With four, we were fairly packed in; with six, we began to suffocate. What would it be like if two more arrived...?

At last our four horses set off at a good trot and all went well, without too much jolting, for about a league. The countryside was superb, its vegetation different from what we had seen before. Gum-trees still predominated, as they do everywhere in Australia, but here they grew more thickly, were larger and seemed to carry more foliage: they belonged to a third sort of the multifarious species of the genus. The road, well-defined and indeed quite well made for three or four miles from Albury, wound round the slope of a hill. It was enclosed on both sides by a wooden fence and, up to a certain distance from the town, we saw a few pleasant farms and country houses. As usual in Australia, wherever there is enough room, the distance between the fences was about 200 feet, but the surface paved by the actual road was only just wide enough to allow two vehicles to pass. On both sides of this causeway trees pressed in as though it were cut through a forest, and heavy wagon-wheels had ploughed veritable furrows in the soft earth at the sides of the road itself. Australians call them *tracks*.

Nothing less resembles a road in France than a road in Australia.

In proportion as we travelled farther inland, every trace of civilization disappeared and soon a violent jolt announced that we had left the made road altogether.

There we were, hurtling at full speed through the virgin forest, brushing under branches and between tree-trunks.

Suddenly catapulted from my seat, I was hurled into the arms of the traveller sitting opposite: the Count soared up to the roof where his top-hat was flattened like a pancake: my neighbour disappeared under the seat as he threw the child into its mother's lap. This lady, to fortify herself for the journey, was carrying two great flagons of eau-de-cologne which she had been applying to each nostril alternately. Flying from her hands, they broke on the head of the second passenger and we were all rendered embarrassingly fragrant for the rest of the journey. The unhappy man, whose head had been anointed, swore like one possessed.

It took us some minutes to recover from the shock, but we had thirty-six hours to travel in this fashion. To counter the terrifying lurches that followed each other in rapid succession, we wedged ourselves into position as well as we could.

Nothing can give any real conception of a two hundred-mile journey through the bush in a virgin wilderness, without roads worthy of the name, in impossible coaches slung on leather springs (steel ones won't stand up to it), and pulled at full speed by four spirited horses. Never stopping for a moment we brushed past overhanging branches, tree-trunks and yawning ruts at the gallop, while the infernal machine threatened to overturn every minute. This last kind of accident happens often enough, and when they hear in Melbourne or Sydney that the *royal mail coach* has overturned somewhere or other, one may listen to such a typical conversation between two Australians as the following:

'They reckon,' says one, 'the mail-coach went over again last night.'

'Aw! Anyone killed?'

'No. Jock, the driver, broke his leg. There were only four inside. One bloke was blinded in his left eye; another had four ribs broken, another a dislocated wrist, and both right wheels ran over the fourth bloke's legs. They'll probably have to amputate.'

'Aw! All right! That's not too bad at all. It could have been worse.'

Iron men, almost indifferent to pain and endowed with indomitable energy, the people of inland Australia have more to do than sorrow over the misfortunes of others. Despite their apparent coldness, however, they are very good-hearted, and no people on earth are quicker to reach into their pockets to help those in trouble. When there is a disaster anywhere – among their neighbours, in England or even in France – the Melbourne *Argus* and the *Sydney Morning Herald* open subscription lists which very quickly add up to hundreds of pounds sterling. Doubtless the reader will remember the great floods which ravaged the French Midi some years ago, and perhaps the distress caused by the Kanaka revolt in New Caledonia. In both cases our consuls received considerable sums collected by public subscription in the Australian colonies to help the victims of these calamities.

We wallowed on through the bush, a prey to horrible torments, and pounded into the condition of so many rubber balls, bounced continually back and forth between the seat and the roof. All things come to an end, however, and after four hours of this battering we stopped for dinner at an inn beside the road. It was about mid-day and the somewhat violent involuntary exercise we had taken had sharpened our appetites. In the dining-room built onto one end of the inn, we were served with roast mutton chops and the inevitable boiled potatoes, without which no English or Australian dinner could ever be complete. Some excellent fresh butter and a piece of very good colonial cheese – I swear it – ended this simple meal and restored our strength.

As there was still a quarter of an hour to the time of our departure, I had a look around the inn and its surroundings. The road, a little more visible here than it had been since the vicinity of Albury, wound away through the forest that enclosed the hotel on all sides. It was wonderful weather, the air bracing and absolutely clear. Under the rays of the winter sun the landscape took on that blue tint peculiar to Australia. Indeed all nature's colours in Australia are quite different from those in Europe. With us the general tone of the countryside is always a more or less deep green. Here there was nothing of the sort. The leaves of the trees were of a bluish colour, intermediate between silvery grey and azure. On the finest trees, branches grew only high up near the top of their trunks. Bushes, also with bluish foliage, were scattered here and there over land covered only sparsely with tufts of grass. The ground where we stood was lined with veins of quartz which the eye could trace very much further than a European would expect. It was the beginning of winter and the country looked dry; but after the rain in spring this rich, reddish soil is carpeted with grass on which the squatter's sheep graze in their thousands. A strange country where both the fauna and flora follow rules opposite to the normal ones, where the forests are shadeless and the birds songless!

But the most striking aspect of this part of the country is the everlasting sameness of the vegetation: eucalyptus! everywhere and always eucalyptus! It may be the land of gold and of sheep, but the poet should shun it – unless he would die of immeasurable boredom.

Yet on a clear night the Australian bush creates a different impression. The curious, sparse foliage of the trees takes on a silvery hue in the pale moonlight that elongates their shadows on the ground and gives even to this country a certain poetry. However, the air of melancholy always prevails. One ought not to see Australia only by night, though there is no other land in the world where the nights are so clear and splendid.

These remarks apply to most parts of the continent, but in mountainous districts the country is often very picturesque. Likewise the tropical, northern areas reflect their geographic position and the vegetation is quite different.

After a couple of hours our rickety old coach ground to a halt for the second time in a little hamlet at the foot of a hill. It consisted of a blacksmith's shop and two or three huts, built of tree-trunks split in halves and stripped of their bark, which served to cover the roof. The word 'Post-Office' was painted in large white letters on one of these shacks. Behind the smithy a little *creek* gurgled between steep banks, and this wayside village had quite an attractive air. It lacked only inhabitants.

It grew colder as night approached and we got ready to make ourselves as warm as we could. For a moment we discussed the possibility of sleep, but the appalling jolts which continually threw us on top of each other ended this debate in the negative.

It should be remembered that the country we were passing through had been, scarcely thirty years ago, an utter wilderness; and nothing was more surprising than to discover at each stopping-place hotels which would not have disgraced a small provincial town. In place of a refined cuisine one is always sure to find an enormous platter of mutton or *corned beef*, a good glass of beer or brandy according to taste, and to top it all off, a good bed. Here and there in the distance a wisp of smoke indicated a *free selector's* hut. Sometimes, beside a little stream, we passed some road-workers' white tents or a picturesque encampment of immigrants with their big-wheeled wagons, pulled by ten or twelve strong horses under the charge of a single driver, who wields a twenty-foot long whip with uncanny skill.

Our journey was – according to the point of view – both a horrid and a delightful experience. At times novelty and the magnificent, though rather cold, weather made us forget we were crammed in a horrible contraption which Australians dignify with the pompous title of *royal mail coach*, together with a

41

foul-mouthed drunkard and a young government surveyor going to rejoin his field team at Yass.

We left Billabong at seven o'clock. It was already dark and we had tried everything humanly possible to avoid quarrelling. All went well for a quarter of an hour for the roads are a little better made in or near growing townships: but soon the darkness became deeper, clouds arose and it was obvious that a splendid day was about to be followed by an abominable night.

A sudden jolt made us aware that we had run off the road.

We had also changed drivers: the new man was as bad-tempered, rude and surly as the first had been friendly and polite. It seemed as though he were deliberately seeking out the worst patches of road: the bumps became really frightening and more and more frequent. The arrangements we had made in the coach brought about so much confusion that they were soon a dead letter. Sleep was out of the question and conversation languished in the gloom. However, we tried to keep our spirits up and bursts of laughter were heard now and then when the lurches threw us into each other's arms. But we could not always laugh, and gaiety was quickly extinguished when torrents of rain, penetrating every cranny of our jerry-built box, began to make life even more insupportable. It grew colder still as hail and snow succeeded the rain: we were approaching the mountains and the temperature proclaimed the fact.

At last, after four hours of torment, the driver stopped at Tarcutta to change horses. It was about eleven o'clock. The passengers got out to take a cup of tea or swallow a glass of brandy, each according to his taste and capacity. As for me, I was so shrivelled with cold that I stayed curled up in my corner, as did Madame de X.

The horses were un-harnessed and we thought we were going to have a few minutes' rest, but the driver ordered us out as we had to change coaches. Then followed the tedious business of transferring infinite loads of baggage, floundering back and forth between the two vehicles in mud that reached up to our thighs! Speaking in English to Madame X, who understood nothing but Portuguese, the driver asked her to get out. The unhappy lady refused to budge, but she was finally made to understand that we had to change coaches. No sooner had she stepped into the muck, than the wretched driver realized that the new vehicle was too small. We had to carry all the luggage back again and resume our original places. We lost all patience! It was impossible to get our sodden feet warm again and it was only with the greatest reluctance that we were persuaded to re-enter our prison.

In a few minutes the fresh horses were harnessed and we returned to the inn where our fellow passengers were waiting, refreshed and in a better state to continue the journey. They resumed their old places in the coach, whose interior was lit up by a candle-end the young man had been enterprising enough to procure. We packed ourselves into position, wrapped ourselves up and, in short, arranged everything as comfortably as possible. The drunkard drew out of his huge overcoat pocket an ill-defined shape which, on examination, proved to be a bottle of *wisky* (brandy made from grain), upon which he bestowed a brotherly kiss. We each pulled our travelling-hats down over our eyes and the young surveyor blotted out the picturesque scene by extinguishing the candle.

At last! we were off. What a lurching start! Everyone tried in vain to shut his eyes and silence reigned in the gloom. It was broken now and then by the mumbling of the drunkard, who thought he was on a ship at sea and called out at every bump:

'Come on then, roll on, old tub!'

Outside the wind howled dismally. The hail had stopped, but rain streamed in everywhere through the gaps in our raw-hide curtains and the cold grew more and more biting. In the end we got used to this state of affairs and consoled ourselves by thinking that tomorrow morning at Gundagai we would be able to sleep off the exhaustion caused by this stage of our journey.

Suddenly, however, the infernal machine stopped!

The driver, cursing and swearing, appealed to the passengers to get out and help him mend the harness. Understandably, no-one budged.

'Shake it up in there,' he bellowed, 'or do you want to stay here till tomorrow?'

At last the drunk got out to give him a hand, but he was too intoxicated to understand what was wanted. The driver again demanded help and the young surveyor decided to brave the storm. In about five minutes these gentlemen resumed their places. They were soaked – and frozen to the marrow: which seemed to have quietened down the drunkard a little. The candle was lit and the sot immediately improved the situation by returning to his inner man the warmth lost during the five minutes out in the rain. He saluted his spouse even more lovingly than on the earlier occasion when we had changed stages at Tarcutta. I could not help noticing that the contents of the said help-meet had clearly diminished: apparently darkness favoured their mutual embraces.

We set off again, only to stop in another ten minutes. Another breakdown. This time the drunk swore that nothing would make him get out. The driver abused everybody, but no-one inside the coach stirred a finger. In the end he repaired the harness by himself and we started again after another quarter of an hour.

After this we were hoping to have peace till Gundagai and, as no other passengers had reserved seats for the next stage, everything led us to think we had a good chance, at least, of not having our sufferings increased. Moreover, as we were approaching a more thickly-populated mining district, the road began to improve. The jolting seemed to become less frequent and less severe. True, we wallowed through holes full of water from time to time, but things were not too bad. It was three o'clock in the morning and exhaustion, piled upon wretchedness, had begun to close everyone's eyes, when the coach stopped again: an enormous Irish nurse, with a child suspended from her neck, appeared at the door. It was raining cats and dogs, and the driver had no time to waste.

'Move over;' he ordered us, 'this coach is built to carry eight passengers.'

Imagine our despair in the face of this invasion. But alas! we had to accommodate it and, although there were already six of us where there was room for only four, by reducing ourselves to our lowest common denominator we managed to re-arrange ourselves again.

Merciful Christ! What a squeeze! It was Pelion piled upon Ossa and the nurse on top of the lot.

The drunk bellowed with pain when someone stood on his corns and consoled himself with a last application to his beloved bottle. The child screamed, the nurse gasped, the driver swore: it was an indescribable cacophony. To compound our misery, the swaying and bumping redoubled as the road was unformed at this point. Luckily we were so tightly crammed together that we could hardly feel the lurches.

After four hours in this painful condition, we rolled at last onto the bridge at Gundagai and crossed the Murrumbidgee, the great tributary of the Murray. This bridge is nearly a mile long and the river steamers, coming to load inland wool for Echuca, sail up-river as far as its arches.

It was daybreak. I woke after being asleep for scarcely two hours. I scanned my fellow travellers' faces, but I could not see the Count. At length I perceived a contused arm in the corner of a seat and, on closer examination, realized that the said arm belonged to a body, which body was completely overwhelmed by another enormous torso belonging to the fat Irish nurse. I realized then that our additional complement of passengers had not affected me too directly. The worthy female had installed herself quite comfortably on her neighbours' knees, and the drunk had slipped gradually under the seat where he lay in a profound slumber.

At last we had arrived. It was seven o'clock in the morning and the coach stopped in front of the Royal Hotel in the middle of the little township of Gundagai.

These twenty-one hours on the road had certainly put us through the mill.

Monsieur de Castelnau, instructed by the experience, devoutly swore never again to set foot in the conveyances which carry Her Britannic Majesty's mail across her glorious Australian realm. He regretted, now, that he had not closed with the Albury publican's offer; and he resolved on the spot to stay two or three days at Gundagai, and then to cover in a private conveyance the eighty miles that still separated us from the terminus of the New South Wales railway line.

After a day of fatigue and a night of insomnia, the best thing to do was to go to bed. We did so immediately while the hotel's Chinese cook prepared an excellent dinner. I must say here that we were very agreeably surprised to find, in this little town of 2,000 inhabitants, a hotel so thoroughly well run by a proprietor so personable as Mr Fry. Nowhere on our whole journey, in the greatest cities or in the worst holes, were we made more comfortable. It is true to say that no other country on earth offers more of everything needed to make a good meal, or offers it more cheaply, than Australia; but there is no other country either where the cuisine is so elementary, not to say abominable.

At a *sixpenny* (twelve sous) *restaurant*, or at the Royal Hotel in Sydney or Melbourne, you will be faced with exactly the same dishes. Everywhere the menus are identical and, what is worse, they never change throughout the three hundred and sixty five days of the year. Invariably beef, mutton and poultry, boiled and roasted, roasted and boiled; the everlasting dish of potatoes and sometimes some soggy boiled vegetables: the meal ends with a kind of hash, an incredible concoction rejoicing in the title of *pudding*. At the *Royal Hotel* you are served from silver platters, and you pay five francs for a repast you would have been able to get for sixpence with an iron fork. That is the only difference.

However, the yellow cook at Fry's hotel in Gundagai treated us wonderfully.

After dinner, in spite of the mud, I went out to look around the town. It nestles on a hill above the right bank of the Murrumbidgee, and at its feet are spread fertile alluvial plains, often covered by the river in times of flood. Formerly the town stood at a little distance from the river on the plain itself, but it was destroyed by a shocking catastrophe in June 1852. In one of those sudden floods that make the Murrumbidgee so dangerous, most of the houses were engulfed and swept away and nearly a hundred people lost their lives. Since then Gundagai has been re-built on higher land above flood level, and some of its public buildings would not disgrace a sub-prefecture in France. The branch offices of several city banks are housed in really monumental style; the churches of several different religions are represented, and the hospital occupies a fine, well laid-out building.

In the middle of a rich district where gold and other metals are mined, and where agricultural development extends further day by day, this township is destined to become an important centre.

I extended my stroll through the town to the bridge which, with its approaches, cost nearly a million francs.

A bridge worth a million francs, a hundred leagues inland,

in a country that was unknown scarcely half a century ago! One wonders if one is dreaming! In the face of such achievements it is impossible not to admire the practical genius of our cross-Channel neighbours who know how to make such good use of their capital.

During the night we had passed an important mining centre, Adelong, about twenty-five miles from Gundagai in the middle of a very rich goldfield. There too may be seen concrete evidence of the practical bent of the colonial governments. For some years alluvial gold-digging had attracted a considerable population to Adelong and there had been, at one point, what Australians call a *rush* (from the English verb, *to rush*). At that time the floating population of the colony moved headlong towards this supposedly very rich field. But when the alluvial gold on the surface was exhausted, the easy work of washing 'pay dirt' perforce gave way to hard labour with the pick. The precious metal had to be gouged out of the quartz reefs in which it was locked. This type of mining demanded considerable capital and more exacting labour: sometimes the reefs had to be followed to a great depth. When this stage was reached, most of the miners shifted camp to *rush* anew to some other part of the country where alluvial gold had been discovered, only to repeat the same process there. This phenomenon still repeats itself frequently, for the soil of Australia holds great quantities of the precious metal. Adelong was following fatalistically the general pattern.

But since some of its quartz reefs were very rich, it would have been absurd to abandon them for lack of capital. The government therefore offered a reward of 25,000 francs to the first company to strike a payable reef at a depth of not less than 800 feet. This inducement had the desired effect: attracted by the bait, the companies formed in the early days of the field made new appeals to their shareholders and continued the work they had been on the point of suspending. One of them discovered a reef at 1,000 feet and claimed the reward, which served to pay a dividend. Since then several other mines have found the gold-bearing reefs they were seeking and are continuing to work at a profit. Farmers have just settled round these mining centres, and the countryside is acquiring from day to day a less wild appearance. When the mines have been worked out, Adelong

47

and Gundagai will become large agricultural centres where the plough has replaced the miner's pick.

Without such governmental forethought, Adelong would have been abandoned and this rich district would have become once again a sheep-walk for the flocks of a few squatters. Instead of the six or eight thousand people it supports to-day, it would have held perhaps a hundred thousand sheep. The squatters would certainly have gained but the colony would have lost. Indeed if each sheep in Australia represents a commercial value of six shillings or seven francs fifty centimes a year, that of an able-bodied man may be reckoned at £200 sterling a year, or about 5,000 francs. If we put the adult male population of the district at 2,500 it can be calculated that, with sheep the value of annual production would be 7,500,000 francs, and with men 12,500,000 francs. On the other hand the first colonists in the area attracted others who helped to swell the number of producers and the quantity of goods turned out.

It is easy to understand that only a local government, in close touch with the needs of the colony and administered by men chosen from among its intellectual élite, could make such offers to industry. Government must be on the spot, first to weigh the competing claims of this or that part of the territory, but even more to encourage at the right moment the development of the country's resources by private enterprise.

Perhaps this is one of the reasons why our overseas colonies, compared with those of Great Britain, make so little progress. First, they generally have for governors ex-naval or military officers who have not always been distinguished in their former service for administrative competence. These gentlemen arrive brimful of good intentions and determined to do all in their power for the good of the colony they have to govern. But they are quickly forced to learn the difference between a military administration, where discipline over-rides all contentions, and a civil one where opposing interest groups jockey for position and influence. They have thus to serve, as it were, an apprenticeship in the art of government, for if they behaved as they have been accustomed to do on their quarter-decks or at the head of their regiments, they would antagonize all the different interest groups to no useful purpose. A year or two passes before they can understand the country and its problems, and by the time they are beginning to give really worthwhile service to the colony they are governing, their term of office expires and they are recalled to France.

It is the same with subordinate officials in our colonial administration. Strangers to the colony and its needs, mere birds of passage, they stay at most for three years and necessarily have no other ambition than to get home to France as soon as possible.

Moreover, no public works can be begun until the plans and specifications have been sent to France where they may remain for months, often for years, before being approved by the ministry.

And yet people are surprised that our colonies don't flourish, and complain that they cost us more than they are worth!

Chapter Five

After a day's rest at Gundagai, the proprietor of our hotel put at our disposal a vehicle to carry us on as far as the little township of Yass. The vehicle was no other than one of the regular mail-coaches, but it was reserved for the trip for our sole use. We expected to need it for only a day as it was only an eight hours' run to our destination and a made road covered almost the whole distance between the two towns.

The weather was fine, and the country through which we were passing looked absolutely splendid. The road wound along the mountain-side and in the many valleys and gorges spread out below us we gazed at huge gum trees, their trunks as smooth and straight as the masts of a ship, which must have reached a height of more than a hundred feet. The frost of the past few days had touched their slender leaves with silver, and the golden morning sunlight shone on the peaks of the mountains, which our four horses were climbing at a smart trot.

Soon we reached the highest point on the road and began to descend on the other side. The view spread out before our eyes was magnificent. Mountains stretched away as far as the eye could reach, and in the bed of the valley below us the Murrum-bidgee carved its winding course through the fertile alluvial soil it had built up over the centuries. We could have fancied we were in Europe when a turn in the road revealed the tip of a steeple and, soon afterwards, a white-walled church surrounded by a few houses. It was the little village of Jugiong* nestling at the foot of the mountains.

We stopped there for lunch and then continued our journey, following the course of the river. Then we traversed some rich,

---

* A printer's error in the original – 'Jugions'.

thickly-wooded country and at about five o'clock in the evening our carriage rolled under the arches of the iron bridge that crosses the Yass River. A few minutes later we alighted at the Commercial Hotel.

It was a Saturday; it was cold, and the main room in the hotel was full of more or less sober people making an infernal din. The sounds of an untuned piano, accompanied by a bad violin and an accordion played in a different key, penetrated the hotel. Evidently there was a dance in some nearby hall. Unluckily I had caught a feverish cold the night before and, in spite of my wish to go and make a study of Australian manners, I was constrained soon after dinner – which was very bad – to taste instead the pleasures of sleep.

But there was such a shocking racket in the adjacent room that it was impossible to get any sleep, and I wished to the devil these unlucky drinkers whose quarrels troubled my rest throughout the night.

If there is a weakness firmly entrenched in Australian customs, if there is a vice from which the whole Anglo-Saxon race so admirable in other respects, suffers, it is the vice of, drunkenness.

In Australia it is possible to find a reason, in the strict sense, for this unhappy state of things. The nature of life on stations in the interior tends to encourage it. It is not unusual, for example, for a man to take a job on a station where he will stay for a whole year or two. During that period it is much if he should enjoy, even at long intervals, the company of his fellows. For the greater part of the time he must ride the plains, making sure that the mobs of sheep and cattle in his care are not getting mixed, that none of them are missing and that the fences of the *paddocks* are kept in good repair. In this way he will pass his days among the sheep and his nights under the stars, wrapped in a blanket, his saddle for a pillow, while his hobbled horse grazes peacefully nearby. Days and whole weeks will slip by thus before he returns to the head-station, even then only for a short visit, before leaving again to resume his solitary life.

After that it is scarcely surprising if these men, with the wages for a year or two's work freshly in their pockets, spend a few days in Sydney or Melbourne in drunkenness – *on the spree* – until they have only enough money left to return whence they came. What is really surprising is that this life of absolute solitude does not drive them mad. On the contrary, once accustomed to this life in which they enjoy limitless freedom, it is rarely that they will submit to a city existence. It seems as though society oppresses them, as though the air they breathe in town is heavy. They are irked by the idea of having to dress like everyone else, of having to imprison their neck in a stiff collar. If only they could still walk the streets of Melbourne, as they did twenty years ago, in their picturesque bush clothes: flannel shirt, riding-breeches, soft Wellington boots, a great broad brimmed felt hat on the head and a coloured handkerchief carelessly knotted around the neck! But no, the usages of civilized society oppose that. 'To the devil with towns and civilization!' they cry, quickly taking the road back to the *bush*, as soon as there is nothing with which to continue the *spree* which drew them to the big city.

Few, very few Frenchmen would be able to stand this solitary life in which a man spends half his existence alone with his sheep and his thoughts: it would drive them mad. The Germans themselves, who are met with all over Australia, rarely undertake it. Generally it is left to the English and especially the taciturn Scots. The Germans are usually farmers supplying, with the Irish, a large contingent to the ranks of the *free selectors*. They succeed, as a rule, better than the Celts, being more patient and sober and not easily cast down by reverses of fortune, however drastic.

I woke next morning almost in delirium, in the grip of a severe fever, and went outside to see if fresh air would do me any good. It was just like winter in France. There had been a severe frost during the night, and between the thin sheet of ice on the ground and my fever it was all I could do to keep on my feet. Then large flakes of snow began to fall. So I went hobbling along to the river. From there I looked back to the town, shrouded in a blanket of snow, and saw below me a river steamer at anchor. In place of screw or side-wheels, it was propelled by a single enormous paddle wheel at the stern. I learnt later that the flat-bottomed river-steamers in Australia are nearly always built in this way.*

* La Meslée might possibly have seen a river steamer at Albury or Gundagai and confused the towns in his memory. River steamers never reached Yass, and most, in fact, had paddle wheels at the sides.

We reached Gunning in the evening. As travelling on Sunday is against the law, there was no train for Sydney and we were forced to spend a night in this place.

At ten o'clock next morning, after having packed all our luggage once more, we found ourselves comfortably installed in a first-class carriage and bowling along towards Sydney. The country we passed through was much more broken, picturesque and rich-looking than that bordering the line from Melbourne to Wodonga. On the other hand the New South Wales railway carriages seemed to me less well made than the Victorian ones, for the cold penetrated the compartment despite all we could do. Perhaps it was just the effect of the feverish cold which was still with me. The line passed through Goulburn, one of the most important and prosperous towns in New South Wales and the centre of one of the richest pastoral districts in the colony.

To-day, however, the agriculturist is beginning to displace the big grazier. As the population grows these latter are forced further inland, giving way to the *free selectors* who encroach gradually on their domains. Hence the constant struggle between the opposing interests of the *squatter* and the *selector*. The first, established on his land as lessee from the government, must make way for the second to whom the same government grants freehold property in the soil. The squatters have no recourse against their enemies, who usually select the richest parts of their *runs*, other than to evade the law or to buy for themselves the land which they have previously leased. But government policy is not really hostile to the squatters, who still lease immense areas of land at a very low rent, though it does aim at establishing on the soil of the colony an influential class of small landed proprietors. Of necessity this class increases all the time and to-day the plough cultivates plains which, until a few years ago, only pastured the numberless flocks of the big graziers. These move off to found new stations, far beyond the reach of their enemies, for whom it is vital to remain within reach of markets for their products.

Everywhere in the Australian colonies the same phenomenon is apparent: the history of the world is being repeated there, on a small scale and in very short epochs. First comes the squatter, a true nomad who plunges into the wilderness to people it with his myriad flocks; in his tracks follows the miner in search of the treasures locked in the soil, and finally behind him comes the farmer to replace them both. Villages spring up, then towns, and all the superstructure of modern society arises where a few years ago there was nothing but a wilderness, traversed by a race of primitive beings on whom the breath of civilization seems to fall as a fatal plague. In fact the aborigines have almost completely disappeared in the province of Victoria. There are still a few hundred in New South Wales, and in the other colonies they have been driven back by civilization into remote retreats. Their frenzied adoption of our vices is what decimates them so rapidly. Spirits have killed more of them than warfare for, except in Queensland and northern Australia, they are very inoffensive; and since they do not attack the whites they are not exposed to reprisals. The situation is different in Queensland and in the vicinity of goldfields in the northern areas: there the natives are still to be feared. They seldom attack Europeans, but seem to nourish a peculiar hatred for the yellow inhabitants of the Celestial Empire who are inundating the *placers** of this part of Australia. They are cannibals, and more than one fat *celestial* has participated in their feasts in the form of a roast. But these savages, like their southern brothers, will undergo the fate which seems to be reserved for the unproductive races of the earth: they will wither, fade and disappear. In the whole course of our journey of more than two hundred leagues, we saw not a single representative of the race which wandered freely over the whole country scarcely half a century ago.

Goulburn, through which we were passing at this moment, is today the seat of two bishoprics, one protestant and the other catholic. These two religions have most adherents in the Australian colonies generally, although there are people of every religion and sect from disciples of Confucius to the worshippers of Brahma. All these faiths exist side by side without the country suffering in any way, and the principle of the separation of Church and State is maintained with the greatest rigour. It is understandable that this should be the situation in a country which harbours an infinite number of different religions and sects. If one of them were favoured by the State, it would be

---

* La Meslée has confused American with Australian vernacular terminology here. On American goldfields *placer* meant a deposit of gold-bearing sand or gravel in the bed of a stream.

necessary, in strict justice, to do as much and in the same proportion for each of the others. However, in the midst of this
liberty there still persists from the past some puritan customs,
enforced by law in England, which all the sects in Australia
must observe. In particular everybody is obliged to observe
the sanctity of Sunday, as they say in England. On this day the
streets are deserted and towns seem dead. In the afternoon
the parks fill up with people from far and near, and extempore
evangelists harangue great or small circles of listeners on the
burning questions that agitate the religious world. In the shade
of a great fig-tree one fanatic denounces Catholicism, hurling
at its pulpit curses from the Apocalypse. A little farther on a
puritan damns to eternal flames everyone whose beliefs differ
from his own, whilst another species of visionary consigns the
puritan to the Devil, along with all Catholics and free-thinkers.
Sometimes politics are mixed with religion. The Irish, who are
generally Catholic and of a very lively temperament, are in-
furiated by the insults lavished upon their religion and, if the
police did not exert their authority, they would willingly des-
patch to another world the heretics who allow themselves to
mock their beliefs.

Let us return to our journey which, indeed, was nearing its
end for the locomotive was speeding across the countryside.
Goulburn was far behind and we stopped for some minutes at
the Mittagong station for dinner. Monsieur de Castelnau, my
young pupil and I got out and entered the refreshment room
where, following the universal custom of such establishments
everywhere in the world, we were served with such scorching
hot broth that we had the greatest difficulty in swallowing it.
Whilst we were attacking a fowl, we hit on the idea of tasting
the wine of the country.

'Waiter! a bottle of Albury wine.'

'Sir, we are not licensed to sell any kind of alcoholic drink
whatever.'

'What!' cried Monsieur de Castelnau, 'what can people drink
here then, when they are thirsty?'

'We have coffee, tea, lemonade, Seltzer water, . . .'

'That stuff! Do you want to make yourselves a laughing-stock
to the whole world?'

'No, sir, it is the same in every railway refreshment room in

New South Wales: they are all run on strict temperance principles. It's a government rule.'

'But, heavens, if it is warm, people can't drink coffee or boiling hot tea. That would not be very refreshing?'

'There is lemonade, *gingerbeer*, . . .'

'Never mind! how much is it? . . .'

And thereupon we ran to take our seats as the bell warned us that the train was starting again for Sydney.

Ruminating on this curious custom, which cannot fail to astonish foreigners, we passed through a pleasant-looking countryside and gradually neared the end of our journey. Having climbed to the highest point on the line in the mountains between Goulburn and Sydney, we descended rapidly onto the plain. The country-side was covered with farms, meadows and well cultivated fields that reminded us of Europe. The vegetation in this part of the country is quite different, moreover, from that on the other side of the range. The trees are less lofty, greener and more luxuriant.

It was dark when we reached Redfern station. This is the starting-point of the main New South Wales railway-lines. The station is situated on the edge of the city in the suburb that bears its name. The two main thoroughfares of Sydney, George and Pitt streets, end in a square one side of which is occupied by the station. Opposite stands a large building constructed during the rule of Monsieur Macquarie, one of the most celebrated governors of the colony. To-day it is devoted to public charity and bears the name of the *Benevolent Asylum*. George Street continues to the right towards the suburbs of Forest Lodge and The Glebe, where it takes the name of Paramatta Road. Once famous for its convicts, Paramatta is now celebrated for its oranges. Times have changed. To the left a wide street separates the station yard from the Benevolent Asylum, skirts the old city cemetery and connects the suburbs of Redfern, Strawberry Hills and Surry Hills with George Street, Sydney's *Rue de Rivoli*.

Behind the station, surmounted by two towers, stands a large building which, from a distance, looks like some public edifice. Strangers often take it to be the station itself, but it is the *Exhibition Building*, constructed to the plan of one of our compatriots, Monsieur Jules Joubert, later Secretary to the commission of the colonial government at the 1878 Paris Universal Exposition. This building, which is used once a year for an exhibition of local products, is situated on the left of the Railway Station in the middle of large public gardens, Alfred Park, frequented especially on Sundays by the local residents. In the winter the city lets this huge hall for great public balls, such as that given to raise funds by the committee of the Catholic St Vincent's Hospital. In these balls Sydney people of every class and religion take part. In the confusion of one of those extraordinary waltzes of which the Australians have the secret, the great lady jostles her cook whose *sweetheart* has escorted her to the ball for the modest sum of thirty francs.

A Melbourne lady told me that once, when she needed a chambermaid, she had put an advertisement in the *Melbourne Argus*. There were many applicants for the job. She was offering quite high wages, fifteen shillings (18 francs 75) a week. One girl asked if she could have every evening off from eight o'clock onwards: another if she could have an hour off every morning for her *piano lessons*. But best of all was a beautiful, tall girl of nineteen or twenty, dressed in the height of fashion, who conducted with her the following conversation:

'What wages are you offering?'

'Fifteen shillings a week.'

'That would suit me, but madam will let me have my evenings free after eight o'clock?'

Madame grimaced but the girl pleased her and, as there were other servants in the house, she gave her one evening off in three and the whole of Sunday afternoon and night.

'Does Madam expect me to answer the front door-bell?'

'Of course. Who else would you expect to do it?'

'Oh well then, madam, I am very put out. The position suits me, the wages are not bad, but I really could not think of answering the front door-bell. My *sweetheart* is a doctor, and if he should see me he would be too ashamed to want to marry me!'

'What is more,' this lady added, 'she has since married her doctor. I saw her not long ago, superbly dressed, riding in a carriage-and-pair in Bourke Street, and she actually had the impertinence to bow to me.'

Chapter Six

*The city and suburbs of Sydney – Port Jackson harbour – A walk to the
Heads – Botany Bay and La Pérouse – The Paramatta* River – Mr Pie's
orange orchard*

There is quite a difference between Melbourne and Sydney. The
first is a city built wholly in the one style, as though created at
a stroke by the wand of a magician: the second, already nearly
a hundred years in age, retains some old fashioned houses and
streets. At Melbourne man found a flat, monotonous plain
devoid of vegetation, and replaced it with city streets a mile
long and a hundred feet wide, surrounded by suburbs bowered
in greenery of his own creation. At Sydney he found a magnificent site on a uniquely beautiful harbour, and he has been content, like the birds, to nest in the bosom of this marvellous
natural phenomenon. These are the essential differences between
these two rival cities which dispute the honour of being the
capital of Australia.

Sydney streets are longer, but narrower and more sinuous,
than those of the capital of Victoria. It is clear that the town has
grown gradually and that later generations have had to accommodate themselves to the idiosyncrasies of the first inhabitants
who had their own taste in building. George Street is the great
business thoroughfare, the *rue d'Ouvridor*, of this city which
disputes with Rio-Janeiro possession of the most beautiful
harbour in the world. This street was a track when Sydney was
no more than a hamlet, straggling along the banks of one of the
many creeks that run into the harbour of Port Jackson. Many
of its citizens still remember the time when *teamsters* used to
pull up in the middle of George Street to load their cumbersome
drays, pulled by teams of six or eight bullocks which had hauled

---

* Contrary to more recent practice, La Meslée uniformly spells Parramatta
with one 'r'.

station products from the bush. Times have changed today. The shrill whistle of the locomotive has replaced the crack of the *stockwhip* [1] and to find a typical *bushman* one must go far out into the station country.

Melbourne passed from infancy to adulthood without experiencing adolescence. The little village on the banks of the Yarra-Yarra went to sleep one evening: during the night mountains of gold sprang from the bosom of the earth, and next day the fishing village of a few hundred souls woke up as a town. In the space of a few years, a few weeks I should say, it was transformed into a city whose population increased every hour. Its rival's story was very different.

Situated at the mouth of a creek in one of the innumerable little coves that open off the wonderful Port Jackson harbour, Sydney grew only steadily. George Street, at first a track into the bush, little by little took on the appearance and name of a street. Around this central artery grew an increasing network of less important roads. As the colony's resources were developed, and as free immigration brought to it an increasing number of energetic workers, the streets lengthened and suburbs began to form around the city. The discovery of gold, when it was already a considerable town, at first decreased but soon increased its population, slowly but steadily.

But Sydney's size and wealth do not spring essentially from the gold discoveries. Without gold it would have become what it is today, a little more slowly perhaps but none the less surely; for its whole development flowed naturally from the immense resources of its hinterland, for which it will always remain the chief port.

But these differences, which strike the visitor after only a few weeks' stay in the two towns, are not the only ones. The two colonies and their inhabitants also exhibit their own characteristics. In the capital of Victoria the twenty years of gold-fever have been succeeded by a mania for speculation, and commercial life is plagued by a perpetual series of booms and slumps. Cramped by the narrow confines of their colony, the Victorians have invaded neighbouring provinces and are to be found wherever some new industry is being established. Thus

---

[1] A very short-handled whip, twenty feet in length, used by bushmen to control bullock teams or in droving cattle.

Victorians, for the most part, have been the first to found new stations beyond the Darling and even in the far west of Queensland. They too, or rather their capital, have, so to speak, created the sugar industry in this northern colony, where their enterprise has been outstandingly successful.

In Sydney, by contrast, there are generally more old-established fortunes than in Melbourne: credit plays a less important role and the people are much less given to gambling on the stock exchange. For many years their Victorian neighbours have bestowed upon Sydney the rather ungracious nickname of *Sleepy Hollow*. It hardly merits the title today, for in the past five or six years it has gone ahead enormously. Its population now is almost equal to that of its rival, which for many years held the first place among all Australian cities. Within ten years Sydney will have passed Melbourne, for the hinterland which sustains it is very much greater, in both extent and natural resources, than Victoria's. Moreover, shrewd government policy is very rapidly extending the rail system between Sydney and the rest of the colony. The trade of the great Riverina district, between the Darling and the Murray, for long a goose laying golden eggs for Melbourne merchants, is going more and more to their rivals as Sydney forges ahead. By the time of the next census in 1891, it will have regained its old position of leadership among Australian cities. This position was really pre-ordained by its situation on the most wonderful natural harbour in the world, where whole navies could anchor in perfect safety.

In itself, Sydney is far from being what most people would call a beautiful city. Except for the government offices, the banks, the post-office, the town hall and the Anglican St Andrew's cathedral in the central part of the city, the buildings are quite unimpressive. There are still relics of comparative antiquity which, I hasten to add, tend to disappear day by day. The city fathers of the Australian metropolis never weary of condemning these reminders of a past, more remote in appearance than it is in fact. The monuments of early colonial times are continually being demolished to make room for more tasteful edifices attuned to modern needs. The rather commonplace inner suburbs cannot compare with those of Melbourne for regularity and neatness of plan: but on the other hand the exclusive suburbs of Pott's Point and Woollahra* are absolutely ravishing. Stylish villas, equipped with every comfort wealth can command, are dotted about among a confused mass of greenery. Most of them have views of some reach of the harbour, and nature's most attractive landscapes serve as backdrops for these elegant homes, tastefully surrounded by lawns and gardens where flowers of every clime flourish in the brilliant sunlight.

On the other side of the harbour, which is no more than a kilometre wide at this point, stands the heavily populated suburb of St Leonards.* It is a sort of Sydney Brooklyn. The whole cluster of suburbs to the north of the harbour is known collectively as the North Shore. They have become so populous in the last few years that there is serious talk about connecting them with the city by a suspension bridge, high enough to allow ships with even the loftiest masts to pass beneath it. This gigantic project, which will cost ten or twelve million francs, will certainly be carried out in future years, for the North Shore is continually becoming more important.

In a position very like that of St Leonards, but further up the harbour, there is another suburb called Balmain whose population has doubled in the last ten years.

The railway line from Redfern also connects many suburbs, some of them very fashionable ones, with the city. Ashfield, Burwood† and Homebush shelter Sydney's social élite, while Newtown,† Petersham and Macdonaldtown† are almost exclusively working class areas.

Other suburbs, built and inhabited by people in easy circumstances, stand on the coastal slopes overlooking the Pacific Ocean, and are connected with the city by steam-trams: Randwick, Waverley, Bondi and Coogee Bay. The last two are crowded on Saturdays and Sundays by thousands of trippers who come to breathe the fresh ocean breezes.

Of all cities on earth Sydney is perhaps the best provided with gardens, parks and other means of public recreation. They are to be found everywhere and most of them are quite large. Pride of place goes to the Botanical Gardens, one of the most beautiful in existence, were trees and plants of temperate climates

* Printers' errors in the original – 'Woolkara' and 'St Leonard'.
† More mistakes, perhaps by the Parisian compositor: in the original – 'Bouwords', 'Neutoron', and 'Macdonnaldtoron'.

grow side by side with those of the tropics. These gardens occupy the slopes of an almost perfectly semi-circular bay, above which stands Government House. The buildings for the Universal Exhibition of 1879 were constructed along one side of the gardens. Great ships, carrying merchandise to Australia from the four corners of the world, lie alongside the wharves in an adjoining cove. Here the five and six thousand ton steamers of the *Orient Line* and the *L. and P. Company*** unload cargo and passengers, returning to Britain loaded with bales of wool and other colonial produce.

From Circular Quay an unbroken line of wharves and piers extends for more than a league round the foreshores to the head of Darling Harbour at Pyrmont Bridge, which connects that suburb and Balmain with the city. It is around these wharves and port facilities that old Sydney displays its ancient buildings, some of which crash to the ground daily under the demolisher's hammer. One could easily lose oneself in the maze of narrow streets on Miller's Point, a part of the town which has preserved an altogether European air. It would be easy to imagine oneself in the slums of an English port. The area is full of sailors' taverns and wharf labourers' *boarding-houses*. Anyone who happens to be wandering in these lanes at sundown, when work is over for the day and the occupants have all returned to their houses, is quickly surrounded by children. They swarm out of every door, in all ages and shapes and sizes. They are usually only scantily clad, but their faces never betray the pinched and miserable expression of the London or Liverpool urchins. They look exuberantly healthy, and if their clothes are dirty and full of holes, it is due more to an excess of liberty than to poverty. In fact real poverty does not exist in Australia: no-one, except those who choose to be so, is truly wretched or truly poor. Every man willing to work can earn his eight or ten francs a day, and unless he is a drunkard or in the grip of some other vice, his life is easier and freer than it would be elsewhere. In a country where extremes of temperature are unknown, where it is never cold and where jobs are plentiful, whoever is willing to work need never be hungry.

There are some certainly, as there are everywhere, who hate work and devote themselves from an early age to every kind of

* Presumably a misprint for 'P. and O.'

debauchery. These help to swell the ranks of the *larrikins*, that plague of Australia's large cities. The *larrikin* is one of a species very difficult to describe, a soul-mate of the Parisian *voyou*, of the London *street arab* and of the *hoodlum** of the great cities of the United States. They come in all ages from childhood up to about thirty, and are sure to be in the thick of any trouble one encounters. Torrents of the scabrous language, with which they adorn their conversation, pour from their mouths along with the noisome smoke from their short-stemmed pipes. They never utter a word unaccompanied by an oath, and never address anyone without insulting him. They are practically always depraved, brutal, drunken liars, and often thieves.

These specimens usually hang about street-corner hotels and they almost invariably choose the evening to insult passers-by, accosting unaccompanied women or – what they regard as the acme of delight – kicking insensible and plundering some wretched Chinaman. This sort of thing goes on wherever there are not many policemen, and especially in the neighbourhood of parks and in the suburbs. In Sydney the evil is already great; but certain parts of Melbourne, Collingwood among others, are literally infested with this dirty breed. As corporal punishment has been abolished for some years past, the discipline of the lash, perhaps abused in earlier times, no longer acts as a deterrent. But the *larrikins*, for whom prison holds no great terrors, have become so arrogant that there is talk of re-introducing flogging.

The *larrikins* of Melbourne and Sydney are by no means the same sort of people as their equivalents in other countries. They are not poor, far from it. One should see them on Sundays, topped off with a soft felt hat with the brim pulled down over the face, dressed almost fashionably, and wearing a loud silk tie with the end floating free. They have an everlasting pipe in the mouth and, to judge from appearances, plenty of money in the pocket. They harass both city and suburbs, and unhappily their numbers are increasing. The weaker sex is also quite well represented in this tribe, and by all accounts the *larrikiness* is much worse than the male of the species. Even on Sunday evenings when the crowds are coming out of church services, Bourke Street in Melbourne and George Street in Sydney do

* A misprint in the original – '*troodlum*'.

not present a very edifying spectacle. The fine flower of the larrikin gangs disport themselves among the faithful, and one often witnesses scenes which would be amusing if they were not so out of place.

Apart from this element – which is to be found to some extent in all countries – the people of Australian cities are generally well disposed towards law and order. Anyone accustomed to the proliferation of town sergeants, guardians of the peace and police commissioners in our French cities, would think Australian police organization absolutely primitive. In Sydney it is much if now and then one catches sight of a single constable. Yet if the *larrikins* did not get up to mischief now and then, the police would have very little to do for there can scarcely be a more law-abiding people in the world than the Australians.

It would take at least several days to see Sydney and all its suburbs, for these latter are scattered about on both sides of the harbour right up to the entrance of the Paramatta River. Although containing only 230,000 inhabitants, Sydney covers a much greater area than Paris. People generally do not live in the city itself; they go there each day to work and return to their suburban homes in the evening. Contrary to the French practice of accommodating several families in a single multi-storey building the Australian, like the Englishman, lives in his own house in some suburb a little way out of the city. Even working people adopt this style of living and they quite often own their own homes – an achievement in which they are greatly assisted by the *building societies*. These institutions advance, at fairly high rates of interest, the funds to build a house on land actually owned by the worker himself. Re-payment is made over ten or twelve years in small weekly instalments, no greater than an ordinary rent would be. At the end of this period, during which he has paid back both the interest on the loan and the principal, the worker becomes the owner of his own house and garden with no more rent to pay to anyone. The building societies are very popular, especially with people settled permanently in the country, and so successful that in an average year they pay dividends of 12 or 15 per cent to their shareholders. It is obvious that this method of housing is quite expensive, but that disadvantage ought not to weigh too heavily against the gains, in hygiene and other spheres, it brings within everyone's reach.

Of all the middle-class suburbs the North Shore is now, perhaps, the most exclusive. The heights of St Leonards and Willoughby enjoy uniquely beautiful views and summer temperatures cooled by the sea breeze. But to see Sydney at its best, to admire at leisure the wonderful panorama of the harbour, one should take the road along its southern shore to the 'Heads' of Port Jackson. Dear reader, if ever chance places you on Australian shores and you would like to spend a day or two in the capital of New South Wales, do as we did and go to South Head.

No matter which way you turn, you are confronted with the most glorious views. Before you the great blue ocean rollers break into a seething mass of white foam at the foot of the cliffs. Farther off North and South Head stand like two advanceposts, guarding the entrance to that incomparable harbour whose waters are bounded by a labyrinth of verdant headlands, on which human beings have built their nests. Over there the water seems to be cut off by a great bluff, but it is merely diverted to twist around for many miles inland between banks of sandstone covered in evergreens. That is Middle Harbour and to its right, at the head of another deeply indented cove, stands Manly the future *Trouville* of Sydney. Manly is built between two beaches, one in North Harbour on the edge of the bay and the other, vastly more extensive, facing the ocean.

In the distance can be seen the sinuous northern shores of the harbour and, first of all, George's Head which juts out almost between North and South Heads. Two batteries were built there recently, one at the top of the bluff and one at water level, recessed into the rock itself. In addition to these batteries defending the harbour mouth, there are forts armed with cannon of heavier calibre on the end of the cliffs which enclose it on the south.

In the background of this picture stands the city of Sydney and the North Shore suburbs and, still further away, the waters of the harbour begin to mingle with those of the Paramatta River. The observatory, silhouetted against the skyline in the midst of a park, dominates the town and the tower of the Holtermann villa crowns the North Shore. Nothing could surpass the beauty of the whole panorama: the water seems to pink the shoreline like lacework. There are nothing but capes, peninsulas, cliffs and islets, surrounded by a dancing sheet of water, as placid as a lake, on which scurry a fleet of white-winged yachts, and some fast steamers plying constantly between the two sides of the harbour. Sydney is indeed *the Queen of the South*, the Australian city beautiful, destined to future greatness.

Having gazed our fill at the spectacle of Sydney and its harbour, we followed the road along the cliff-top right to the fortifications at South Head. At our feet the sea pounded furiously on the rocks and the roar of the breakers rose to our ears. A passer-by drew our attention to a part of the cliff-face which, twenty years before, had witnessed one of the most terrible disasters ever recorded in the annals of the sea.

The *Dunbar*, with a full complement of immigrants, reached Sydney after a voyage of more than three months. They had sighted land and everyone was celebrating the end of the journey. But, in the darkness of a misty night, a sudden storm broke on the coast and the *Dunbar*, mistaking the exact position of the harbour entrance, was hurled against the cliffs of South Head. In a few minutes all was over. Of the four hundred passengers in the ill-fated vessel, only one managed to save himself by clinging like a limpet to the rocks where a great wave had thrown him. After twelve hours in this terrible position, he was rescued next day with the aid of ropes, half dead from exhaustion and hunger.

Since then a second lighthouse has been built to mark the entrance to the harbour more clearly. Without this precaution, other ships might easily have shared the fate of the *Dunbar*, at this place where there is an apparent break in the ramparts of the cliff.

As to the fortifications, they seem well placed and soundly constructed. They are armed with cannon of the maximum calibre and range, and ought to be quite sufficient to repulse an enemy audacious enough to try to penetrate the harbour.

Sydney's natural attractions are augmented by sites of historic interest in which France has her share. If he has time, no Frenchman should fail to visit Botany Bay to see the resting-place of the ashes of some of the comrades of La Pérouse, the first navigator from our country to visit these shores. Father Le Receveur, a priest of the Dominican Order, is buried a few paces from the monument, erected later, to the memory of one of the greatest discoverers to honour the name of France. This was the last place touched at by the unfortunate La Pérouse, before he sailed away to perish on the reefs of Vanikoro. King Louis-Phillipe sent an expedition to erect here a memorial column, surrounded by a little iron-work fence, quite near the telegraphic cable-station which now connects the colony with New Zealand.

On holidays the entire population pours out of the city. Some go to Botany Bay; others go to 'picnic' at the many beauty spots in the harbour, which is covered with pleasure-boats and steamers packed with all classes of people. They set out after breakfast in the morning and return about six in the evening after a day in the open air. Quite a few are not so fresh and sprightly on the morrow, and have to rest for a few more days to recover from the fatigues of their holiday, perhaps because they had not enough wisdom to drink moderately. The *larrikin* element is particularly prominent on these occasions, and sometimes it creates disorders which the police cannot handle. But nothing can give the foreigner a better idea of the easy-going ways of all classes, than to land in Sydney in the middle of a public holiday. Omnibuses, ferries and trams overflow with people in holiday attire, all making their way to favourite resorts. There are no rags and no beggars: everyone has the means to dress decently and have his share of the fun. Well-being is universal. Orange-sellers reap a great harvest, and these days make the fortunes of the publicans at Manly Beach and Botany.

Since oranges have been mentioned, it would perhaps be a good idea to invite the reader to accompany us on a trip to Paramatta. We shall go by river and return by rail, seeing on our way most of Sydney's suburbs.

The steamer leaves from a wharf at the foot of King Street and, passing by Balmain, heads towards the mouth of the Paramatta. Wherever one looks the views are absolutely unparalleled: a series of enchanting vistas unfolds as the steamer sails on, right up into the narrower reaches of the river. The foreshores are covered with houses, with villages rising in the distance: the slopes have long been enriched with orange orchards and all kinds of fruit trees. The steamer ties up at the wharf about a mile from Paramatta. An omnibus connects the landing-place with the town, the road winding through properties where camellias flourish in every garden. We were at the height of the season and the views on both sides of the route were ravishing.

Paramatta recalls memories of the early days in New South Wales. The first governors lived here in a building at the entrance to a splendid park called the Domain, and the first efforts at farming were made in the neighbourhood of the town. Today it owes its importance to the district's agricultural wealth, and above all to the great trade in oranges which are exported to all parts of Australia and New Zealand. Mr Pie's orange orchard, situated a few miles from the town, is famous throughout the colony. We hired a carriage to the place and a gardener explained how the work was carried on. The orchard is very picturesquely situated in the basin of a ravine,'surrounded by steep rocks sheltering it from the strong winds that blow at certain seasons of the year. The gardener pointed out a dozen magnificent trees, growing in the very depth of the gully, which it seems are the finest orange trees in the country. As is usual in Australia, the farmhouse at the entrance to the property is surrounded by a verandah to protect it from the heat in summer. The season had just begun. Before leaving, we accepted the invitation to eat some oranges of our own picking. If ever, dear reader, you should taste this delicious fruit, ripe to perfection and just plucked by your own hand at Paramatta, and if ever you should savour its delicate flesh on the spot, you will know that oranges bought in the world's best markets are insipid by comparison.

4

5

4. The ruins of Jones' Hotel, Glenrowan, after the fight between the police and the Kelly gang
5. A squatter's station

6. The Eastern side of the Circular Quay, Sydney

Chapter Seven

Departure for Queensland – The Australian Navigation Company's Alexandra *– Moreton Bay and the mouth of the Brisbane River – The city of Brisbane – The Botanical Gardens – Ipswich – Toowoomba – It rains Counts – How small the world is – Return.*

Our time in Sydney passed quickly. The count de Castelnau was in a hurry to leave for the colony of Queensland and, despite his loathing for sea travel, he had decided to take ship for Brisbane. The port of Newcastle is only a few hours from Sydney, and if the railway thence to the north of New South Wales had been finished and connected with the Queensland system, he would perhaps have made the journey in this way, but there was still a gap of a hundred and fifty leagues. Having learnt from experience what an Australian *coach* journey means, the Count had conquered his antipathy for the sea, and our passages had been booked on board the *Alexandra* of the *Australian Navigation Company.* This firm carries mails, passengers and goods between the major Australian ports, from north to south and between all the colonies. Its headquarters are in Sydney and it runs a fleet of magnificent steamers, ranging from 600 to 1,500 tons, luxuriously fitted out and capable of the reasonable speed of eleven or twelve knots.

As far as the stronger sex was concerned, the company aboard the *Alexandra* was quite interesting, but I never found out whether there was a single woman in the ship. One of the passengers was a member of the Queensland parliament, a rich squatter who owned many huge sheep and cattle stations, and who 'was worth',[1] a complaisant neighbour told me, the enormous sum of £500,000 sterling (12,500,000 francs). This Australian Croesus had happened to be in Melbourne at the time of an

[1] In English a man possessed of a certain fortune is said to be 'worth so much money'.

agricultural show, and had bought there a couple of pure-bred bulls for 1,200 guineas. He had seen to their embarkation in Melbourne and was keeping an eye on them himself. Like the English and the Americans, Australians willingly pay the most exhorbitant prices for pure-bred stock whose *pedigree*[1] is authenticated. Here, where sheep and cattle form the basis of the national wealth, it is impossible to exaggerate the importance of improving the breeds.

Among the other passengers was a swashbuckling figure, six feet in height. He sported a superb but somewhat uncultivated beard, which gave him a rather barbarous air. What a fine brigand he would have made in some melodrama! He was, I heard, an ex-miner, who had made a huge fortune on the Gympie goldfield in the Australian bush. He too was a member of parliament for some other goldfield and, like our Monsieur Roche-fort,* he was in perpetual opposition to all governments. He offered to treat all on board to champagne, and he consumed a considerable quantity of it himself. He was accompanied by a furtive looking little sneak who never left his side for a moment, while absorbing an endless number of 'grogs' and other potions of the same sort. at his patron's expense. This individual even borrowed money from the politician now and then, in order to pay for a round of drinks himself.

The person who gave me this information about our fellow passengers was a tall, straightforward, intelligent young man of about twenty-eight. The son of a wealthy squatter, he was just on his way back from England where he had spent three years at the University of Oxford. He made a striking contrast with the other passengers. Well bred, well built and impeccably dressed, he belonged to a different world from the other people around us. I learnt later that his father had begun life in Australia as a shepherd on an up-country station. Helped by good luck, he had gradually accumulated a few hundred sheep. Then he had set out for the north and successfully established himself in the vast solitudes of the Warrego† district. Before plunging into the interior, he had married the cook on the station where he

---

[1] Genealogy.

* A prominent journalist and politician, exiled in New Caledonia for a time for his part in the Paris Commune of 1871. He escaped in an Australian ship and returned to political life in France.

† A misprint in the original – 'Wanego'.

had been employed as a shepherd, and this brave woman had agreed to share with him the manifold hazards of the wilderness. At that time, when the blacks had not yet disappeared, the district was something less than agreeable when it was not downright dangerous. But fortune favoured the bold, and the ex-shepherd became a rich squatter who dreamed of better things for his son. He sent the boy to *Brisbane Grammar School*[1] where, by using his natural gifts diligently, he won the main prizes, and finally a Queensland Government scholarship of £100 a year for three years for the most brilliant student in the colony to complete a course at the University of Oxford or Cambridge. He was now returning, laden with academic distinctions, to take his place among the intellectual élite of his country. He had been admitted to the bar, he told me, and was planning shortly to begin practice in the colonial capital.

On the morning of the third day out from Sydney, the *Alexandra* steamed into Brisbane River. The day was perfect: not a cloud in the sky, just hot enough to be pleasant and just enough breeze to give a delicious freshness to the air. Such weather exists only in a tropical winter and, with the natural beauty that surrounded us, it made one think spontaneously of an earthly paradise.

From its outlet into Moreton Bay right up to the capital, the Brisbane River flows through relatively low-lying country. The vegetation was quite different from that in the southern colonies. Mangrove trees grew in the water to some distance out from the banks, and everything proclaimed that we were arriving in a tropical country. Wherever the land had not been cleared, the trees were interlaced with an absolute tangle of liana creepers. Here and there rose some *free selector's* hut, always surrounded by banana trees whose huge leaves had been slashed by the wind. It was clear that these trees grew here only with some difficulty, the climate not being hot enough to suit them completely.

The river wound along through the rich alluvial flats in which it had dug its bed: not until its junction with Breakfast Creek did the first signs of rising ground appear. On a little knoll where the two streams joined stood a charming country house, built in the colonial style with wide verandahs on all four sides. Magnificent green lawns stretched right down to the water's

---

[1] The *lycée*.

edge and a pleasure boat was moored to a little stone pier. Two small children, a boy and a girl, gambolled about on the grass or let themselves tumble down it together to the foot of the hill. From here on to Brisbane the river's course became more tortuous: as it was only two hundred yards wide at the most, our experienced officer needed all his skill to pilot our 800 ton steamer safely to the Company's wharf, where we tied up at about eleven o'clock in the morning. A cab took us to the *Imperial Hotel* in George Street, where a good English-style dinner awaited us.

There are good reasons why Brisbane is by no means such a large and prosperous city as Melbourne or Sydney. From a commercial viewpoint, it is not very well situated. Standing on a bend in the river that bears its name, about thirty miles from the sea, it cannot be reached by large modern ships. The depth and breadth of the channel are not great enough to accommodate vessels of more than about twelve hundred tons. Consequently port charges are high, for sailing-ships must be towed up the river from Moreton Bay and big steamships have to unload their cargo at the river's mouth, whence it is carried to Brisbane by lighters.

In 1825,* when Sir Thomas Brisbane was Governor of New South Wales, Brisbane was founded as the headquarters of the Moreton Bay penal establishment. Until Queensland was separated from the mother colony and opened its doors to free immigration, Brisbane was scarcely anything more than a convict depot. Since then it has grown steadily as its immense hinterland has been opened up and developed.

Immediately behind the town rises a very fertile tableland called the Darling Downs. Today it produces millions of sheep, thousands of cattle, quantities of wheat and of all the other cereals and fruits that flourish in temperate climates. Brisbane's prosperity depends largely on the Downs, with which it is now connected by rail. This line, which penetrates more than a hundred leagues inland to the centre of the pastoral district of Maranoa, forks at Toowoomba on the highest part of the plateau, and ships to Brisbane all sorts of products from the huge area it serves.

At the present moment the city and suburbs contain a popu-

* Actually in 1824.

lation of about 35,000 people. As in Sydney and the other colonial cities, no-one lives in the business centre: the suburbs extend in all directions, along the riverside and over the surrounding hills and valleys.

For a good view of Brisbane, people climb to the summit of Spring Hill near the observatory. From this vantage-point there is a superb panorama. The town is spread out below on a bend of the river which snakes across the plain. At your feet lies the aristocratic suburb of Kangaroo Point, joined to the city by a *ferry*, which crosses the river at Petrie's Bight near the Government wharves. Farther away a large bridge connects the city with the important suburb of South Brisbane. To the right the line of the horizon is etched by the blue peaks of the great coastal range, and to the left the suburban houses of Farm Valley cover the plain. The elbow of the river is partly hidden by the trees in the Botanical Gardens and in the adjoining reserve where Government House stands. Nearby a great domed building dominates a park which is, in some sort, a part of the Gardens. That is the Parliament House of the independent colony of Queensland, independent not only of the neighbouring colonies, but equally of the metropolitan country itself, which is content merely to send out a Governor to whom Queensland pays the salary of a hundred and twenty-five thousand francs a year. Like her sisters, the colony is governed by two chambers. The first, the Legislative Assembly, is composed of members chosen by different electorates under a system of restricted suffrage.* The Legislative Council, on the other hand, is made up of members nominated for life by the Governor on the advice of the Executive Council.

Each colony has its own system of government. Some, like Victoria, have adopted universal suffrage; others have both houses of representatives elected only for a limited period. England has deemed it good to allow the Australian colonies the right to manage their own affairs. They allocate their own revenue as seems best to them, and when their revenues are insufficient, they may raise loans on the London money market in exactly the same way as any foreign power; but the imperial government never underwrites these loans.

* Marin La Meslée, writing of Australia in 1876, was out of date here. Queensland enacted adult male suffrage for all enrolled electors in 1872.

If a loan bill, for no matter what sum, is passed by the two chambers which make up the legislature of each colony, and approved by the Governor, the imperial government places no limit whatever on the market interest rates. But it is up to the colonial governments themselves to justify their borrowing at the bar of public opinion. These public loans are generally taken up at an interest rate of $4\frac{1}{2}$ or 5 per cent, but against an unusual type of security; for they are almost always guaranteed by the future value of the public works for which the money is being raised. Three quarters of the borrowed funds are devoted to building new railway lines. Additional security for the loans is provided by the vast areas of unoccupied government land whose value is constantly increased by new lines of communication. Thus these government loans are usually fully subscribed almost as soon as they have been floated.

Queensland, one of the richest Australian colonies, has by the same token the heaviest burden of public debt – amounting to £12,192,150 (304,803,750 francs). This is an enormous figure for a population of only 221,964 inhabitants, representing a debt of 1,373 francs and a few centimes per head. If the French national debt ever reached this rate, the total figure would be approximately a formidable fifty-one thousand million francs. Notwithstanding the great wealth and natural resources of our country, which are astonishing to foreigners, France would hardly be able to support the weight of such a burden. Unlike the colony of Queensland, she no longer has the disposal of hundreds of millions of acres of land which, at the price for which the Marquis de Rays* sold his holdings on the coast of New Guinea, would suffice to cover the debt of the colony ten times over.

At the moment there is talk of building a transcontinental railway line across Queensland to a recently discovered harbour named Point Parker, on the Gulf of Carpentaria. It is a fine project which has, moreover, a good chance of being realized.

Brisbane would not be the town to profit least from the

* Charles de Breil, Marquis de Rays, was a French nobleman of ancient lineage and great villainy. In 1880 he fraudulently founded a colony, with himself as the (absentee) 'King', at Port Breton in New Ireland. Many settlers died. The survivors reached Australia. De Rays was imprisoned in 1884 by a French Court.

advantages to Australian commerce, which the construction of a *Transcontinental Railway* would bring.

The city's main thoroughfare, Queen Street, is already becoming rather crowded with business activity, and the shops are gradually invading the parallel streets nearby. In years to come the business quarter of the city will cover the whole area between the Botanical Gardens and the foot of Spring Hill. Some people are already predicting that the beautiful Gardens will have to be destroyed, in order to widen the river and build wharves in their place. It is to be hoped that the economic benefits to Brisbane, from such an act of vandalism, would be small enough to prevent its being committed. During our stay of nearly six weeks in Brisbane we often visited the Gardens, and it was always a fresh delight to walk along the great avenue of *bunya-bunyas* that borders the river. There too I met again those old acquaintances from Mauritius, flame-trees, with their exotic scarlet flowers that for a whole season of the year replace the leaves, and create such a beautiful effect among the surrounding greenery. I noticed also, growing beside some tree from New Zealand, a specimen of the traveller's tree, the *Ravenala* of the botanists, which is a native of Mauritius. This tree, which is provided with a little store of water at the base of its leaves, never has, despite popular belief, saved the life of any traveller dying of thirst in the desert. On the contrary, it grows in swampy country and is never found in arid lands.

In any city, except Paris, Rome or some other great metropolis with innumerable attractions, a visitor with no great business to attend to cannot fail to be bored after quite a short time. Brisbane is quite a pretty town, it is true, but it bores you to death.

We resolved to get out of it for a few days and next morning we left the *wharf* on board the *Emu*, a reasonably comfortable paddle-steamer of the American type, which I saw again some years later on the run between Manly Beach and Sydney. Having rounded the point formed by the Botanical Gardens, we sailed under the arches of Victoria Bridge and up the river, whose banks were dotted with pleasant villas and plantations of maize and sugar-cane. Everywhere the soil was extremely fertile and the vegetation luxuriant. The climate is not quite hot enough to be ideal for sugar-cane, but some small growers have done well with it in the neighbourhood of Brisbane. It can be seen at its best in the northern districts of the colony, where it grows prolifically and forms the main crop.

Early attempts at cane-growing were not very successful. Probably they were made by people who understood nothing about this kind of agriculture, and even less about the process of sugar refining. The unhappy results of these first efforts inhibited the progress of the industry for a long time afterwards. It was not till after our visit that sugar-growing really took its place among the staple industries of the colony. Profiting by past experience, those who had managed to survive the early disasters appealed for help to the authorities in Mauritius and the West Indies, and the situation was quickly transformed.

Today several companies have been formed in Melbourne, principally to exploit the alluvial lands that flank the northern rivers. In the southern part of the colony, as on the north coast of New South Wales, sugar-mills have been built on the main water-courses and *free selectors* have begun to take up farms around them. The farmers grow the cane and the mills turn it into sugar. According to well-informed opinion, this system gives the best results. The farmer is not obliged to find the considerable capital required to install crushing machinery on his own farm – something that only those rich enough to maintain a great plantation can afford. Each small working-owner of a twenty-acre block can thus grow his own cane without crippling overhead expenses. The mill buys his crop, at so much per ton of cane, or according to the richness of the *cane-syrup*, and his expenses are reduced to the simple costs of farming – something to which he must give all his time and care. If it were otherwise, cane-growing would be impossible for small farmers: only large companies could undertake it with any chance of success. On the river flats of North Queensland the industry is organized in this latter way; but in New South Wales and on the banks of the Brisbane River small farming is the general rule.

Our steamer continued its leisurely course towards Ipswich: the river meandered capriciously back and forth across the plain. But as we advanced, the countryside changed in character and cultivated land disappeared. A forest of huge trees, entangled with lianas, began to clothe the banks of the river and, rounding a sharp bend, we came upon a great, walled establishment resembling a convent or a monastery. It was, we were told, the lunatic asylum and bore the euphonious name of Woogaroo, a word borrowed from the dialect of the first inhabitants of the district, the Australian blacks. Here, as everywhere else, the native people have disappeared before the white invaders, leaving no trace of their existence other than some sonorous place-names which the newcomers have respected and retained. The Woogaroo Asylum is built in absolutely virgin country on the right side of the river, whose high banks at this point protect the institution from the terrible floods that sometimes ravage the area.

After steaming for thirty miles through this beautiful scenery, we reached the junction between the Brisbane and the Bremer* rivers, on which latter stream the town of Ipswich stands.

To reach it, we had still to sail fifteen miles up the Bremer. This river was narrower than the Brisbane, the forest coming right down to the water's edge. Here and there a flock of brilliantly coloured little parrots, blue, red and green, flashed across our path and perched in the trees, making the air ring with their discordant cries. These birds are very beautiful, and they do much to enliven the landscape; but their call is so piercing and disagreeable that one would cheerfully dispense with their presence. The river, already narrow, grew still more so as we approached Ipswich, where it was no more than a deep stream which our boat could navigate only because it was fitted with a rudder at both bow and stern. We reached the wharf at three o'clock in the afternoon, after a journey of fifty miles, perhaps a little less than eighteen leagues.

Some years ago Ipswich was a very important town, but it has been declining almost daily since the railway connected it with Brisbane. Up till about ten years ago, all up-country trade was funnelled through this town: wool, wheat, hides, everything was loaded aboard the small boats that tied up at its wharves. But since these products can now be despatched direct to Brisbane, Ipswich's trade is gradually dying. However, its population has not declined: the agricultural resources of the district still maintain nearly six thousand people in a condition of relative prosperity.

* La Meslée spells the word 'Broemer'.

After strolling round the main streets, we set out for the railway station; but we missed our way and found ourselves at the foot of a hill on which stands the lycée of Ipswich, *Ipswich Grammar School*. Tired of walking, we stopped where an old woman was knitting, on a flight of steps leading into a house. We asked her permission to sit down for a moment and began chatting. In a few minutes she was interrupted by the arrival of an old gentleman, who wished us a friendly good-day.

These old inhabitants of Ipswich had been in the country for thirty-five years. They had come out at a time when the district was peopled only by fierce, man-eating tribes of Aborigines who have since disappeared. The old man told us how one day the cannibals attacked the village, then inhabited by only about twenty settlers, who defended themselves energetically. After a struggle that raged throughout the whole day, the miscreants succeeded in taking prisoner a very fat settler. Many others perished at the hand of the savages during the fight.

On the evening of the battle, the blacks took their prisoner to the top of the hill where Ipswich Grammar School now stands. They killed, roasted and ate him, in full view of the horrified colonists who could do nothing to save him.

'We saw them dancing round their victim,' the old Irishman told us. 'We heard them chanting their savage yells, as they argued with each other over the tit-bits. But what could we do? There were four hundred of them, and only ten of us were left.'

Recounting the story, with the enthusiastic corroboration of his wife, seemed to excite the old man; and he appeared to enjoy telling us about his early struggles, and painting a picture of the success which had crowned them.

'I came here a full thirty-five years ago, not worth a penny, and for the last twenty years I have been married to the good mate you see before you,' he added, pointing to the old lady who smiled at her happy memories. 'Well, I took my pick and shovel and went into the wilderness, for that is all it was in those days. I sowed, planted and ploughed. Later I was able to buy a plough and my crops grew heavier. I always had a good market at the Moreton Bay convict establishment. Over the years other settlers arrived: the land around me was cleared, and one day I saw the railway line pass by my front door. That was fifteen years ago now. To-day all the land you see on both sides of the line is mine. My children are well established and, at the age of eighty-five, I can still walk three leagues in a day without becoming too tired. I have worked hard, and to-day I am much better off than I ever dreamed of being under my father's roof, when as a boy I used to mind our animals in the fields of old Ireland.'

Could anyone help admiring the energy of this hardy race, for whom twenty years had been almost enough to snatch from barbarism these countries destined to a limitlessly expanding future?

We returned to Brisbane as night fell, and a few days later a new excursion was mooted; but this one would have been better described as a journey, since we were thinking of nothing less than a visit to Toowoomba, about a hundred miles from Brisbane. The Count planned to push on from there to the flourishing little town of Warwick, in the centre of the Darling Downs, and thus to visit all that part of the colony which is reputed to constitute one of the richest districts in Australia. At that time the railway did not go beyond Warwick, but to-day it extends to the Queensland border, a few miles from the New South Wales town of Tenterfield. This line, however, is only a branch of the great western railway which runs inland from Toowoomba. At the time of our journey in 1876 the main line terminated at Dalby on the Condamine River; but since then it has been pushed forward vigorously and the iron road now connects the prosperous little township of Roma, centre of a pastoral district, with the capital of the colony. From Roma it must swing north to the township of Blackall* in the Mitchell district, to form the first section of the great transcontinental line mentioned above.

Twenty-five years ago at most, the vast stretch of land crossed by this railway was a wilderness, as wild and desolate as the country in which the ill-fated explorers, Burke and Wills, perished from the torments of thirst. A few native tribes wandered over it, leading a miserable existence in summertime, and living by hunting the kangaroos and opossums that infest it. A few years have sufficed for the tough and industrious squatters to transform the whole countryside. To-day the finest cattle-stations in all Australia are found there. The squatter reigns

* A misprint in the original – 'Blackhall'.

as absolute sovereign over his innumerable horned subjects, wandering at will over stations any one of which is as large as one of our French departments.

To reach the tableland, the railway runs for some thirty miles through the rich alluvial plains watered by the Bremer and Brisbane rivers. After passing Jimbour Station, one of the most celebrated properties in the whole of Australia, it climbs the steep escarpment of the Little Liverpool Range. Construction of a railway up such a steep slope does honour to the engineers who were responsible for it. The iron ribbon snakes around spurs and along the face of cliffs and hillsides, which plunge downwards into deep gullies where gigantic eucalyptus grow far below. One wondered how the engine could pull the long string of carriages up such steep grades.

Thus we reached an altitude of nearly 3,000 feet above sea level. From this point we looked out over a magnificent panorama of heavily timbered country. The views were wonderful: nothing could equal the natural grandeur of these mountains. The trees towered to a height of 260 feet above the valley floors, and in the distance we could see the plains we had just crossed. To the south a rich valley, where sugar-cane and tropical agriculture make fortunes for the *settlers*, lay at the foot of the mountains. The rivers looked like long silver ribbons, strewn haphazardly on a green carpet. Unhappily, this superb vista was revealed to us only at intervals through breaks in the clouds. As we climbed higher a thick mist, soon to be transformed into torrential rain, formed around us. The nearer we got to our destination, the worse the weather became, and in another hour we were engulfed in a veritable deluge which robbed us of the finest views.

At Toowoomba, where we arrived at about four in the afternoon, the rain had preceded us and had converted some streets into torrents and others into absolute rivers of thick, red mud. It was urgent to shelter in some hotel and we were directed to one near the station, the Royal Hotel, said to be the best in the town. We reached it in an unspeakable state: soaked to the marrow, and bespattered with mud to the eye-balls. We were frozen into the bargain, for it was bitterly cold. We were shown into a little room where someone had hurriedly lit a good fire, but it took a long time for us to get warm.

Outside, it sounded like one of the forty days of Noah's flood. Shivering by the fire in the chimney corner, Madame X*** passionately declared that this was the last excursion she would ever make in Queensland. The good lady was afraid of catching a fever. As for her son, though he was already steeped to his ears in mud, he hankered for more, rushed out into the hotel yard, and came back five minutes later, unrecognizable. He had been inspired to roll on the ground, and he came in again wrapped in a veritable cocoon of red slime. It was not in his nature to do otherwise.

While the Count and I were trying to revive our spirits a little before dinner, and Madame de X*** was cleaning up her son, there was a knock on the door and the landlady came in. She was a thin Scotswoman, five feet eight tall and with a very dry exterior. The inner woman was of quite a different character for, unless appearances were deceptive, she probably applied herself most liberally to the bottle.

'Sir,' she said to the Count in a husky voice, 'there is another French count in the next room, who wants to know if you would like to see him.'

'Good heavens,' said Monsieur de Castelnau, turning to me, 'I swear, by Noah's flood, it is raining French counts in this hole of Toowoomba! Who can this stranger be?'

'Show him in.'

A moment later a tall, well-bred young man, dressed in bush fashion with sturdy riding-boots, made his entry.

'Be so good as to excuse the picturesqueness of my costume, Monsieur de Castelnau,' said he, 'but you see me as I have just arrived from Woodstock Station. In the *bar-room*, where the weather forced me to seek shelter, I heard it said that a French gentleman had just arrived at the hotel. Knowing of your visit to Brisbane, I immediately wondered who the traveller might be. My slight doubt was dissipated when the landlady, in speaking of her new guest, let slip the words *"French Count"*, and I took the liberty of announcing myself.

'I am Count Pierre de B***.'

'Well, please dine with us Monsieur de B*** and we shall have plenty of time to talk, for we are all dying of hunger, and I imagine that your ride in the rain must have given you an appetite.'

Monsieur de B*** needed no urging: he was a charming conversationalist, full of gaiety and not lacking in spirit. He was in Australia for his sins, which, it seemed, were many and great; and he was now a *boundary-rider* on P. A. Jennings' Woodstock Station. An excellent horseman, endowed with considerable energy, he had taken to this free life and was quite happy, he said, among the sheep.

After chatting for about two hours, he left us and rode off again into the rain.

This chance meeting, in the depths of a lonely country, with a cheerful and friendly French gentleman, made us forget the vile weather, which looked as though it had come to stay. We left Toowoomba next day without going any further.

It was written that Queensland should be a land of unexpected meetings for all of us. Scarcely had we returned to Brisbane, when a distressed French ship entered the river. She was the *City of Lille*, commanded by Captain X***, whom I had known in Mauritius. While being very concerned for the poor captain, whose ship in all probability was about to be condemned, I felt very happy at the circumstances which had brought us such pleasant company: Monsieur X*** was a first-class musician.

For some days there had been another French vessel in the river, the *National* out of Havre, a fine ship of 800 tons, skippered by a little dark man who was a *bon viveur* and very good company.

I went aboard the *National* the day after our return from the rain-soaked expedition to Toowoomba. The captain bade me stay to dinner and informed me of the *City of Lille's* arrival – something of which I knew already. The captain of the disabled ship came aboard while we were still at table.

He was not a little astonished to be greeted with the words: 'Tell me, Captain X***, do you realize how small the world is? How are you?'

'What, it's you!' he replied, recognizing me at once. 'What are you doing here, then? Things are not going very well with me, as you can see!' And even while shaking me warmly by the hand, he could not repress a cry of pain. During the storm which had reduced his ship to the condition of a hulk, a wave had hurled him, with unheard of force, against the cabin wall and almost broken his leg. He had stayed at his post till the end, however. Only when the ship and her crew were safe and sound in the river did he think of his wounded leg, which by then was all puffed-up and hurt horribly.

I stayed on for more than a month in Brisbane, devoting the days to my young pupil, who became more and more incorrigible in proportion as he was more and more spoilt, and spending my evenings aboard the *National*. There the time passed quickly, too quickly, for these gentlemen were both excellent hosts. Sometimes we left the poor invalid, whose leg was recovering only slowly, on board, and went to waste an hour or two in a room in Elizabeth Street which had been dignified by the title of the *Queensland Theatre*. Shakespeare's masterpieces were performed on a stage three yards square, and the ghost of the King of Denmark could be seen. making his exit behind a backdrop representing Mount Vesuvius in eruption. Hamlet, dressed like an undertaker's mute, philosophized on the vanity of the human condition, while contemplating a hollowed-out pumpkin, in which an artist had cut out the jawbone, the nose and two huge round eyes. Other performances were in keeping with this. At last winter drew to an end and we left the capital of Queensland on board the steamship, *Governor Blackall*,* which landed us in Sydney.

* The word is again misprinted in the original as 'Blackhall'.

PART TWO

A Journey to the Cobar Copper Mines and to the Darling River

Chapter One

Standing in the bustle and din of a Sydney street the stranger, whom chance or wanderlust has led to the enchanted shores of Port Jackson harbour, cannot fail to be astonished by the evidence of his own eyes. In wealth Sydney has already left the cities of the old world far behind. Occupying a leading position as regards population, it looks forward to the future promise of a position in Australia, comparable to that which the city of New York holds in America. There exist to-day circumstances, similar to those which created the United States of America, that are going to assist in the future creation of a United States of Australia.

In the Australian colonies, a well-conceived system of settlement and development will assuredly lead to results like those exhibited in the New World. Actually such results have already been realized in most of the colonies – proportionately to their populations – and surpassed in New South Wales. Anyone can readily gauge the success, which has crowned the efforts of the colonists in that province, by casting an eye over the statistics published annually in its government *blue book.*

One cannot form a just idea of the progress of the colony by staying in Sydney. It is a great city, which in many respects resembles all other great cities: but to appreciate properly the development of the country's natural resources, one must go and judge on the spot. A few years, nay, a few months are sufficient to transform a whole countryside. Anyone who should read to-day the Count de Beauvoir's delightful description of Australia,* and who should then go straight off to the country

* The Marquis Ludovic de Beauvoir, *Australie: Voyage autour du Monde etc.*, Paris, 1869 (3 volumes). There was a three volume English edition in

for a month or two, would not be able to recognize it. What is true to-day will not be true to-morrow. Take, if you will, a map of the Australian continent – not a French map, be it understood, for these have not been corrected in any way for a quarter of a century. In the midst of but recently unexplored territory, a mass of little black dots indicates the formation of farming, mining and pastoral centres. Railways run across the great inland plains, and in a few years they will have reached the confines of that huge desert area, of which the first explorers painted such a discouraging picture.

Already New South Wales has 1,200 kilometres of railway in use, and more under construction which should be open to traffic by 1884. Victoria, which for long led the way in this field, possesses more than 2,000 kilometres of lines. The colony of Queensland is even more ambitious than her elder sisters, as is South Australia, which dreams of building a transcontinental line to which the main lines of the neighbouring colonies would be linked. The people of the last-mentioned province have already thrown a telegraph line across the continent from Adelaide to Port Darwin. For some time they have been thinking of building alongside it a railway, which would considerably shorten the length of the journey to Europe, and would make Adelaide a vast *entrepôt* for the products of the whole of the interior of Australia. England herself is concerned with the need to improve communications in the only remaining Crown colony on the southern continent. The British parliament recently approved plans for a railway joining Perth, the capital of Western Australia, to the port of Albany on King George's Sound at the southern extremity of the colony. As for the other British possession in the area, New Zealand, as mountainous as Switzerland and whose occupation dates from only 1840, possessed 1,169 miles (1,557 kilometres) of railway line in 1880.

This colony, scarcely forty years old, was created by England in a country inhabited by tribes of savage cannibals who had to be fought for some years. It has a population of nearly 500,000 people of European origin and of about 42,000 Maoris. The total value of its import and export trade has reached a figure

1870. De Beauvoir, at the age of 21, accompanied the Duc de Penthièrre, a prince of the House of Orleans, on a world tour. They landed in Melbourne on 10 July 1866.

of 312,500,000 francs, and its revenue in 1880 was 82,084,800 francs. On the other hand, its national debt of 759,000,000 francs is the greatest burden of this sort carried by any of the Australian colonies. But this comparatively enormous debt is guaranteed by the value of the railways and public works that were built with the money, and in addition by the immense tracts of unalienated government land. New Zealand is considered the most prosperous colony in Australasia.

Even little Tasmania has a railway line from Launceston to Hobart Town, linking the northern and southern parts of the island.

In the early spring of 1880, that is to say at the most favourable season of the year for inland travel, I received from Mr Russell Barton, manager of the great copper mine at Cobar, an invitation which I hastened to accept. He proposed to make a trip of three hundred leagues into the interior, even beyond the township of Bourke on the River Darling. At that time Bourke was still considered the *Ultima Thule* of New South Wales. Mr Barton was planning to stand for election to parliament. It could not have suited me better, for this excursion would enable me to travel through the station country at shearing time and see the pastoral industry at the height of its activity. I had no intention of letting such a chance slip, as I should be able to see all aspects of outback life and to study its social, economic and political ways. There was even a further attraction. Beyond Wellington, the western terminus of the railway, our journey was to be made in an excellent *dog-cart* with four horses – a vast improvement on the infernal machines of Cobb and Co. If it had been necessary to fall back on those *coaches*, I believe I should have refused.

My host had also invited one of his friends on the trip: he was one of the directors of the company and a director too, I believe, of the newly discovered mine at Nymagee which we were to visit first.

We had to meet each other at Wellington and set out from that township towards the end of August.

The distance from Sydney to Wellington is 238 miles. The railway line traverses that part of the country which was first settled, the Nepean and Hawkesbury valley. It is quite a pretty, open countryside reminiscent of Europe. Soon after

89

leaving the little town of Penrith, the line crosses the Nepean on a splendid iron bridge. The river, forty or fifty yards wide at this point, waters a very fertile district. Beyond the Emu Plains siding, the country changes in character: a line of tall mountains rises like a veritable wall, shutting off access to the rich tablelands and plains of the interior. To climb the first escarpment, the railway engineers designed a very ingenious zigzag system which enables relatively high speeds to be maintained. This zigzag section is not as complex as that at Lithgow, where the line descends on the other side of the Mountains. As the altitude increases, the horizon extends to embrace the entire plain below, enclosed in a vast circle of hills ending at the entrance to Sydney Harbour, which can be seen with a good telescope. The line continues climbing along the mountainsides in this way and then keeps to the top of the ridge for about thirty miles. One after the other we passed through charming little villages like Woodburn, Lawson and Mount Victoria, where wealthy Sydney people maintain attractive country houses for their summer holidays. People appreciate the mountain climate keenly: European fruits grow there freely and in winter the temperature falls to freezing point. The pretty little town of Mount Victoria, in a sense the centre of the district, boasts a hotel that would not disgrace a provincial town in France. Sometimes trains from the mountains reach the station in Sydney with snow from Mount Victoria on the carriage roofs. Whenever this happens the city's idlers, who have never seen snow, hurry to the station to watch the arrival of the 'mountain train'.

Beyond Mount Victoria the line continues to follow the crest of the Blue Mountains till it begins to descend the western slopes. Here we came to the second zigzag, the masterpiece of Australian engineering.

It seems miraculous that human brains and brawn should have been able to conceive and construct the zigzag along the fearful face of this escarpment. The mountainside falls away dizzyingly here, and when the engineers made their first preliminary surveys, they had to be lowered down the precipice by ropes to measure their angles. Later, to build the three viaducts that carry the line, the workmen in their turn had to work on the foundations, while dangling suspended by ropes from above. The wild and rugged landscape contrasts with that enjoyed by the traveller between Lawson and Mount Victoria, where he looks out over an ocean of variegated greenery. The locomotive slowed down to negotiate this difficult section of the line. We passed through a short tunnel and the train stopped. Before backing down to the beginning of the second leg of the zigzag, the driver sounded a strident blast of the whistle, that re-echoed eerily from the abyss, to warn the men working lower down on the line of the train's impending arrival. The coaches skidded on the rails but were controlled by powerful brakes. One shuddered to think what terrible accidents could occur on such gradients without these safety precautions. The train stopped a second time, negotiated the third zigzag, and soon we were bowling along on the valley floor. Alongside the line flowed a little stream with flowering bushes growing on its banks. To see the crest of the mountainside, more than a thousand feet above, one had to lean right out of the window. In fact, until the train entered the Lithgow valley, it was not easy to catch a glimpse of a patch of blue sky.

Here we were in one of the colony's main industrial centres: the coal, iron and shale mines of Lithgow, Esk Bank and Hartley are all situated within a radius of a few miles. New coal deposits are being discovered almost daily. As I intended to spend a few days touring the Lithgow district on my return journey, I continued straight on towards Wellington. West of the Lithgow and Bowenfels valleys, the country is still fairly mountainous until the village of Rydal. Beyond this point lie the rich plains around Bathurst, one of the largest inland towns in Australia. I did not stop to see it. Next the railway traverses a district, once prosperous with rich gold mines, but now for the most part deserted. It was the gold discoveries that led to the closer settlement of this part of the country, and the consequent development of its great agricultural potential. The plains of Bathurst and Orange are, indeed, famous throughout the colony for wheat and other cereals, and the country around these two flourishing towns is sprinkled with well-run farms.

It was near Bathurst that Hargraves discovered, in 1851, the first goldfield to be exploited in New South Wales. The follies of Melbourne were then repeated in Sydney: everyone deserted the city for the diggings, in the hope of making a fortune.* New veins of gold were discovered almost every day, and the whole ground surface of the district was quickly transformed by the miner's pick. There followed the same process which is still taking place in the vicinity of other past *rushes*. Once the surface gold had been worked out, people were thrown back on the other resources of the country and *free selectors* established themselves round the abandoned diggings. The soil, which once contained gold, to-day grows wheat and the whole country has benefited by the change.

Between the abandoned goldfield of Ironbark† and the township of Wellington the country is rather broken, but the soil appears to be very fertile. In my compartment a group of farmers, who had boarded the train at Orange, talked about their hopes for the coming harvest and I heard them bemoaning the water shortage. It would be a good harvest, they said, but what would it be like if only there were more rain! That was the gist of the conversation. In fact, as far as the general appearance and fertility of the soil are concerned, it would be impossible to find anything better in the world than the whole country round Bathurst, Orange, Wellington and Dubbo. However scanty the rain may be, the vegetation looks splendid, and every kind of agriculture gives a fine return. In spite of recurrent droughts the farmers in the district are all, if not wealthy, at least comfortably off. Nearly all of them began without much capital: it was much if they could raise something towards the expenses of setting up the farm. With agriculture they combined small scale sheep and cattle-raising, and many of them have grown quite rich.

When we were there the country looked green with spring, and the wattle trees in flower gave an almost gay appearance to the monotony of the bush.

At length we arrived at Wellington.

Mr Barton had been unexpectedly detained in Sydney and could not reach us until the day after the next.

At Wellington I fell in with an interesting man who knew the surrounding district like the back of his hand, and who gave

---

* Hargraves' discovery of gold near Bathurst in 1851 was, of course, the *first* significant find in Australia not, as La Meslée implies here, one that post-dated the Victorian discoveries.

† A misprint in the original – 'Pronbartes'.

me much valuable information about it. He was associated with one of the biggest firms engaged in the business of transporting stores to the inland stations. Mr Heaton had personally traversed, in both senses of that word, the whole western part of the colony practically right out to the South Australian border. His company had the contract for supplying stores to, and transporting copper from, the Cobar and Nymagee mines, which are situated a couple of hundred miles further inland in the very centre of New South Wales. We had a long chat about the country and its future, and Mr Heaton wound up by proposing a visit to the Wellington Caves. I readily accepted and we set off in a cab after our midday dinner.

These natural limestone caverns are situated a few miles from the town on the banks of the Bell River, a tributary of the Macquarie. We had the foresight to take with us enough candles to light our way through the underground passages.

The entrance to the caves is at ground level on a rocky hillside, and passing through it is not at all difficult. It amounts simply to allowing oneself to slide downwards on one's heels for two or three minutes into the midst of a great chamber with a very lofty, vaulted roof. Mr Heaton, for whom it was not the first visit, led us through a succession of caverns of which the most remarkable was *the pulpit room*, so called because of a great, free-standing column of limestone, somewhat resembling a pulpit, which dominated one end of the chamber. Next we rounded this pillar and climbed down into another cave forming a sort of lower storey to *the pulpit room*. Opening off this cavern on all sides were many smaller ones, better described perhaps as alcoves or large niches. One of these, with a very narrow entrance, was remarkable for its echoes. Every sound was magnified to an extraordinary degree and the faintest noise produced the most delicate reverberations.

The Wellington Caves were discovered, I believe, by Sir Thomas Mitchell on one of his celebrated exploring expeditions. Many fossils, especially of animals of the marsupial order, have been discovered there. An old German savant, whom I met that same day at Wellington, Dr Böhme, has devoted his life to research and has penetrated further into the caves than anyone else. Having descended by ropes to the bottom of a pit at the far end of the lower level of the caverns, he discovered, just above the water level, a narrow funnel into which he could burrow for only a few metres. There he discovered some very interesting and important fossils belonging to several species of marsupials.

On returning from our expedition to the caves I met the old doctor at the hotel, and in the evening he took me into his home, a little retreat surrounded with flowers and vines, just outside the town on the banks of the Macquarie River. I spent a few pleasant hours with the old scholar and inspected his magnificent collection of precious stones. From the zircon and topaz to the diamond, every variety was represented by natural, unpolished specimens of great value. The learned geologist had lived for almost twenty years in that part of the country. He knew every nook and cranny of it and maintained that it had immense mineral riches. Yet he spoke judiciously, and with solid evidence, to make good his claims. In addition to his impressive collection of precious stones, he had made one of mineral samples in which gold, silver, lead, tin and copper were most plentiful. The most superb specimen of all was a blue sapphire, almost the size of a small broad bean, which at first I ignorantly mistook for a diamond. This stone, like a couple of rubies, emeralds and one or two very beautiful topazes – half a dozen in all – had been cut: the rest of the collection were still in their natural, unpolished state.

'I have still another collection like this,' the old doctor told me, 'but I do not keep it at home. Cut off as I am in this lonely hut, I would not be able to keep it safely. What I have shown you this evening will soon be going to join the rest in the bank, where they are deposited.'

'I have found all these stones,' he added, 'within a radius of ten or twelve miles, and I am convinced they are not the only ones. Australia is truly a privileged country: nature has denied her nothing. Gold occurs all over the country, which holds other, and incalculable, mineral wealth locked in its bosom.'

Before we parted Dr Böhme offered me a glass of his own home-made wine. It was a sort of tokay, with a very delicate bouquet, made from a vine growing over his hut. After sipping it, I had no doubt but that the favourably situated hill slopes along the banks of the Macquarie River will one day grow excellent wine.

I left the old philosopher as night fell, delighted to have met, among people who talk only of sheep and cattle, a man whose conversation was so illuminating. What on earth had happened to bring to live among these stock-merchants a sixty-five year old man who, to say the least, was not one of them? As we have already noticed, Australia is a land of contrasts where nothing should be too astonishing!

The next day Mr Barton arrived and we set out for Dubbo. The horses were fresh, the road excellent and the air bracing. We quickly passed out of Wellington which is built at the junction of the Bell and Macquarie Rivers.

From the moment of our departure my companions did not utter a word. Mr Barton was fully occupied in driving the horses – a task of some difficulty. They were magnificent animals, Australian-bred of course, which pulled us along at a great rate. As for Mr Linsley, he remained plunged in thought and never once opened his mouth. Perched on the driving seat beside Mr Barton, I was happy to inhale the clean morning air and look at the country we were travelling through. It might almost have been a rural landscape in France or England, and the illusion would have been complete if there had been hedges growing round the cultivated fields, instead of the eternal wooden fences one encounters from one end of Australia to the other.

We passed by a beautiful property on our right: the homestead was hidden by clumps of greenery, and some alpacas were grazing peacefully in a beautiful paddock nearby. This station belonged to one of the richest squatters in the country, Mr Gardner, quite a character, they say. Certain it is that he showed very good taste by building his house on the river bank near the foot of some hills on which grew an absolute forest of colonial pine. It was the first time I had noticed any appreciable change in the terribly monotonous appearance of the Australian vegetation: and that was a real pleasure. The colonial pine is by no means a beautiful tree, but it has the advantage of being a useful one. In the outback part of the country where we were to travel, almost all the houses were built of its wood. Newly sawn planks of colonial pine give off a very pungent, resinous odour which is said to be good for the health, but which makes living in a newly built pine house quite unpleasant for the first few weeks. After a while one gets used to it, as to everything else.

Between Wellington and Dubbo the country looks splendid and its soil is so rich as to beggar description; but the district is said to be liable to bad droughts in summer. It is well wooded and eucalyptus is not the only scent wafted from the trees. About a mile out of Wellington the road came to a dead end. Beyond that point there was only a *track*, or rather a network of *tracks*, through the *bush*. The horses maintained a good pace on this ground which was easy on their hooves: we could have been bowling along over turf in an English park. Like a good driver, Mr Barton was not afraid to make his own *track*. By so doing, he avoided the ruts gouged out by the heavy wagons which carry everything to and from the inland stations. From the top of a slope we had just climbed, we saw in the gully below an encampment of *teamsters*.

There were drawn up four huge wagons, loaded with packing-cases, scrap-iron and all sorts of merchandise. The teams were all harnessed and on the point of resuming their journeys. Three of the wagons were pulled by teams of sixteen horses, magnificent animals as beautifully built as those strapping Normans used by the General Omnibus Company in Paris. The fourth was drawn by eighteen oxen, yoked in pairs. Step by step the column moved off. The noise of all those animals' hooves on the ground, and of the *teamsters* urging on their beasts with whip-cracks and shouts, issued suddenly from the bottom of the valley and excited our horses so much that Mr Barton could scarcely restrain their friskiness. By the time the four wagons were fairly under way, we passed them at a fast trot.

It is a great strain on the teams to drag the enormous bulk of these wagons over fairly soft ground, especially when the load weighs up to four or five tons. Once started, they keep moving, without fatiguing the draught animals, at a steady pace and stop only when they have covered a distance of ten or twelve kilometres. Unless the season has been so dry as to make the soil harder than usual, *teamsters* hardly ever exceed this distance in a day. From the time of their departure from Wellington, they take nearly two months to reach the banks of the Darling. But when rain has dissolved the heavy alluvial soil on their route alongside the tributaries of the great inland river, they may have to take ten or twelve months on the journey. If people on the distant stations, and in the little hamlets that are beginning to take shape here and there, run out of necessary provisions, they have no other recourse but to fall back upon the nearest inhabited centres. A horseman can always get through where a heavy wagon would be bogged. After covering the thirty-five miles between the two towns in less than five hours, we reached Dubbo in the afternoon.

Near the approaches to the town there is a very fine property owned by a Frenchman, who for some years has been successfully cultivating many species of vines. It would be difficult to find land more propitious for this kind of agriculture. The stratum of rich, chocolate coloured, volcanic, surface soil is everywhere several feet deep. People complain generally of the dryness of the atmosphere but, except in extreme and prolonged droughts, these conditions are rather favourable for vine-growing. As soon as a few drops of water fall to moisten the deep bed of humus, grass springs up as if by magic. The Chinese, who are the best gardeners in Australia, grow all sorts of fruits and vegetables and perform horticultural miracles along the banks of the Macquarie. To-day on the outskirts of every Australian town, great or small, one comes across these beings who look as though they were suffering from chronic jaundice. They are our vegetable purveyors, and without them these delicious necessities for European tables would be beyond the reach of most people.

Chapter Two

Dubbo is a much more important town than Wellington: it is also better built and a busier trading centre. It stands in the middle of a rich valley watered by the Macquarie River, which flows along at the foot of some hills that define the limits of the town. The surrounding district used to be essentially pastoral, but the approach of the railway is already tending to transform it into one of the richest farming areas in the colony. Thus the township of Dubbo is undoubtedly destined to future greatness. It is easily accessible from every direction, and its position marks it as the future *entrepôt* for all the products of a wide area.

Since the time of my journey, the *Great Western Railway* has reached Dubbo. The line planned to connect it with Bourke on the Darling has been extended as far as Nyngan Station on the Bogan River, about thirty leagues short of its destination. In another four years it will be completed, and the western *Ultima Thule* of New South Wales will be joined to the capital by a steel ribbon three hundred leagues in length. Such is the astonishing rate of progress in this great colony, as it moves with giant strides towards a glorious future. Next day, when harnessing was finished, we left Dubbo at the gallop, drawn along by four superb beasts: the groom rode a little distance behind us. After driving across the bridge over the Macquarie, I glanced back at the town, the last one we were to see before reaching Cobar, eighty leagues away in the middle of the waste.

It was a very beautiful morning in the first days of spring,

* In the original Dandaloo is spelt throughout with two 'l's' – 'Dandalloo'.

and though the preceding winter had been drier than usual, the soil had retained enough moisture to encourage new growth. Everywhere the *bush* was a mass of flowering trees and shrubs whose perfume filled the air. Can anything on earth be more enjoyable than a drive through the bush, in a well-sprung vehicle, pulled by four mettlesome horses?

Before taking us to Nymagee, Mr Barton wanted to visit a newly discovered, and reputedly very rich, copper mine near the hamlet of Dandaloo on the Bogan. Our first stop was at a *bush* inn, set in the midst of Narromine* Station on an elbow of the Macquarie River. In the neighbourhood of Dubbo our route was clearly marked between two lines of fence, which indicated that this rich district was completely occupied by *free selectors*. Here and there cultivated paddocks surrounded some farmhouse almost hidden under a blanket of creepers.

About a mile from the Macquarie River falls, near the little village of Minore,† we passed a funeral procession. A cavalcade of about fifty people, all carrying hats swathed in long crepe ribbons whose ends flapped in the wind, was following a light cart bearing the coffin draped with a black pall. This long file of horsemen, winding silently through the trees and exhibiting all the trappings of mourning and mortality, made an unforgettable impression on me. The English do not often raise their hats at funerals; but this encounter on a lonely track in the heart of the Australian *bush*, when we were the sole spectators, moved us all profoundly. Without exchanging a word or a glance, the three of us took off our hats at almost the same instant. This simple ceremony in the midst of the wilderness had an air of solemn melancholy, very different from the aura of pomp and circumstance that surrounds the obsequies of the great.

A few miles from the place where we passed the funeral, the Minore *public house* appeared on the top of a rise and we stopped there for lunch. From Minore to O'Neill's Hotel, the track runs through splendid country hugging the banks of the Macquarie. On the way we met four big wagons coming from Cobar, loaded with copper ingots smelted at the mine. Like most buildings in this part of the country, O'Neill's Hotel was made

---

* In the original, spelt 'Narromin'.
† Actually a cattle-station at the time.

of colonial pine. It had only one room for travellers, a sort of dining-room where I lay down on a sofa, and a bar. We arrived early and, having nothing better to do, Mr Linsley borrowed the publican's gun in the hope of bagging a kangaroo or some wild ducks along the river bank. An hour later he came back empty-handed. At dusk some wagons, the first one's I had ever seen loaded with wool, arrived at the inn. In a few minutes the *teamsters* made camp between the hotel and the river, and soon after it grew dark.

I think I have already remarked that Australia looks best by moonlight, and this was borne in on me again by the beauty of the night, the first I had spent in the solitude of the *bush*. The moon shone but feebly, for it was still in the first quarter, and the shadows of the enormous white gum-trees that cover the Macquarie valley were outlined on the ground only vaguely. Here and there twinkled the camp-fires of the *teamsters*, who were preparing their evening meal a few paces from the wagons loaded high with wool-bales. The inn formed the backdrop to this scene and in the drawing-room Mr Barton, Mr Linsley and I chatted gaily about our trip, which had started so promisingly. At the same time we paid our respects to the cooking of Mrs O'Neill, who had levied toll on her poultry-yard for the occasion. After dinner things became more lively. The bar filled with happy *teamsters*, one of whom owned an accordion with which he began an impromptu concert. Soon the night resounded with the notes of the national tune, *Rule Britannia*. The camp dogs joined in and the noise woke a flock of *galahs** (grey parrots with rose-coloured breasts) roosting in the trees by the river. They flew off into the darkness, mingling their discordant shrieks with the sound of this strange concert. To the accompaniment of the accordion, the *teamsters* went on singing songs until nearly nine o'clock. Then silence reigned supreme.

We left *O'Neill's public house* at the first glimmer of dawn. To reach Dandaloo we had to follow a track which had been travelled only once before. Some of Wright, Heaton and Company's wagons had marked the route, after a fashion, only a few weeks earlier. We were about to plunge into the real wilderness. Wherever the *track* was indistinct, or invisible, we should simply have to rely on Mr Barton's great experience of

* Consistently mis-spelt 'gallahs' in the original.

the *bush*. There would be no-one on these lonely plains to show us the way. As far as the Narromine out-station, seven or eight miles from the inn, we might possibly meet an odd bullock-driver; but beyond that point we should have to cover thirty miles of country, which was without marked roads and completely unknown to any of us.

As far as Australia is concerned, it would not do to take the word 'road' literally. Roads in the ordinary French sense of the word, exist only in, or close to, big centres. As one goes farther inland 'roads' become simply wide spaces; sometimes bounded by fences, more often marked by nothing but a few trees felled almost at ground level here and there, and by the wheel-marks made in the soft soil by wagons loaded with wool or copper, which last passed that way. But this description applies only to main roads between townships, villages and a few big inland stations. On minor roads, one has simply to trust to one's lucky star to find traces of some earlier traveller's *track* to suggest the right way. When no visible signs exist, there is no other recourse but to go straight ahead. If the country is lightly timbered and fairly open, it comes down to a question of experience. With good horses and one of those solid vehicles specially built for the *bush*, one may still get through fairly easily: there is a chance of reaching some lonely station before nightfall. But if, by ill luck, the country is more or less cut up with swamps, or covered with dense thickets of belah[1]* or mallee[2]† the inexperienced traveller runs a good risk of losing his way, and may well die of thirst. It has happened often enough.

Beyond the limits of the soil that forms the bed of the Macquarie valley, the magnificent gum-trees that grow in those rich lands give place to a much poorer flora. The country is covered with that species of gum referred to above, the *box* tree, which is found almost everywhere in the interior of Australia. Here and there in this monotonous landscape one sees an occasional tree crowned with dense foliage, whose deep green tint contrasts vividly with the greyish colour of the surrounding vegetation. This beautiful tree is the *kurrajong* which,

[1] A tree of the casuarina family that grows in swampy areas.
* Mis-spelt 'ballahs' in the original.
[2] A large shrub with very hard wood, which inhibits all other kinds of vegetation over the large areas where it grows.
† Mis-spelt 'mullee' in the original.

unfortunately, is tending more and more to disappear from the land. As useful as it is beautiful, the *kurrajong's* spongy outer bark has a slightly sweet taste and is endowed with excellent nutritive properties. More than one poor *bushman*, at his last gasp from hunger, owes his life to finding this tree in the midst of the lonely *bush*.* Stock are very partial to the leaves as well as to the bark, of this precious tree.

Our expertly driven vehicle covered the miles quickly, and new specimens of Australian flora appeared from time to time. The journey began to grow interesting. At about eleven o'clock we drove out onto plains stretching to the horizon and covered with dwarf trees, *myalls*, that were nothing like the eucalyptus to which we had been so long accustomed. Generally low-growing with blackish trunks, their branches droop like those of a weeping-willow and are covered with leaves that are silvery coloured on one side. It is an odd fact that these drooping branches seem all to have been cut off at the same level, about six feet from the ground.

'You are surprised by this curious phenomenon?' asked Mr Barton. 'You will see much more of it before we get back to Sydney'.

'Can you tell me the reason for it?' I asked.

'The explanation is very simple,' he replied. 'The stock are very fond of *myall* leaves which have an aromatic and nutritious juice. When the grass is dead or dried out by the heat, especially during a drought, the beasts fall back on *myall* leaves which they crop off to the highest level they can reach. Since all cattle are more or less of the same height, it is easy to understand how all the branches above a certain level remain untouched.'

Mr Barton had hardly finished his explanation when a horseman appeared in the distance on the other side of the plain. A few minutes later he approached, glanced keenly at us and abruptly reined to a halt.

'Hulloah, Mr Barton! How are you? You're going to Nymagee, I suppose?'

---

* La Meslée is confused – and confusing – here. Kurrajong is indeed a splendid stock-food. However, the tough, fibrous *bark* is quite inedible by man or beast: the *roots* do provide water and can also be cooked, as can the leaves, to provide respectively a turnip-like and a 'green' vegetable.

'Ah! It's you, X***! It's good to see you again! What are you doing here?'

'Since you have created towns in the desert,[1] I also must create roads to connect them with the rest of the civilized world. Do you imagine, perhaps, that your Nymagee miners are goind to spend six months without a word of news from their *sweethearts*? Joking aside, I am looking for a more direct route to start a coach-run between Dubbo and Nymagee. . . . Hey! What's wrong? Look out for your horses!'

Mr Barton had no time to answer. One of the rear horses suddenly went mad and rained against the fore-board of the dog-cart kicks that threatened to smash it to pieces. The cart began to sway and jolt and, but for our driver's presence of mind, the horses would have bolted away with us through the scrub. Mr Linsley and the strange horsemen leapt to the ground in a flash, one to the head of the frightened beast and the other to that of the two leaders. Immediately it was their turn to jump dementedly, and the howls of anguish they let forth revealed the cause of this strange incident which could have been fatal to us.

When the strange rider approached us, Mr Barton had pulled our vehicle to a stop on a slightly rising piece of ground which was, in fact, nothing less than an ants' nest – crammed with those huge, black ants whose bites are hideously painful. Mr Barton hastened to press forward beyond the range of their attacks. With the danger over, we burst out laughing at the absurdity of the situation. There was poor Mr Linsley, stroking the frightened horse with one hand whilst, with the other, he scratched frantically at the fleshy part of his left calf to which half a dozen *soldier-ants* were clinging implacably. He got rid of them in the end and climbed back to his seat. After exchanging a few more words with Cobb and Co.'s scout, we continued on our way to Dandaloo. All's well that ends well.

Towards two o'clock in the afternoon Derribong Station appeared at the end of a great *myall* flat, and we reached the banks of the Bogan River. The character of the landscape had changed completely. In the Macquarie valley the river flowed

---

[1] The recently founded township of Nymagee owed its existence, in effect, to the exploitation of a copper mine in which Mr Barton owned half the shares. He was thus, in a sense, the township's founder.

through broken country whose rich soil supported the finest trees I had seen in the whole course of my journey. The Bogan, by contrast, had carved a deep bed for itself in wide alluvial plains. Mimosa trees had replaced eucalypts and the appearance of the country was quite different.

A few miles beyond Derribong, we passed Dandaloo Station and stopped in front of John Richardson's inn. There Mr Barton's eldest son, and a very knowledgeable old mining captain, had been waiting for us since the previous evening. Ted Barton had ridden from Cobar on horseback and the old captain, Lane, with his son, had harnessed his two best horses to his best *buggy*[1] and made the same journey in short stages, camping out in the *bush* every night.

There was company at the worthy Mr Richardson's hotel. Entering the dining-room, we found the table set and the police inspector for the western district, Mr Layard, and his son, confronting a superb roast turkey. We were among friends and those who were strange to each other quickly became friendly. Ted took me to see the town. It consisted of a hut to house the police officer of the Dandaloo district, a sort of barn that served as the post-office, a blacksmith's shop and the inn. Close by on the river bank was built the station homestead in a garden containing all sorts of fruit-trees – peaches, apricots, grape vines and so on. The garden, homestead and out-buildings, extending over an acre or more, were all enclosed by a thick, earthen wall ten or twelve feet high. Its function was to protect the house and garden from the river in times of flood. On the other side of the road which had brought us into Dandaloo were the *cattle-yards*, large, heavily-fenced enclosures into which the beasts are driven to be tallied and drafted. The finest animals are then sent to market, or to other stations, in charge of men, known as *drovers*, who have no other trade. Sometimes these drovets take the herds entrusted to them to the other end of Australia, to stock some new run in the outback part of another colony. At other times they move overland to the environs of Melbourne, to sell their stock there, after journeys that often last several months. All the Australian colonies are criss-crossed by strips of public land, reserved by the government. These are actually 'roads', several miles wide, known as

[1] A light, four-wheeled, American-type vehicle.

travelling stock reserves,[1] and their existence allows squatters to send their sheep and cattle from one end of the country to the other without causing loss to the stations on the drovers' routes.

The Dandaloo inn-keeper was also a *free selector*, whose *selection* adjoined the station *cattle-yard*. He showed me some splendid wheat from his last crop, which had averaged a hundred bushels to the hectare,* for the sowing of little more than a bushel of seed. The rich alluvial land of the Bogan valley is very fertile.

Early next day we left the hotel to go and visit the copper mine I mentioned earlier. There were eight in our party: Mr Barton, Mr Linsley and I in the excellent *dog-cart*-and-four, Captain Lane and his son in their *buggy*, and Ted Barton, Mr Richardson and a groom riding their horses alongside us. After a few miles the geological nature of the country changed suddenly. The ground began to rise above the level of the alluvial plain, the soil took on a reddish tint and we crunched along over gravel. Veins of quartz appeared here and there, and porphyritic rocks were scattered everywhere. New kinds of vegetation grew in this stony ground. The well-marked road wound along between colonial pines, flowering mimosas and occasional eucalypts which seemed ill at ease among these quite different species. This part of the *bush* struck me as very pretty. The terrain was somewhat broken, and one could easily have believed we were following a well-kept avenue in a park, where the most graceful shrubs had been planted among clumps of fir-trees.

Frightened by the noise of our cavalcade, two huge birds started up suddenly and ran across the road a few yards in front of us, soon disappearing in the *bush*. They were *emus*, the ostriches of Australia, and the first I had seen in their natural state. The emu is by no means as large as the ostrich of the Cape of Good Hope, and it is commercially useless. It is a great, ungainly bird, set on stilt-like legs three or four feet long, and covered with long, hard, grey feathers quite devoid of beauty. It enlivens the solitudes of the *bush* and is generally left to roam at will, safeguarded by its uselessness. Its eggs,

[1] Reserves for stock being driven about the country.
* About two and a half acres.

on the other hand, are much sought after: a little smaller than ostrich eggs, they are of a beautiful, deep green colour instead of white like the former. They have a slightly rough surface like shagreen, and *bushmen* who have time to kill and a taste for handicrafts carve on them designs which are sometimes quite fascinating. Every Sydney or Melbourne jeweller has carved emu eggs on display, mounted in silver and usually in the form of a cup.

From what Mr Barton told me on our way to the mine, it was possible that there could be some dispute over the ownership of the land on which it was situated. To this hint Mr Richardson added that the self-proclaimed owners had stationed near the workings two men well known in the district as retired pugilists. We could rely upon being warmly welcomed. Perhaps these two worthy watchdogs would try to stop us from going down the shaft, in which case there might be a scuffle and I should have a chance of studying a new side of colonial life.

After a drive of about an hour and a half, we came on a lonely hut some yards from a mound of rocks richly veined with copper ore. The shack was roofed with sheets of gum-tree bark. We had arrived.

Drawn out of the hut by the unaccustomed noise, the two guards stood there, following our every movement with their eyes. One of them, a great, strapping fellow well over six feet tall and built like a Hercules, regarded us with an air of detached curiosity. Evidently he did not understand the position very clearly. Where on earth could they have come from – these people dressed in city clothes and driving that stylish *dog-cart* with its superb four-horse team? Certainly they had not come from Sydney a hundred and fifty leagues into the bush to have a picnic!

With the excuse of asking for a drink of water, but really to sound out the intentions of the two *bushmen*, Mr Linsley left our party and walked up to the hut. A moment later we were astonished to see our friend and the big fellow warmly skaking hands and giving every sign of being on the best of terms with each other. Mr Linsley came back towards us with his strange friend who, it seemed, was none other than an old school mate, born and bred in the same village of Windsor on the banks of the Hawkesbury.

In the Australian *bush* social distinctions disappear; and when two men meet again after some years, no matter what may be the difference between their positions in society, they treat each other upon a footing of complete equality. The old *bushman* and the wealthy city business-man behaved as though they were still at school. The one was Johnny and the other Jack, just as it had been thirty years before when they used to play together at their national game of cricket in the Windsor park.

While Mr Linsley was chatting with his great boyhood friend, the old captain and his son lifted up some planks which were covering the mouth of the mine shaft. The big watchdog saw what was happening. He dropped his conversation in the middle of a sentence and lumbered towards the mine entrance. Without a word he calmly replaced the planks our friends had just removed, and planted his massive, iron-shod boot on them.

'No-one goes down there,' he said laconically.

I was quite expecting him to take a revolver from his pocket, but I was disappointed: apparently this American usage has not reached Australia.

Mr Barton stepped forward and tried to make him see reason. Mr Linsley kept harping on the theme of old boyhood memories. Ted remarked that they were two against eight, and that if it came to fisticuffs, they would infallibly be routed. Nothing would do.

'No-one goes down there,' he repeated.

His comrade came to stand at his side and held himself ready for action. I sat on a tree-trunk a little way off and watched the developing stages of the dispute, all the more deadly because no tempers were lost.

'Come on now,' said Mr Barton, 'let's get it over. I have not come here to waste time in futile argument. Leave us to our own business, and you carry on with yours.'

'My business is to stop anybody whatever from going down this mine,' the man answered bleakly, 'and no-one is going down it.'

The situation was beginning to look nasty, when hoof-beats were heard and two troopers from Dandaloo appeared on the scene. That changed the complexion of things as though by magic.

After some minutes of palaver, the great watchdog himself brought the discussion to an end.

'Gentlemen,' said he, 'be so good as to witness that I have done my duty to those who are paying me to guard this shaft. I yield only because the presence of the police makes the argument unequal. Do whatever you want to.'

While Lane, the old mining captain, went down the shaft to examine its walls, we yarned with the two *bushmen* who invited us into their hut. It was built of pine-trunks, cut in halves and nailed to each other: the interstices between the uneven wooden slabs were filled with clay. The roof was composed of sheets of gum-tree bark, held in place by poles laid cross-wise over them. Other sheets of bark, nailed to four posts sunk in the ground, formed the table. Some stools, made on the same pattern, and a bed of equally primitive construction completed the furnishings of the hut. The two *bushmen* entertained us most hospitably, inviting us to regale ourselves by sharing a meal with them. This consisted solely of a platter of *corned beef* and a slice of *damper*, a sort of wheaten cake cooked in the embers of the fire.

While we were chatting in the hut, Mr Barton, Richardson and the old captain, Lane, had gone off into the bush to settle some point, and to inspect another piece of ground a few miles off where, according to the Dandaloo publican, very promising indications of copper reefs could be followed on the surface. We had stopped near the place where Richard Cunningham, brother of the famous English botanist Alan Cunningham, was killed by savages on one of the first inland exploring expeditions. To-day the aborigines have almost completely disappeared. In Tasmania the last representative of the native race died about ten years ago. In the colony of Victoria their numbers are negligible, and the government seeks to protect and civilize them as well as it can – a labour in vain, for infanticide and addiction to alcohol are stronger than the attractions of the gospel and civilized life. The once free natives of the Bogan have been reduced to a nucleus of about fifty souls, living more wretchedly than ever before on the fruits of the chase and shanty alcohol. In fact, if you happen to come across some representative of this unhappy people near a *public house* where you are staying in the *bush*, you may be certain he will come to offer you some *boomerangs* or other missiles in exchange for a few glasses of grog. They will come and pluck you unceremoniously by the sleeve with their dirty hands, and babble in half-English, half-savage jargon:

'Captain! Me throw *boomerang*: him fellow plenty come back. You give it grog.'

You throw him sixpence to get rid of him, and he will demonstrate the use of this curious weapon. It flies from his hand first in a horizontal direction, then suddenly soars upward, all the time spinning in the air at an incredible speed, and describes a semi-circle before returning to fall at the native's feet.

The same thought always occurs to visitors when they first see an Australian native throw this weapon, a terrible one in his hands. From where did the aborigine get the boomerang? They are essentially the most degraded and savage beings, probably nearest in the scale of evolution to those great apes which Mr Darwin wants to present as the ancestors of all humanity; yet they have a weapon whose trajectory in space seems to defy the laws of mechanics and physics! It is an unanswerable question which scholarly research has succeeded only in making more mystifying.

While we were enjoying the two *bushmen's* hospitality, our friends covered a good deal of country searching for their mine and returned about two hours later. The Dandaloo inn-keeper wished us a good journey, and we climbed back into the *dog-cart*, shaking hands with the two hut-keepers who, only a couple of hours earlier, would so willingly have exchanged punches with us instead. Ted Barton had been depressed by the arrival on the scene of the Dandaloo policeman: he would have liked a small fight to break the monotony of the bush journey, which held no novelty for him.

'The country we have to cross to reach the next *public house* at Caroline is very little known,' Mr Barton told me. 'The land is no good for sheep or other stock, and the whole area is visited only occasionally by some prospector looking for signs of gold or copper. There are some indications of the latter all over the district, but,' he added, 'we want something better than indications. Later, when a bigger population reduces labour costs and when transport is speedier, it will pay to exploit these metal deposits; but to-day one has to discover something big, something that will give the shareholders a profit from the start. In two days we will be at Nymagee and you will see something pretty good there, but for something really astonishing, just wait till we reach Cobar.'

It was about five in the evening when we drove out of quite a dense scrub into a big clearing, in the middle of which stood the Caroline *public house*. Behind it was a large paddock, all sown with seed. Our arrival frightened a couple of kangaroos grazing quietly on the plain in front of the inn. They moved off in a series of extraordinary leaps: then, after a hundred yards or so, they calmly sat back on their tails and watched curiously as we climbed down from our vehicle at the door of the *Hit or Miss Hotel*.

There is a strong sporting flavour in the name of this hotel, lost in the middle of the bush ten leagues away from the nearest human habitation. It seemed, indeed, that the whole surrounding country abounded in game: we were not far from the Bogan, and kangaroos, *wallabies*, and wild duck were plentiful. The *wallaby* is simply a smaller species of kangaroo. The Australians make from kangaroo or wallaby tails a soup which, according to their account, rivals the famous turtle soup which the English love so much. As for wild duck, there is no need to insist upon its attractions: it is a perfect game bird. The emu, the Australian ostrich, was also very plentiful in these parts; as was another species of long-legged large bird with pale grey plumage, called the *native companion* – the companion of the aborigines. Why? No-one has the faintest idea.

The bush also swarms with *opossums*, whose beautiful fur is in so much demand to-day in Europe. These animals are seldom seen in daylight and can be hunted only at night. *Opossum* hunting is a veritable treat for small boys of twelve or fifteen. They set out in a party of half a dozen or so, some armed with guns and some with sticks, and accompanied by a few terriers, the best kind of dog for this work. When friend 'possum' has been found in some gum-tree, if it is not too big, they will climb up and quite easily capture the animal alive. Otherwise they must shoot him from the ground. But Jack Possum is hard to kill and it often happens that, even when quite dead, his long claws will still cling to the branch on which he was taking a stroll in the moonlight when the deadly bullet struck him.

In our party Mr Linsley enjoyed the reputation of being a real Nimrod: his aim was deadly, his hand steady, and as there were plenty of kangaroos about, we counted on putting to the test his talent as a marksman. The *Hit or Miss* publican owned an absolute arsenal – shot guns, revolvers, and long-range rifles, all of the most up-to-date type and in first class condition. We had then only to choose our weapons, and the Caroline kangaroos had only to present themselves as targets.

A few minutes after we arrived, our party split up. Ted Barton left us to go on ahead to Nymagee, where he had to stay for a while with friends at a nearby station. Ted had friends everywhere: he was a tall young man of twenty-two, as strong as an oak, who worshipped only two things – freedom and horses. Like so many young Australians born and bred on up-country stations, accustomed to a life of untrammelled liberty with no other law than his own whims, he had no love at all for city life. He went sometimes to Melbourne or Sydney, but he was no sooner in the midst of civilization than he hastened to return to his horses and his freedom. He was typical of a breed met with only in Australia and then, nearly always, only among people of Anglo-Saxon ancestry. To meet us at Dandaloo, he had set out six days before and covered a hundred leagues on horseback: he was preceding us to Nymagee and, to get there, he had to make a detour that would lengthen his journey: he had forty leagues to cover and would arrive the day after the next. Thence he had to follow us to Cobar and to ride, sometimes in advance, sometimes beside us, the same distance that we should be travelling. During the five weeks that our trip lasted, he was scarcely ever out of the saddle, and he rode for more than four hundred leagues without seeming to suffer from it. Indeed, from one end of the year to the other, that was his life, and he was happy only while he gripped between his muscular legs the flanks of one of those excellent Australian horses which, like their masters, never seem to tire.

It was just as well that he left us as, if he had not, I do not know how we should have been accommodated with beds; for the *Hit or Miss* inn had never before put up so many travellers at once. There were only two minute bedrooms and a kind of

parlour, furnished with a certain elegance that I had not
expected to find in what was virtually a shack, lost in the heart
of an almost completely uninhabited countryside. Tasteful
designs, beautifully executed in crochet and tapestry work on
the chairs and the two or three armchairs, bore witness to the
presence of the weaker sex. I wondered how women could
condemn themselves to this life of perpetual exile in the heart
of Australia, with no other company than that of their husbands
and children. This is the kind of life, I said to myself, that would
never answer the purpose for a Parisian woman, and I know
scarcely a woman in all France who would resign herself to it.

Twilight came on while I was musing thus, and two or three
aborigines arrived at the inn. They were repulsively ugly and
unspeakably filthy. Of course their first words were to ask for
a glass of grog. Before giving them anything, I asked the
publican about the ways of these savages, and particularly
about how they made fire. He told me they did so by rubbing
two pieces of wood together. I then promised my blacks a good
glass of rum if they would make fire for me in this way.

I expected to see them take two dry sticks and rub them
slowly together till they caught alight but it seems that the
operation requires careful preparations and the use of certain
kinds of wood. For some minutes my two blacks searched
around for the right material and in the end, after examining
many pieces of wood, they found what they needed.

First one of them took a piece of *wattle*, a kind of mimosa,
and after stripping off the bark he smoothed it down with his
tomahawk.* Then, choosing another piece of extremely hard
wood known as *ironbark*, he whittled it to a point.[1] He then
placed two or three dry leaves on the piece of wattle, and set
about rubbing its smooth surface energetically with the point of
the *ironbark* stick. In a few moments wisps of smoke curled up,
the fire caught and rapidly spread to the dry leaves, which took
the place of the tinder of our ancestors. The exhibition was over.

It was not in the least difficult! Only – one had to know how
to do it.

There was once an emergency in my life when I tried hard

---

* Misprinted 'tomawak' in the original.
[1] Before the introduction of the tomahawk, the natives used pieces of quartz
to smooth the wood.

to make fire by rubbing two sticks together, but I sweated away for half an hour on end without success. If such an occasion overtakes me again, I shall at least know how to set about it.

If, instead of two savages, we had had a whole tribe, we should have been able to make them do a *corroboree*, a kind of wild, warlike dance, common to all the aboriginal tribes of Australia; but in our whole journey it proved impossible for us to arrange for this interesting spectacle.

Once satisfied, the blacks went off to camp among the trees while we returned to an excellent dinner at the hotel – fresh eggs, a delicious ham and a superb roast fowl. We did full justice to the repast and then made the best arrangements we could for the night, for there were five of us and beds for only two. The innkeeper's wife and daughter installed us on sofas with kangaroo and *opossum* skins, and thus we slept the sleep of the just.

At five o'clock in the morning we were up with the sun. Two hundred yards away at the edge of the forest a herd of kangaroos, scattered among the trees, was just emerging into the clearing to browse on the fresh, dewy grass. Two big emus, high on their stilt-like legs, strutted round among them, and the forest rang with the piercing shrieks of pink and grey *galahs* and yellow-crested white cockatoos. A flock of the latter, which had landed in the middle of the clearing, speckled the green of the grass with hundreds of white dots.

Now or never was the moment to put to the test the marksmanship of our travelling companion. The host of the *Hit or Miss* brought him an excellent Snider rifle and some cartridges. The kangaroos were scarcely two hundred yards away, and could be shot at without our even leaving the shelter of the hotel verandah. Mr L*** slipped a cartridge into the rifle, raised it to his shoulder, took careful aim and fired. . . .

An old kangaroo who was browsing quietly, raised his head at the report, sat up on his tail for a moment and stared in our direction: then he resumed his grazing, without concerning himself further with what was going on around him. The flock of cockatoos flew off, shrieking raucously, and the two emus moved back towards the fringe of the trees to see what made the cockatoos call so wildly.

'Missed,' said Mr L***, through his clenched teeth. 'I must have misjudged the distance.'

'I say, publican, your rifle at least shoots true I suppose?'

'It certainly does sir! I often use it myself and rarely miss a shot: it is an excellent weapon. I'll answer for it.'

Mr L*** raised the gun again, covered the kangaroo, took careful aim and fired. . . .

The old beast leapt once, a few feet.

'I hit him that time!' cried Mr L*** triumphantly.

But the marsupial bounded away for about twenty yards and sat up again on his tail.

'How clumsy you are!' said a female voice behind us suddenly, and the innkeeper's sister, a provocative, twenty-year-old brunette, showed her pretty face on the verandah.

'My dear young lady,' stuttered the disconcerted L***, 'one must know one's weapon to be sure of one's aim, and it is harder to estimate distances here than on a rifle range where every yard is measured off.'

'Wait a minute, give me the rifle,' she said laughingly. 'Perhaps I shall have better luck than you.'

L*** handed her the loaded weapon: she raised it to her shoulder and fired.

The big kangaroo made a single bound in the air and fell on the grass. He was dead.

'Bravo, miss,' cried L*** enthusiastically, forgetting his discomforture in the face of this beautiful shot. 'What a pity that the shooting galleries in Sydney should not be open to women! You would win many prizes.'

The girl laughed, thrust the weapon into his hands, and ran off across the clearing. A moment later she called out in her clear voice.

'He's dead all right. It's an *old man*. What a beauty!'

We joined her immediately. The dead animal was a superb specimen nearly five feet tall. He belonged to the largest and most formidable species of red-backed kangaroos, which sometimes reach a very great size. It is true that these animals never attack man: they flee from dogs set on their scent, moving fifteen to twenty feet at each jerky leap and trusting to speed for their safety. However when brought to bay, they must be treated with considerable respect and dogs often fall victim to their prowess: with one kick from its hind leg, a kangaroo will rip open a dog's belly. There are few cases of men being killed: however, some have been eviscerated in this fashion, and others stifled between the little front legs that serve the animals as arms.*

We took the dead beast to the inn. The girl suggested cutting off the tail and making some soup straight away. But the horses were already harnessed and we had twenty-two leagues between us and Pangee, the station belonging to Mr Barton's friends, so that even if the soup had been already cooked, we could not have had the pleasure of drinking it.

It was a beautiful morning, cold enough at first to be quite bracing, but the brilliant sunlight was gradually making the air pleasantly warm.

We had to ford the Bogan River as we left the inn. The water was low and the crossing occasioned us no difficulty whatever.

On the far side the nature of the country changed completely. Instead of the quartzy ground and charming park-like land we had traversed the previous afternoon, with its thickets of colonial pine interspersed with flowering wattles and bright green shrubs, we were driving over immense alluvial plains, devoid of trees, but separated from each other by belts of stunted gums. The soil was very rich and produced excellent pasture. From time to time we saw a flock of emus, which watched us pass by without troubling themselves any more over us. It is true that we had left the settled districts completely behind. As far as Dandaloo one still meets with a certain number of colonists, but the further we went towards the west, in this huge area between the Lachlan and the Darling, the sparser the population became. Hardly fifteen years ago it was completely uninhabited: there were not even any sheep, as people were afraid of drought and had not yet formed a valid estimate of the country's capabilities. Now the full development of its resources is no more than a question of time. The railway, projected between Bourke on the Darling and the colonial metropolis, will lead to rapid changes. Colonization proceeds apace because of the considerable inducements offered to immigrants, and administrative difficulties are almost

---

* La Meslée is, of course, wrong here. No man has ever been hugged to death by a kangaroo.

unknown: the method of establishing settlers on Crown lands only sometimes involves wasted time.

Now that we had said goodbye to civilization, we came across human habitations only at rare intervals. There was the occasional inn, generally about ten leagues' distance from the next one, or even the isolated sheep or cattle station. These inns are meeting-places for the men who work for the squatters, and there they often squander in a few hours the wages of many months' labour.

Between Buggabuddah and Pangee our route traversed country interspersed with waterholes known as *Gilgi Holes*: around these little natural reservoirs the grass was thick and green, the trees seemed to support denser foliage, and many flocks of birds took wing at our approach. Among them I noticed a fine cockatoo whose crest, and the underside of whose wings, were of a superb rose colour: the most beautiful species of cockatoo I had ever seen. Flocks of tiny parrots, known in France as love-birds [inséparables] and called by the aborigines *budgerigars*,* flew across our path at every moment; and we drove past, almost close enough to run over them, about half a dozen baby emus, fat as turkey-cocks, following a great male bird with such an imbecile air that he did not seem to be aware of our presence.

The horses began to tire, for the road was bad enough and the journey long. We stopped in front of a roadside inn which was said not to enjoy a very good reputation. Walking up and down on the verandah, to my unbounded astonishment, was a man who looked about thirty, dressed in the height of fashion down to his gloves and his gleaming top-hat. He would not have cut a bad figure on the *Boulevard des Italiens*.

Who on earth could this stranger be? And what in the world was he doing in such clothes, in a bush shanty a hundred leagues from civilization?

In general bush-dwelling Australians do not take much trouble about their appearance even when paying visits – which they seldom do – for they hardly have time to worry about such matters.

The day was drawing to a close and we still had ten miles to go across country which was getting worse, interspersed with

* Spelt 'budgerygahs' in the original.

belts of *mallee* – a species of shrub with very hard wood, which is quite useless and around which nothing else will grow. So Mr Barton urged on his horses, who responded as gamely as they could to their master's voice. At last, at nightfall, we drove into the yard of Pangee Station where a warm welcome awaited us.

We had scarcely stopped before we were surrounded by the owner, Mr Donaldson, and four or five young men who were serving under him their apprenticeship to *bush* life and to the management of a sheep and cattle station.

Chapter Three

Pangee Station – Mr Donaldson and the ladies *– Shearing – Observations on large outback stations in Australia – Classing and despatching the wool – Leaving Pangee – Nymagee – A death warrant – Off to Cobar.*

We were received with the greatest possible warmth at Pangee. As the arrival of visitors at an up-country station is quite an event, they are assured of the most open-hearted hospitality. Moreover these gentlemen knew Mr Barton. Only Mr L*** and I were strangers to them.

We were immediately shown to our rooms where we found enough water for all our needs – a rare thing in country where water is often more precious than beer or wine, and far from pure or fresh. And God knows how much dirt had accumulated on our hands and faces after a day's journey on the dusty roads. Our clothes were covered with it, our hair was grey with it, and our eyes were full of it. It was an unspeakable pleasure to steep myself in that limpid, cool water. It came from a splendid lagoon, half a league long and three hundred yards wide, on the banks of which the homestead was built.

Dinner was announced a few minutes after our arrival.

Entering the dining-room, I was agreeably surprised to find a lady doing the honours of the table for the numerous company gathered there. I recognized some of them: Lane, the old captain and his son, who had managed to arrive a few minutes after us, and the district police inspector, Mr Layard, whom we had met at Dandaloo and who had preceded us to Pangee. Half a dozen young men attached to the station completed the party, which was made still more agreeable by the presence of the ladies. Mr Donaldson, the owner-manager, was a good conversationalist and a charming host: everything about him was frank and free, and I must say that he was a gentleman in every sense of the word.

It was a very lively dinner party. We could have been at the table of some rich merchant in Sydney, and no-one thought of the distance separating us from the rest of the civilized world.

I admit that I was surprised by this first taste of station life. But it would be a mistake to think of Pangee as a typical outback property. Few places like it could be found except for some nearer the city: farther out life is generally quite different. Instead of a well-built homestead with large rooms and a numerous staff of young men of good family, come out to gain colonial experience, you find as a rule mere shacks, dignified with the title of head-stations, and people who are sometimes hospitable but often ill-bred and boorish. The presence of women always brings about a complete transformation of the atmosphere at a station. They bring with them that feminine charm which imperceptibly softens the manners of even the roughest male. But I marvelled again at the courage a woman must have to come out and bury herself among sheep and cattle in the middle of nowhere.

The next day was a Sunday and we spent it most agreeably. Mr Donaldson showed us around his domain with the utmost urbanity. The homestead stood beside the magnificent sheet of water mentioned above. Pangee was centred on this large main building, built of colonial pine and surrounded by a wide verandah, like all the other homesteads in that part of the bush. In front stretched a big garden of vegetables, flowers and fruit-trees, mostly of European varieties. At the back was a big yard in the centre of which stood a row of rooms for the young men of the station and, further away, some additional huts for shearing-time when a large number of *shearers*, *teamsters* and all sorts of temporary employees are gathered at Pangee. One side of the yard was bounded by the stables and station storehouses, while an immense shed stood on the opposite side near the lake. This was the *shearing shed*, so placed that the wool could be washed, either on the sheep's back or after it had been shorn, without its having to be transported for any distance, and without any time being wasted.

A little beyond the station buildings the lightly-timbered plain beside the lagoon, covered with dozens of white tents, presented a most lively spectacle. As the station had not built

119

enough huts to house all the workers needed for the shearing, the hands simply camped in the open air a little distance from their work. In spite of the sanctity of the day and the horror which the English seem to have for working on Sunday, one teamster, less religious than his fellows, was getting ready to leave the station.

Sixteen sturdy horses stood harnessed to his fully-loaded wagon. He cracked a long whip over their heads and ordered them to start. At their master's voice, the noble animals threw their weight forward, strained with their mighty legs, and the load, a veritable mountain of expertly packed bales of wool, lurched off towards Wellington.

'Jack,' shouted some of his mates as he moved away, 'you will have bad luck, leaving on a Sunday: you'll be lucky if you are not bogged on some flat for a fortnight.'

Despite the predictions of the superstitious teamsters, Jack was not bogged at all: on the contrary he got through very quickly. We saw him again in the railway yards on our return to Wellington five weeks later. He had already despatched his wool and re-loaded with machinery for the Nymagee copper mine.

Before we left Pangee on the next day, a Monday, Mr Donaldson took us to inspect his *shearing shed*, one of the largest and best-equipped in the district. At Pangee the shearing shed, the barn for cutting off the wool from the sheep, was a large, roofed building divided in two down the middle by a long gangway, down which the sheep were driven. In front of each shearer was a little gate, arranged so as to let only one animal at a time through it, and opening off the central race. The shearers were all equipped with long wool-clippers, called *shears* in English – whence comes the term *shearers*. Whenever he was ready each man opened the gate before him and dragged out a beast, closing the gate again on the other sheep in the race. With a few blows of the shears, executed with an extraordinary skill born of long practice, he stripped the fleece off the wretched sheep while holding it in a vice-like grip between his legs. The operation over, he pushed the animal through an aperture in the wall of the shed, into an enclosure from which it would be drafted with others of the same breed, age and sex, and then driven off to a *paddock* kept for this or that special class of sheep. The shearers did not waste an instant. One sheep had scarcely left a man's hands before he had seized another victim. Meanwhile boys of fourteen or fifteen moved up and down the shed, gathering up the fleeces from the ground and taking them to the far end of the building to place on a table before the *sorter*. This man's task was to classify the fleeces according to the quality, length, springiness and cleanliness of the wool. He rapidly separated the scraps of neck, belly and leg wool from the fleeces proper. A child picked up the scraps and threw them anyhow into an immense bin, which reached from the ground to the roof of the shed. The fleece was then rolled up and also thrown, according to its quality, into one of five or six bins set on both sides of the sorting table.

From these bins packers took the wool and placed it in bales, beneath a press worked by a lever. When the wool had been thus rammed into the bales, they were sewn up and hoisted by a little crane into a store adjoining the wool-shed. Next the bales were weighed, and then another little crane loaded them onto wagons waiting at the store-house door. A tarpaulin was made fast over the load, and a team of sixteen or eighteen bullocks or horses immediately hauled the wagon off on the road to Sydney.

When the wool has to be washed before packing the process takes longer, for the fleeces must be spread out individually on sheets of cloth, to dry thoroughly in the sun before being pressed into the bales.

These successive operations are all carried out at high speed. The workers do not waste a moment, for they are paid according to the number of sheep shorn and the number of bales pressed and sewn up. No sound is to be heard but that of the shears, swiftly relieving the sheep of their winter coats. The men hardly speak to each other: that would waste time and there, as everywhere among the English, *time is money*. It often happens, during the headlong process of shearing a sheep, that the point of a blade pierces the animal's flesh, lifting a great slab that causes a painful wound. In such a case, before shoving the beast through the chute mentioned above, the shearer takes a brush from a pot beside him and daubs the cut with tar. This cauterizes the wound which heals in a few days.

In this rapid fashion the squatters manage in a few weeks

121

to shear fifty, a hundred, two hundred thousand or more sheep, and to send their wool to Melbourne or Sydney in time for the great public wool sales in those cities. Some send it direct to London, where buyers from all over the world come to bid for favoured lots in that huge *entrepôt* known as the *London Docks*.

When the season ends the *shearers*, who are usually small farmers, return to their homes, only to come back at the right time in the following year to one station or another. Some make fifty, sixty or seventy pounds sterling, according to the number of sheep shorn, in a single season. Some of them squander in a few days *on the spree* in roadside shanties, or in Sydney or Melbourne, the last penny they have earned.

It was only thirty-five miles from Pangee to Nymagee, but the country became steadily rougher as we approached the latter place.

We reached it in the afternoon, and there I was confronted with a completely new and very interesting sight. The road came out on the top of a hill from which we looked down over a valley encircled by mountains, and in the middle of the valley there stood out, like a buttress, a rocky knoll. The Nymagee copper mines were located on its flank.

Only a few months before, the whole district had been virtually uninhabited. An old shepherd had come to build a hut in the waste where he lived a half-savage, half hermit-like life, on his chosen fifty-odd acres of ground. Whenever he happened to have any money he went off to a *bush pub* and never left it until, having drunk his last penny, he was thrown out of the door by the publican. One fine day this old drunkard stumbled over a magnificent specimen of copper ore. He took it to Cobar, which was already a flourishing centre, and the rumour spread that he had found a rich copper mine. Speculators got wind of it, came to visit the scene of the find, and offered the old shepherd eleven hundred pounds for his Nymagee property. The old toper, who thought he might become a millionaire at one stroke, refused at first, protesting that people wanted to ruin him: but he accepted in the end. Within a few months the scene was transformed as if by magic. People rushed to the find and, by the time of our visit, development was proceeding rapidly. Wooden cottages were replacing the tents of the first arrivals, hotels were built, and the company's brick blast-furnaces stood already at the foot of the knoll mentioned above. A little distance from the workings a huge dam had been dug and was waiting only for a series of good rains to fill it. Water, indeed, is the prime necessity for any undertaking in up-country Australia, and to procure it no expense ought to be regarded as too great. With a water supply assured, mining operations would follow.

As to the mine itself, I am no expert on such matters. I can say that I climbed down the ladders in two shafts to a depth of a hundred feet, and that this tour into the bowels of the earth was enough for me. When I reached the surface after my second descent, I did not want any more.

I took up my quarters in the *Royal Hotel* and we stayed at Nymagee for forty-eight hours.

There I had a very disagreeable experience of *bush* life, especially mining-fields life. About midnight the *Royal Mail coach* arrived, full to overflowing. There were passengers everywhere, inside, on the driver's seat, and even sitting atop of the baggage on the roof. They were miners returning from a newly discovered field which had been abandoned for lack of water. They were all more or less drunk, and throughout the night they kept up the most infernal din I have ever heard in my life.

Never, most emphatically never, have I heard such language as assailed my ears all that night. There were not two words unaccompanied by appalling oaths. As may easily be imagined, it was impossible to sleep a wink. As nothing but a thin partition separated my room from that in which these persons played, drank, swore and blasphemed at the same time, there was no question of sleep. The uproar was crowned by a wretched drunkard who, for two hours on end, played on an atrocious accordion, tunes that would bore anyone to death. Some danced on tables, the thump of punches reverberated through the partition from time to time, and the pandemonium was interrupted only when an argument broke out between two miners. Then the difference was settled by a fight, conducted according to the latest rules of English boxing. During one of the intervals of relative calm, when mosquitoes were keeping me awake, I had the idea of glancing into the room. What I saw is worth describing.

Everyone was dressed in typical Australian *bushman's* costume – flannel shirt, heavy boots, riding-breeches and a leather belt to which was attached the sheath for a seaman's knife. About twenty miners had formed a ring around their two comrades. Some were sitting on the wooden benches of the pub, others were standing, and still others were calmly climbing up on the tables to get a better view. All of them were smoking vile tobacco in vile pipes, which poisoned the air with an acrid stink of nicotine that would have been insupportable at any other moment. But curiosity can make one put up with many things.

The two antagonists, with shirtsleeves rolled up to the elbows and fists held at chest height, stared at each other without uttering a word. Now and then a brawny arm shot out like a steel spring as one of the champions aimed a punch which did not always find its mark, since the other would parry adroitly and retaliate in the same instant.

A blow of prodigious force, too sudden to be dodged by the smaller of the two boxers, struck him below the left eye and sent him weltering in blood to the floor.

'Hurrah! hurrah for you Jack! Well hit!' bellowed twenty voices. The deafening hubbub was accompanied by such thumping and stamping as threatened to smash the tables.

The injured man was up again in a moment, his face covered in blood and dust: his eye seemed to be out of focus, he was a frightening sight. Silently, with clenched teeth, he advanced slowly on his adversary, feinted and, before the other had time to recover his position after dodging the feint, he delivered a terrible blow between his eyes which sounded like the fall of the poleaxe on the skull of an ox.

It was all over. Blinded by the blood pouring from his pulverized nose, and with both eyes blackened by the knock-out punch, the loser staggered heavily backward for three steps and collapsed in a heap.

At this dramatic climax to the fight, the crowd abandoned what little sanity it had retained: the cheering became more frenzied, the row absolutely hellish. Two strapping fellows snatched up the conqueror, blinded as he was by blood all over his eyes and face, hoisted him on their massive shoulders, and carried him in triumph round and round the room. As for the vanquished man, he lay half-dead in a corner while one of the miners and the publican staunched the blood that still flowed from his face. He was hideously disfigured.

'Hey there! boss!' shouted half a dozen men who had just noticed the publican. 'You here, by God! What are you doing down there? Leave the poor cow alone. It's not the first time he has had his head broken: he only needs a new nose . . . Turn on champagne for everybody!!!!'

Thus importuned, the publican carried out his orders. As for me. I stole away without being seen. Otherwise, I should have risked being dragged into the middle of the maddened mob and forced to drink the winner's health.

Bedlam continued till daylight.

After breakfast I was talking with Mr Barton when he asked: 'Have you ever seen a death warrant signed?'

'I? – No.'

'Well, you are going to see me sign one in a few minutes.'

'How is that? As far as I know, you are not a judge of the criminal court. What do you mean?'

'At any moment now, a man is going to come in here. Have a good look at him,' Mr Barton said. 'I am going to give him a cheque for twenty thousand francs. That is his death warrant. In three months, if he is still alive, he will have drunk his last farthing:* and then he will be dry for many a day. He is the former owner of the land on which the mine stands.'

A few moments later I saw a tall old man come in. He walked only with difficulty, and his whole appearance betrayed unmistakeable signs of debauchery and drunkenness. He came up to Mr Barton and greeted us.

'Well, father M***,' said Mr Barton, 'you have come to get the rest of your money?'

'That's right, Mr Barton, and it is none too soon for I am getting old.'

Mr Barton gave him a cheque for eight hundred pounds, which he had just signed, and looked at me significantly.

I knew then what he had meant by his talk of signing a death warrant: and he was certainly not in the least mistaken. The poor old chap had scarcely received his money before he headed in the direction of the *Royal Hotel,* and I saw him there

* Mis-printed 'farting' in the original.

the next morning, a few minutes before we left, in a state that can hardly be described. He had been drinking all night in a vain effort to get to the end of his money.

His death warrant had indeed been signed the day before.

Chapter Four

After our forty-eight hours' rest at Nymagee, we took the road for Cobar, which we expected to reach the day after the following one. We had had to leave behind two of our horses, and to hire two others to make up the team and continue the journey. It happened that there was only one suitable horse in Nymagee, and Mr Barton had been very hard put to it to find a second until someone appeared offering a superb, coal black animal which, it was admitted, had never been harnessed in a team of four.

'Has he ever worked in harness at all?' asked Mr Barton.

'Yes, once or twice.'

'All right. I'll take him.'

The beast was harnessed up with the others and we set off.

At first all went swimmingly and the horse readily followed the lead of his team-mates. Because of his colour he had been named *Zanzibar*, and he was well known in the district as a good racehorse, but as being very vicious if put into harness. Of the last report we were ignorant.

Beyond Nymagee we were plunged more or less into the middle of that immense area extending from the Lachlan to the Darling, the two great tributaries of the Murray, which still appears as a virtual blank on Australian maps. There was a slight change in the plant life. The gently undulating country-side was covered with good pasture, and new species of Australian *flora* began to appear. No longer was the country interspersed, like that near Pangee, with little water-holes called, as we have

127

seen, *gilgi holes*: here, on the contrary, there appeared to be no water whatever. Occasional thickets of *mulga bush*, a shrub with very brittle wood, a blackish trunk and silvery-grey leaves, made a striking contrast with the extremely deep green of the *wilgas*, another species of small, but very bushy, tree which makes a wonderful shelter from the heat of the sun on these endless plains. Everywhere the grass grew tall and thick: now and then there started up, on both sides of the track, kangaroos, emus or some of those magnificent birds the Australians call wild turkeys, which make such delicious eating.

After covering about forty miles, we stopped at a little inn a mile or so from Priory Station, had some refreshments, and set off again. It was about half past five in the evening and would be dark within the hour. We had, then, not a minute to waste if we were to reach the *Shear-legs* hotel, still eight miles ahead. The road, or rather the *track*, snaked back and forth through the densest thickets we had met with so far. There was an absolute jumble of shrubs and undergrowth with a few big trees growing here and there.

As we started to gather a little more speed, Mr Barton cracked his whip over the horses' heads. They leapt forward at a pace which, within half a minute, grew into a steady gallop. Our driver thought he had the team under control and we sped along quickly, raising clouds of dust on the road behind us. But in spite of all Mr Barton's efforts to restrain the team, our pace increased ominously and there was soon no room left for doubt. Our four horses had taken the bit between their teeth and were bolting headlong through the *bush*.

At the crack of the whip, *Zanzibar* had broken into a gallop and drawn the other three horses along with him. Before Mr Barton had time to check them, all four, with outstretched necks and flaring nostrils, were hurtling us along at the speed of an express train.

No human power could save us.

We were at the mercy of the four animals, intoxicated by their own speed and convinced that they were in the midst of an exhilarating contest on the race-course.

It was impossible even to try to stop them!

With a skill and coolness I could not help but marvel at, Mr Barton kept his team on the *track*; but it was soon clear that this state of affairs could not last for long. The way forward was becoming more and more tortuous, and we were in a state of fearful anxiety.

At a sharp bend the vehilce canted so far over that the wheels on the inner side of the curve left the ground. But for our presence of mind, it would certainly have overturned and crushed us: Mr L*** and I instinctively threw our weight over to the rising side and the carriage came down to earth again.

Another turn like that and it would be all up with us.

A hundred yards ahead the *track* wound sharply round the trunk of a huge eucalyptus, standing alone among the surrounding shrubs. . . .

It was too late to avoid it: the horses were now completely maddened and our speed was terrifying.

A terrible crackling, the sudden noise of breaking branches, the flying vehicle abruptly brought to a halt . . . and we realized that we had, literally, been projected into a tree.

Having seen at a glance the absolute impossibility of driving round the gum tree which barred our way, Mr Barton had steered his bolting team into a *mulga* thicket on the opposite side of the *track*. . . . There we were safe and sound, staring stupidly at each other and asking ourselves if the whole thing had not been a dream, and whether we were indeed still alive.

The sight that met our eyes quickly brought us back into the realm of reality.

Chaos was complete.

Horses, carriage and passengers lay in a confused heap. The smash had been such that the lead-horses, suddenly stopped in their mad career, had crashed to the ground. Carried forward by their own momentum, the wheelers had been thrown on top of them: the dog-cart had ridden up crazily over all and we were roosting, without a scratch, among the branches of a big *mulga*.

We were soon on the ground and, helped by Ted and the groom who had by then arrived on the scene, we righted our conveyance and got the horses to their feet. They were trembling with nervous terror but, by some inexplicable stroke of luck, did not seem to have suffered any injury. It was quite otherwise with our vehicle: the pole had been shattered in three places and the fore-carriage buckled. But thanks to our ample supply

of ropes and leather thongs, without which no-one undertakes a
bush journey, the damage was temporarily repaired within a
quarter of an hour, two of the horses were re-harnessed, and we
limped off towards the *Shear-legs* Hotel. It was quite dark when
we arrived. This inn, standing in the middle of a vast, treeless
plain, is the general rendezvous for the whole district at certain
seasons. Two or three times a year horse-races, which attract
a considerable crowd, are run on the flat in front of the hotel.

A race-track in semi-desert country in the middle of Australia!

One has to be English and mad on horses, as people are in
Australia, to entertain such ideas.

Luckily the *Shear-legs'* blacksmith was a highly skilled
tradesman. Our vehicle was repaired so quickly that we were
able next day to resume our journey to Cobar, where we made a
triumphal entry at four o'clock in the afternoon.

Mr Barton was the managing director of this important mine,
which he had bought when it was in a languishing state and
transformed into a flourishing undertaking. Shares issued at
twenty-five francs had fallen to ten francs fifty centimes, but
at the time of our journey they were worth ninety-five to a
hundred francs.

A section of the population turned out to meet him. There
was a short welcoming speech, promising him the unanimous
vote of the electors of Cobar in his candidature for the parliament of New South Wales. His brief and straightforward
response was greeted with frantic cheering, and we proceeded
to the local mine manager's home where we were received with
the utmost hospitality. He had a charming, well-built, brick
house, surrounded by a garden. Mrs A. L*** entertained us
most cordially.

Cobar is situated almost in the middle of that blank space
on our maps between the Lachlan and the Darling, a hundred
miles south of Bourke and a hundred and fifty-two from
Wilcannia, both Darling River towns, and two hundred and
fifty miles from Dubbo which we had left a week earlier.
It already has a population of three thousand inhabitants
and it is still growing steadily. All sorts of dwellings rub
shoulders on the Cobar plain, from the two-storied mansion to
the humble miner's tent and even the miserable bark *gunyah* of
the aborigines, half a dozen of whom prowled around the hotels.

Even more picturesque edifices may be seen there – shanties made from the remains of broken wine or spirit crates and roofed with empty sardine cases or the material of old discarded tins, that once contained preserved meat, vegetables or kerosene. The last are the most highly prized because they are the biggest. These habitations have a distinctive character of their own, in no wise to be found anywhere else in the world.

The mine comprises three main reefs, about two hundred feet from each other, with clear surface indications of their positions. Work has been started on the most westerly reef. In two or three places trial shafts have been sunk to study the lie of the land, and the location of the lode has been fixed within quite narrow limits. The rock, wherever it has been laid bare, presents an interesting sight: it is friable and veined with an accumulation of minerals, chiefly carbonates and oxides of copper, which tint the stone with beautiful blues and greens.

At great expense the company's directors have had brought to the site all the machinery necessary for extracting, raising and crushing the ore. It is then loaded onto an automatic tramway, which takes it from the pile of crushings to the blast furnaces. A double line of steel rails on a kind of viaduct carries the ore over the plain.

All the machinery necessary for making certain pieces of mechanism used in the mine has also been installed at Cobar, and the company pays enormous wages to men in a position to undertake this skilled work.

Operations in the Cobar copper mine are carried out according to the most up-to-date principles of the mining industry. To-day one no longer climbs down those interminable ladders which can be ascended again only at the risk of contracting curvature of the spine. We took our place in a great iron cage, like one of the lifts to be seen in some modern buildings, and descended into the depths of the mine. This cage serves two purposes: as a means of transporting to all levels those in charge of the mining operations and, more importantly, of raising ore that has been won to the surface. The working galleries at each level are laid with tramway lines, the trucks on which are loaded and then wheeled out to the landing-stage opening on the main shaft. The passing lift picks up the fully loaded truck and takes it to the surface, where it runs directly onto a line of the same gauge: thence it rolls off, unattended, down a gentle slope, to discharge its contents on a great mound of ore. After being crushed, the ore is re-loaded and moved in the same way to the blast furnaces, which work continuously day and night.

The cage lowered us first to the deepest level, where we found ourselves in a sort of chamber about sixty feet square. There the reef was composed of very hard and compact copper-sulphate containing, so Dunston* the mining captain told me, about fifteen per cent of pure metal. Unfortunately it was alloyed with a tincture of bismuth, even the smallest fraction of which – actually scarcely a half per cent – is enough to lower by a hundred and fifty francs per ton the price of Cobar copper on the English market. About six hundred yards to the north-north-east a second shaft, sunk to the same level, struck the same reef, a little narrower there but of just the same quality. Where we stood, at a depth of three hundred and twenty-four feet, the floor, ceiling and walls all round us were composed of a compact mass of this brilliant yellow ore, which glittered like molten gold in the candlelight. The fifty-four-foot thick lode was encased between two layers of perfectly constituted steatite of a lustreless hue, which contrasted with the glowing yellow surface, shining like soap, and the harsh texture of the mineralized walls of the cavern in which we found ourselves. On this iron-hard surface the steel picks of the miners sounded metallically, as though they were striking a cracked bell.

After a few minutes' inspection of this deepest level, the captain tugged a cord connected with the surface and, grasping the speaking-tube which descends with the cage, gave orders to have us raised to the next higher level only about two hundred and sixteen feet from the top.

There we explored two long galleries, one leading off from each side of the main shaft – which was known, after the managing director, as the Barton Shaft. A double line of tramway, on which loaded trucks moved one way and empty ones the other, ran to the end of each gallery.

At certain places, to avoid cave-ins, it had been necessary to buttress the wall with props, for the ore at this depth was not

* A misprint in the original – 'Duntar', should presumably read 'Dunston'. See the first sentence of Chapter V below.

7

8

7. Macquarie Street, Sydney
8. Cobb's Coach on a long bush journey

9. The Town Hall, Sydney

as hard and compact as that on the lower level: it was an oxide of virgin copper, absolutely pure and mostly in a foliated form.

There were still two other levels where miners were at work in galleries of the same kind, threaded with tramways and extending for long distances into the earth. Ventilation shafts had been dug to keep the air pure, and I did not notice any part of the workings where the heat was excessive.

For those who may be interested in the subject I am going to describe here the composition of the ore in the lode which, as we have seen, is enclosed between well-defined layers of what the English call *steatic clay*, and the miners call the *country*.

From the surface down to the level of the second galleries at one hundred and seventy feet, the lode is composed predominantly of blue and green carbonates. Between the second and third levels there is plenty of copper-oxide mixed with a large quantity of iron ores, and the sulphates make their appearance. Lower down these last predominate and finally the lode, becoming more compact, forms an immense deposit of yellow ore containing, in nearly equal proportions, enormous quantities of first quality sulphate and copper.

From the surface to the lowest level the lode maintains an average thickness of more than sixty feet, and in one place where Mr L*** and I took measurements, it divided into two layers, separated by a thin stratum of clay, with a total thickness of three hundred feet.

After we had toured the greater part of the subterranean workings, the lift took us back to the surface and we breathed again the pure air of the open plain.

From the top of the hill, the scene was most animated and interesting. Nearby an army of men and boys were sorting and classifying the ore. Others were loading it on the trucks which trundled away towards the blast furnaces, and down there smoke billowing from the tall chimneys bore witness to the work being done. Now and then our eyes were caught by a sudden gleam of light: a furnace was being opened to draw off the metal which, from a distance, looked like a mass of molten gold, flowing into the clay moulds which cast it in ingots of four to five hundred pounds weight.

Using big crowbars, some men were levering heavy lumps of *regulus* to the furnaces, where this first crude product was treated: others were taking the raw copper to the refinery. There the smelters, armed with long-handled shovels fashioned like soup-ladles, filled the moulds to cast the ingots. These were then cooled by being plunged in water, and stacked in stores to await bullock-team transport to Wellington, the rail-head for Sydney.

The Cobar mine has sixteen blast furnaces and eight more under construction, bringing the total to twenty-four of which two are for refining. In a few months when all these are in use, total production of copper will reach a *hundred* tons of ingots per week. On the London market Cobar copper maintains an average value of £60 sterling, say 1,500 francs, a ton.

Quite a simple calculation will rapidly give us the annual value of the copper output of this mine in the midst of the wilderness, at the antipodes of the European world, and a hundred leagues from every modern means of transport. It will be worth the sum of 7,800,000 francs. We should also note that the figure of 1,500 francs per ton is minimal, as copper frequently fetches 2,000 francs or more.

The company, which was moribund about eight years ago, has since paid many millions of francs in dividends to its shareholders and its output is continually increasing. It employs directly a work force of 750 people, but nearly double that number depend on it indirectly for their living. In addition, an enormous quantity of wood is needed to keep the furnaces burning all the year round: the forests are being depleted and this vital commodity has to be brought from great distances away.

During the eight days we spent in Cobar, I had the opportunity of catching a glimpse of the colony's up-country political life. Mr Barton had to present himself to the electors and make his first election speech on Saturday night, a time of leisure for everyone, or nearly everyone.

After dinner the miners' band, comprising seven or eight brass instruments and a huge drum, came to play a tune suitable for the occasion in front of the *White Horse* Hotel, where the future member of the New South Wales parliament was surrounded by a number of friends drinking his health. A considerable crowd of blacks was gathered around the hotel. They made an alarming hubbub, above the noise of which could be distinguished shouts of '*Hurrah for Barton! Barton our member! Barton for ever!*' The brazen notes of the Cobar band dominated the din, and it was in the middle of this crowd, some waving torches, others playing their instruments, and still others simply bellowing, that Mr Barton stepped out from among his friends to the place where he had to deliver his *maiden speech*.

The candidate made his profession of faith from the balcony of a two-storied house that was being built, the first of its kind in Cobar. Then he was immediately put to the question by the leader of a deputation of *teetotallers* who, however, became entangled among the first words of his speech.

Yells of 'Shut up!' and 'Sit on him!' prevented him from continuing, and he was swallowed up in a nearby part of the crowd.

Then a new orator stepped forward, spoke for five minutes on Chinese immigration to the colony, a matter pregnant with perils if closely examined, and wound up by demanding the candidate's opinion on the question. When Mr Barton had answered this and some other questions in a manner satisfactory to his audience, his friends formed a committee which went into action immediately and asked the crowd, by raising their right hands, to vote on the following motion:

'That R. Barton Esquire is the best man to represent the electors of Cobar in the next parliament of New South Wales.'

This was carried almost unanimously.

The band down below played *God Save the Queen*, the crowd dispersed, the dance halls filled up, and Cobar retired to rest very late that night.

One of the great problems of inland Australia is lack of water. The whole undertaking at Cobar was well nigh ruined by this scourge but, since our visit, the government has voted a considerable sum for the construction of huge reservoirs, holding enough water to meet all the needs of the population throughout the worst droughts. For its own purposes the company too has scooped out large open dams for storing rain-water, for, when it does fall, the rain comes down in torrents.

Gradually, as the country's resources are developed, measures to safeguard the land against drought will be taken everywhere, perhaps in the manner suggested above, perhaps by sinking artesian wells which, indeed, have been a great success in the neighbouring colony of South Australia.

Chapter Five

We stayed about eight days in Cobar and, after having taken leave of our kind hosts, Captain Dunston and his wife, we got ready one fine morning to take the road for Louth, a village on the banks of the Darling River. We had to cover about a hundred miles across almost completely uninhabited country. Between Louth and Cobar there was not a single inn or even a *shanty*.[1] We would therefore have to camp out in the open that night, for it was futile to think of covering the whole distance in a single day. Mr Barton had foreseen the situation, and the previous night a man had gone ahead in a cart with blankets, provisions and all the camping gear necessary for us to spend the night comfortably.

After travelling for an hour we noticed that the leader, *Darky*, the best horse in the team, was showing signs of distress: soon he could go no further. We stopped and un-harnessed him. A few minutes later he began to tremble in every limb: his skin became swollen and puffy. Only then did Mr Barton realize that the unfortunate beast was suffering from arsenic poisoning. At Cobar he had drunk tainted water from the dams near the blast furnaces.

Poor *Darky* had to be abandoned. We were then in a pretty plight, with only two horses to take us on to Louth. Provided the weather remained clear and dry, things would not be too bad; but it was the season for spring rains and, if ill-luck decreed bad weather, God knows how long it would take us to reach

---

* Misprinted in the original 'Breewarrina'.

† Misprinted 'Lithgour'.   [1] A 'one-eyed inn' by the roadside.

Bourke,* two hundred miles away and the only place where we could get fresh horses.

But fate was kind. Arriving at a dry watercourse called Buckweroon Creek, we came upon a camp of bushmen who were droving a mob of fifty or sixty horses to sell in the south.

Luck was certainly with us.

Mr Barton immediately bargained with them for two horses which were soon harnessed. We then continued on our way to the camp that had been prepared for us at Karragundy water-hole, where we arrived very late after a journey through pleasant, slightly undulating country, whose apparently very rich soil supported a varied range of plant life. But apart from our encounter with the bushmen, the solitude had been absolute: only a single kangaroo had hopped across our path.

Passing near Wirtigoona Station I noticed a curious geological formation: some natural caverns in a rocky bluff that rose almost vertically from the plain. Mr Barton informed me that the walls of these caves were covered with aboriginal paintings. I should dearly have loved to examine them at close hand, but time was precious as we could not let ourselves be overtaken by nightfall in the middle of the bush, and I had perforce to resign myself to not seeing the Wirtigoona Caves at all.

At Karragundy we found a party of telegraph lines-men camped round the water-hole. There were fifteen of them in all, and they had plenty of horses and some half a dozen wagons loaded with telegraph posts and steel wire. It was a working party employed by the contractor who was constructing the telegraph line between Louth and Cobar.

Our quarters had been prepared a little farther off in a thicket of *wilgas*, those pretty, leafy trees with deep green foliage which I mentioned earlier. The man, whom we had sent on ahead, had built a big bough hut to shelter our camping-place on a thick bed of dead leaves. A quarter of mutton was roasting on a huge fire which lit up the whole camp, and a pewter vessel of boiling water awaited only our arrival to be turned into tea.

The next day we were wakened at the first streak of dawn by the screeching of many flocks of parrots and cockatoos, coming in to drink at the water-hole and then flying off into the bush.

* Misprinted in the original 'Bourthe'.

The fires were lit to make breakfast, the horses rounded up and we left early for Louth which we reached in the afternoon.

Louth is a hamlet of about ten houses including one quite passable hotel. It stands on the left side of the Darling River which flows along between very steep and high banks. The village has no other reason for existence than to serve as a sort of depot for the stations within a radius of twenty leagues or so, and as a point of embarkation for their wool, which is shipped down the Darling to Adelaide,* the capital of South Australia. Mr Barton had come to Louth because he had to make himself known as a candidate for the approaching elections, but we stayed there scarcely twenty-four hours and left for Bourke as soon as his business was finished.

The road to Bourke runs over alluvial plains along the course of the river, though at some distance from it. The stream meanders about so much that the track is often several miles away, crossing great plains covered with grey-leaved, salty-tasting shrubs – which do not make for a very attractive landscape. On the other hand it seems that this shrub constitutes one of the best possible kinds of fodder. Stock, feeding on its salty leaves, grow fat before one's eyes. Moreover the country is nothing if not picturesque: it could be called an image of absolute desolation.

In the evening we reached Yanda Station where we were welcomed just as warmly as we had been at Pangee. The owner, Mr W. Hattan,† arrived on horseback on a tour of inspection at just the same moment as we did. With him was the government assessor who, under the terms of certain ordinances, was examining the country with a view to fixing, for the Crown lands leased by the squatters, rents more in accordance with their actual value.

I was astonished to see dismounting from the horse a little, dark, thin man with a wooden leg, who took a crutch from a hook on his saddle and advanced smilingly towards us.

'Welcome to Yanda Station,' he said, shaking hands with us.

---

* Actually to Goolwa, the river-port near the Murray mouth, about fifty miles from Adelaide.

† Presumably a misprint, as the name is subsequently and reiteratedly spelt 'Hatten'.

'Come in: the mail-man has just arrived and we are going to have a look at the Sydney and Melbourne papers.'

We entered the main living-room of the station, where we found dinner on the table and a pile of newspapers on a console. In a moment everyone was deeply immersed in the *Sydney Morning Herald* or *Evening News* from Sydney, or in the *Argus* or *Age* from Melbourne.

Mr W. Hatten rejoined us a little later. I heard subsequently about the accident in which he had lost one of his limbs, and the story illustrates so graphically the value which bush-dwelling Australians set upon endurance, and their contempt for all physical suffering, that I have no hesitation in telling it here.

Some years before Mr Hatten had set out from the Yanda head station, alone as usual, to visit a distant paddock and check the condition of the stock pasturing there. While galloping after a beast that had strayed in among the wrong flock, he failed to notice a low-hanging tree branch in his path. It caught him squarely on the chest and hurled him violently from the saddle to the ground ten feet away. The fall shattered his leg. His horse, excited by the chase, did not stop for nearly a mile. The unfortunate man lay there suffering agonies, alone in the desolate bush and twenty miles away from any possible help.

He was condemned to die a horrible death from hunger and thirst.

In spite of the fearful pain, he lost neither his head nor his courage. Summoning up all his strength, he set out to drag himself along in the horse's tracks to the place where the beast was browsing quietly on the grass.

Enduring the acute agony, with superhuman efforts he heaved himself forward on his elbows and good leg, dragging the broken limb across the ground, and succeeded in reaching his horse. Ten times he tried to catch the bridle hanging down within his reach, and ten times the horse took fright and galloped away a little further. At last, after hours of indescribable torture, he managed to seize the bridle and succeeded in scrambling into the saddle.

He reached the station in a state of collapse, and had time only to ask for a doctor before subsiding unconscious into the arms of a station-hand.

They had to go all the way to Bourke, fifteen leagues away,

to fetch the doctor who reached the station during the night. The poor man had regained consciousness, and when the doctor told him his leg would have to be amputated, he contented himself with the laconic reply:

'Do it, and do it quickly.'

His leg was cut off then, and after a few weeks he appeared again among the men and resumed his horse-riding as if nothing had happened. He speedily learnt to hold his seat as well as in the past.

A man must really be made of iron to face such trials successfully.

Mr Hatten treated us like old friends and everyone was quickly made to feel at home.

It was a lively dinner with the conversation touching on all sorts of subjects. Politics were not forgotten and the host, in his capacity as an elector, asked Mr Barton's views on the main issues of colonial politics.

Was he a protectionist or a free-trader?

A free-trader! . . . That's the stuff!

What did he think of the Chinese question? Was he in favour of Mongol immigration to colonial shores, or did he think this race should be forbidden to enter Australian territory?

And what about the land laws? Did he not think they would have to be amended?

Thus were all the important questions of colonial politics discussed over an enormous piece of corned beef.

Before our departure next day, Mr Hatten took us over the shearing-shed and out-buildings which were very like those I had seen at Pangee. Here too they shore 50,000 sheep and, in addition, the fleeces were washed in the river before being baled. I went with Ted Barton to see the operation carried out.

The wool is brought from the shed and placed in immense wooden or tin buckets, perforated all round, and immersed almost completely in the water near the river bank. It is put into each of five or six of these buckets in turn and vigorously stirred about in the water, at each stage, with long poles known as *pot sticks*.

When removed from the last bucket, the wool is very white and has lost much of its grease. It is then spread out on white sheets to dry in the sun, after which it is taken back again to the shed to be packed in bales and sent off to a coastal port.

When the Darling is navigable – which is not very often so far up-river – the bales are despatched to Adelaide, thus having only to float down with the stream. But as the railway approaches the Darling, which it will reach in two or three years, the squatters find it pays better to send their clip to Sydney.

Leaving Yanda, we again followed the course of the river, traversing splendid plains covered with a native grass, known as *blue grass* because it grows in bluish coloured tufts. It makes excellent stock feed. The plains were dotted also with tufts of wild indigo in flower, and still another species soon made its appearance. This was *barley grass*, wild barley, which in certain places grew tall and thick. It was particularly plentiful inside the fence which bounds the Bourke common, a huge reserve of 15,000 acres surrounding the town on which anyone, in return for a trifling fee, may graze a few head of stock.

A convent was the first sign that we were entering the township of Bourke. It is built about three miles up-stream from Fort Bourke, which is to-day no more than a memory. At the time of our journey Bourke was one of the remotest outposts of civilization and the most important town, or rather village, in that part of the interior. It has a population of nearly two thousand inhabitants. It is a pleasant enough place with wide streets cutting each other at right angles. It has a considerable trade with the neighbouring stations, and when the iron road gets there it will undoubtedly become a great commercial centre.

In the morning we continued on our way to Mooculta and arrived there for lunch. There we were in Mr Barton's home, among his brothers and his family, and I need not tell you, dear reader, that we were received like old friends. The ladies were charming and we hit it off with them perfectly. We stayed at the station for two days and with Ted Barton I rode over the great paddocks that make up the 'Mooculta Run'. They were covered with barley grass, growing so luxuriantly that we could pick the heads without stooping from our saddles. Mr Barton, who had known the country from the early days of settlement and had explored the banks of the Darling in every direction, had chosen this *run* for his station about fifteen years before, and he had certainly made the best choice of all the country I had seen up till then. The sheep were lost to sight in the tall grass, above which stood out here and there the tops of that curious bush known as *lignum*, a kind of leafless shrub whose succulent stalks are much sought after by stock. Lignum has the additional advantage of resisting even the longest drought.

In the evening we enjoyed a little music in the Mooculta drawing-room and the time slipped by un-noticed. In Australia, even in the heart of the bush, wherever there are women there is almost sure to be a piano. Music is in fact the best way of helping to pass the time in the long winter evenings, which are but rarely enlivened by the company of visitors: albeit, travellers are generally warmly welcomed wherever they call.

The next day we set out for a distant *paddock* used by the station for raising horses. Mr Barton was going to select a team to replace our four animals who could go no further. We had to choose from about sixty splendid beasts, running together in a mob near the banks of the Bogan river, which flows into the Darling a little below Mooculta. When they saw us the mob broke up and neighing horses galloped off in all directions. Two station-hands hurtled after them, cleverly turning the leaders, so that in a few minutes they had rounded up the whole herd to drive it past in front of us at the gallop. Then they drove them back along the track we had just followed. A quarter of an hour later the horses had all been driven into a small stock-yard, with high railings, among the station out-buildings. There, those we needed were separated from the others, who were turned loose to gallop off in the direction of the paddock they had just quitted.

The following day we drove to Brewarrina.

Before entering the village, our route passed through an aboriginal encampment which warrants a few lines of description.

An area about a hundred yards square was crawling with some forty individuals, men, women and children, all of them repulsively ugly and filthy. They were surrounded by a veritable pack of half-savage dogs, a cross between the *dingo*, the native dog of the country, and some domestic breed introduced by the settlers. Completely naked children played in front of what can only be called apologies for huts, made of gum tree bark dried in the sun. Men and women, barely covered in veritable rags and tatters of decomposing woollen blankets, wandered about the camp. In the shelter of the huts, which the aborigines call *gunyahs*, some old hag, half enveloped in an ancient rag, gnawed away at a kangaroo bone, whilst in front of a nearby *gunyah* a young women with a slender figure, skinny and almost naked, stirred up the embers of a fire which was threatening to go out.

As we passed the camp the dogs set up a howl and the men rushed out to run alongside our *dog-cart*, begging us to throw them some money for brandy.

Never had I seen such a degrading spectacle, and I would never have believed that there were human beings capable of living in such a state of nastiness and misery. However it is a fact: seeing is believing.

It might be imagined that the Australian aborigines would gratefully accept the benefits of civilization; but that would be a mistake. They adopt only the vices of our civilization, and these are tending rapidly to decimate them. It sometimes happens that some philanthropist, stirred by the sight of so much misery, removes a child from his tribe to have him reared and educated among Europeans; but in such cases the black child no sooner obtains his liberty than he forgets everything and hastens to return to his own people.

I was told the true story of a young boy who had been sent off in this way to England by some missionaries who paid for his up-bringing there. He exhibited a lively intelligence, made rapid progress, and returned to Australia after having taken his degrees at one of the great English universities.* People talked of him as a prodigy, and the missionaries pointed to him as a striking proof that the most degraded races have just as much aptitude for acquiring knowledge as have Europeans.

One fine day the aborigine disappeared. Search was made everywhere, and it was only long afterwards that he was discovered in the bosom of his old tribe, as naked, dirty and debased as the rest, for he had added drunkenness to all the other vices of his compatriots.

So it came about, more than once, that travellers staying in

* Stories of this stereotyped pattern are legion. However, Marin La Meslée has accepted a very far-fetched version. It is tolerably certain that no Australian Aborigine ever graduated from any university in the nineteenth century, or could ever have had the chance of doing so.

some up-country hotel were approached by a villainous looking black who would ask them for a glass of whisky in exchange for half a dozen verses of Horace or Homer – which he had pat. People were amused by this strange savage who spoke the purest English and embellished his conversation with Greek and Latin quotations, and they treated him to many a glass of spirits – which he would toss down at a gulp without blinking an eyelid.

Despite their degradation and their repulsive habits, the Australian aborigines are far from being devoid of intelligence. They have left a most remarkable proof of this at Brewarrina, in the form of stone weirs built across the bed of the Darling near a bend in the river. There they have constructed of rocks, piled and fitted together, a series of weirs leading into *cul-de-sacs* from which there is no egress. These fascinating works are known as *the native fisheries*, since they are used to trap fish coming down the river. The aborigines go off in a band a little way above the weirs, enter the river and drive the fish along in front of them by beating the water with tree-branches. The fish are thus diverted by the weirs into the enclosed pools where the natives spear them at leisure. These fish-traps have existed for centuries: at any rate that is the opinion of Sir Thomas Mitchell, the celebrated Australian explorer, who discovered them on one of his expeditions between 1836 and 1839. Today the aborigines are content to maintain them in good repair. Naturally this fishing can take place only during droughts, for when the river is high it covers the weirs completely so that, far from being useful, they become a hazard to navigation. The little steamers that sail the Darling at times of high water sometimes go right up to Walgett, near the Queensland border, more than two thousand miles from the river's junction with the Murray.

As Brewarrina was the most distant point we had planned to visit on our trip, we began to retrace our steps and headed back towards Dubbo. First we passed through Golgolgan, a little village of forty inhabitants, thirty miles from Brewarrina and on the Bogan River, which we had to cross. Naturally there was no bridge but only a ford, approached by way of an almost perpendicular descent. Mr Barton headed his team at it. For a moment we thought our conveyance would capsize but in the end, by following a line of small stones that broke the surface of the water, we reached the other side. We still had to climb the opposite bank, however. Encouraged by a brisk stroke of the whip, the lead horses soon scaled the precipitous slope; but it was a different matter for the rear pair who had the whole weight of the vehicle behind them. For some seconds they paused, unable to reach the top of the bank: then, pivoting firmly on their sturdy haunches, with a supreme effort they heaved us over this difficult threshold and we were bowling along once more on the level ground beyond the river.

I admit that I would much rather cross a stream by means of a bridge than in this manner, but in the part of the world where we were, there was no choice.

Moreover the roadside inns were as badly appointed and badly managed as those on the road to Cobar had been well run. Never shall I forget, for instance, the night I spent in the Willeroon Hotel. We arrived quite late in front of a wooden building, just like any other in this part of the *bush*, on the outside at any rate. But the interior presented the most disgusting spectacle: it could have been mistaken for an aboriginal *gunyah*. We were served with dinner, but I refrain from describing this meal. There was food and drink in all the dishes they served – and much else besides. The bedrooms were consistent with the meals: the beds were occupied by vast armies of bugs, fleas and other species of vermin which kept us awake throughout the night. Luckily the river was not far away, so that in the morning we could plunge into the water to assuage the maddening itching with which we were racked.

It was a joy to leave this verminous hole and continue our way towards Canoubah. It was driving across some vast plains at this point that I had the opportunity, for the first time in my life, to witness the phenomenon of a mirage.

At Warren we found another little Australian township with its wide streets crossing each other at right angles, its shops and hotels in which one finds all the comforts of those in great cities. We stayed there only twenty-four hours and the next day, following the course of the Macquarie through well-wooded country, we reached O'Neill's Hotel at Narromine from which we had set out five weeks before.

Nothing had changed. Other bullockies were camped under the gum trees between the inn and the river, but we had not the time on this visit again to go hunting the wild duck along the Macquarie. We had to cover the twenty-five miles to Dubbo before nightfall and we did. Next day we continued on to Wellington, following the line of the railway which was completed some months after our return to Sydney.

About three o'clock in the afternoon we reached the town and drew up in the courtyard of the Royal Hotel. In thirty-six days we had traversed nearly three hundred leagues of country on roads which were only *tracks*, often scarcely visible in the blazing *bush* sunlight. The groom had ridden the whole way behind us and did not seem to have suffered at all by so doing. 'I am not an *English new chum*,'[1]* he said. There was an ironic overtone to his voice, and it was not the first time that I had noticed among the Australians this disdainful attitude towards the young English dandies who come to live among them.

It is a curious but remarkable fact that everywhere in the Australian colonies the *colonials* waste very little love on Englishmen, even though they are their first cousins. It is only fair to add that, if this sentiment is widespread, it is clearly the fault of the latter. Englishmen think of the colonials as an inferior race. They know that they are for the most part the descendants of emigrants by no means chosen from among the fine flower of the British aristocracy. They regard them therefore as their inferiors in birth and often in education; and unfortunately, with the stupidity and self-assurance characteristic of youth, they neglect no opportunity of impressing on the *colonials* the sense of superiority on which they plume themselves.

Strongly independent by nature and with a pride that yields nothing to that of their English cousins, the Australians believe themselves every bit as good as they are. Being simple and forthright in manner themselves, they cordially detest the affected fops who, lispingly and inordinately accentuating their vowel sounds, strut the Sydney streets with yellow gloves, cane and monocle and who – ultimate horror – even allow themselves to court pretty Australian girls, who sometimes prefer them to their own inarticulate compatriots. For it must be admitted that Australian men often desert their girls for the superior attrac-

[1] A newly-arrived Englishman.
* Misprinted in the original, *English nest chums*.

tions of athletic games, horses, races and *cricket*. It is only fair
to add that they are among the best horsemen in the world, and
that they have often proved their athletic prowess on the rivers
and *cricket-fields* of both England and Australia.

All in all the Australians are good fellows. They have excellent
qualities; and who is without faults?

Mr Anthony Trollope reproaches them with being great
blowers, with boasting about their country, the beauty of their
cities, the grandeur of their public monuments and institutions
and the incomparable wealth of their agricultural, pastoral and
mineral resources etc.

Ah, dear Mr Trollope! Let them have their say. They are not
so far wrong after all; for no country in the world, not even
America in proportion to its population, can show such astonishing progress and that, for most practical purposes, in the last
quarter of a century. And then, they are a young people with
the faults of youth. Let them shout, therefore, 'We have done
this! We have done that!' What harm is there in it?

If a future visitor says to them, 'You have done well, but you
must do better still!' you can be certain they will answer,
'All right! God willing, we shall do whatever still needs to be
done!'

At Wellington I separated from my host and our travelling
companion and took the train to Lithgow, which it reached at
night. There I had to visit a few coal mines as well as the Esk
Bank blast furnaces which treat the iron ore that is so plentiful
in the district.

The Lithgow valley is encircled by quite high mountains
which are striated with seams of coal. These are easy to trace,
in many places breaking the surface of the ground. It is said
that the valley will one day become a great manufacturing
centre, the greatest perhaps in the whole of Australia. Within a
radius of about ten kilometres, it already embraces several
small towns: Lithgow, Esk Bank, Vale of Clwyd and Bowenfels.

The first three, which may be said in a sense to form a single
urban area, contain a big industrial population. The Lithgow
coal mines, the Esk Bank iron foundry and blast furnaces, and
the copper smelting plant at the Vale of Glwyd support a great
number of workers. They live there, rather as people do in
Cobar, scattered about the valley in shelters and dwellings of all

147

kinds, from the tent and the humble *shack*, built of boards and sardine-cases, to the two storeyed stone mansion.

As for the last locality, situated in a much richer area, Bowenfels has a woollen textile factory that also maintains a numerous population in comfort, for manual work is well paid.

The coal mines at Lithgow are not very deep. One of them starts at ground level and the tunnel follows the coal-seam directly into the mountain. They produce a very good quality coal which, though inferior to that of Newcastle, has the advantage of cheapness.

One mine I visited belonged to the owner of the Esk Bank blast furnaces, to whom I had a letter of introduction. As he was away, the works manager received me in his place and took me over the mine whose galleries extend under a good deal of the valley, though only at the relatively slight depth of seventy-three feet. The coal was brought out in horse-drawn trucks on tramways which ran through every gallery. These horses were stabled in a great excavation practically at the end of one of the work tunnels. Once taken down into the bowels of the earth, they never see the light of day again until they are no longer capable of working. According to the manager's account, they quickly become accustomed to the new kind of life they must lead, and they survive quite long enough to give useful service.

I noticed, with considerable surprise, that people moved about the galleries in every direction with completely unguarded lamps. I wondered even more when I remembered having read a French work, now famous, by the learned engineer, L. Simonin, *Underground Life: Mines and Miners*. He stresses that, in all coal mines, naked lights must be shielded as effectively as possible from the open air around them, so as to avoid explosions caused by the presence of that terrible gas known as fire damp. I asked the manager for an explanation of this total lack of safety precautions. He told me that there was no such thing as fire damp in all the mines of the district and that, thanks to an excellent ventilating system, there had never been the least accident to deplore.

Back again on the surface, I was taken to see the blast furnaces on the other side of the railway line about ten minutes' walk away. They are not content merely to produce crude iron by treating the ores of the district, but the process is carried much further. Rails for the tramway lines being built between Sydney and its main suburbs were being manufactured there, and at the time of my visit these rails were actually being smelted and drawn out into shape.

Most people have seen this operation or have read descriptions of it: a mass of white-hot iron, shapeless at first, is fed through a series of moving rollers to be flattened and elongated until it takes the precise length, weight and shape required. Then there is no more to be done than to leave the rail to cool and give it a last polishing.

The Lithgow valley, then, has everything necessary to become one day the Manchester of New South Wales, and the inhabitants of the little townships dotted about the district are certainly not lacking in ambition. Lithgow was the last station at which I had to stop, and as I had to get back to work in Sydney, I caught the express train next day. Again we scaled the slopes of the great zigzag and skirted once more the crests of the Blue Mountains, towering above a sea of verdure extending to the horizon. Again I gazed at Govett's* Leap and the immense panorama of the valleys below. The train sped through Wentworth, where I would like to have been able to see the Falls and that curious phenomenon *the weeping rock*, so called because it is a huge, solitary boulder over which the water from a nearby spring flows down in separate, delicate filaments.

At last, after about six weeks' absence, the train deposited me on the platform at Redfern Station and a few days later I was back in harness again at my job in the *Surveyor General's Office*.

* Misprinted in the original, 'Govet's'.

PART THREE

Geographical, Political and Statistical Description

Chapter One

Definition of Australasia – Physical Description of New South Wales.

The geographical expression 'Australasia' can scarcely be found in any French publication, though our neighbours have been using it for a long time now to refer to all their colonial possessions in the southern hemisphere.*

Hitherto the term has been hardly any more than a political expression, but to-day it can be counted a new geographical one. Some English geographers have used it for years past.

As a political expression Australasia refers only to the British colonial possessions in the neighbourhood of Australia, that is to say the continent itself and the smaller islands in its vicinity: Tasmania, New Zealand and their dependencies.

As a new geographic term, Australasia includes also all the Melanesian islands in addition to New Zealand and its dependencies, which formerly constituted part of Polynesia.

Although the British flag still waves only over the main points in this part of Oceania, British influence is paramount in the whole area and the power of the mother country, and even of the colonies, tends to increase gradually but steadily. Southern New Guinea is already practically a dependency of the colony of Queensland, and before the close of the century all the island groups in the vicinity will be equally dependent on one or other of the Australian colonies.

Australia necessarily occupies the leading position in this part of the world. Encompassing between the Indian and Pacific Oceans an area four-fifths the size of Europe, and extending from 10° 39' to 39° 11' 30" south latitude and from 110° 45' to 150° 56' east longitude, it covers, to the south-east of Asia, a

---

* It is curious that Marin La Meslée should ignore Cape Colony, the Falkland Islands and other smaller possessions in the southern hemisphere which were never thought of as part of 'Australasia'.

considerable part of the world's surface, nearly eighteen times the size of France. At its greatest extent from west to east, from Cape Dirk Hartog near Naturaliste Channel to Cape Cartwright, it measures more than 800 leagues; while the distance from Cape York on the shore of Torres Strait to Wilson's Promontory, which juts into Bass Strait on the south, is 657 leagues. The area of the continent is about 5,500,000 square kilometres.

New Guinea is the second largest land-mass in Australasia, but we shall not be concerned with it here since it still does not form a part of the British imperial possessions in this part of the world. It is becoming increasingly important every day, however, and it can hardly be doubted that, before many years have passed, the still independent part of that great island will have become another dependency of the British Crown.

In terms of physical geography Tasmania is an important appendage of the Australian continent, from the south-east corner of which it is separated by Bass Strait.

It is no part of our plan to treat here of physical geography. To do so would, in any case, be a pointless exercise. Since all geography books give the essential facts under this head, we shall content ourselves with listing the main components of Australasia in order to study in turn the political divisions and commercial resources of each.

Indeed everyone knows that Tasmania, formerly known as Van Diemen's Land, covers an area almost as great as that of Ireland. Situated to the south of Australia, it is shaped like a triangle whose base is almost equal to its altitude, these two distances measuring respectively 213 and 225 kilometres. The island is watered by many rivers: its coastline is deeply indented and screened by many groups of smaller islands, about fifty-five in number and all politically dependent upon Tasmania. There is good reason to think that, at no very remote epoch, this great island was joined to the Australian continent, for its general character, its flora and fauna, are exactly like those of the adjoining parts of Australia on the other side of Bass Strait. Gippsland is, indeed, the true counterpart of Tasmania: in both places the terrain has been violently convulsed. Lofty mountains are separated by deep ravines which support absolutely identical vegetation, eucalyptus, orchids and tree-ferns which frequently grow to great heights. The geological formation is the same, volcanic action having had altogether similar results.

To the east of Australia, a few days' steam from Sydney or Melbourne, the three great islands of New Zealand – North Island, South Island and Stewart Island – form the latest addition to the British domain in the South Pacific. Situated between 34° and 48' south latitude and between 164° 16' 30" and 176° 16' 5" east longitude, and covering an area of approximately 190,000 square kilometres, these islands make a splendid colony, one of the brightest jewels in the British Crown. The Chatham, Auckland and Antipodes Islands, and several other small groups in the neighbourhood of New Zealand have one after another been designated dependencies of this fine colony. The South Island is separated from the North Island by Cook Strait and from Stewart Island by Foveaux Strait. On many French maps these islands still appear under their Maori names in the sonorous native language, *Te Wahi Pounamou, Te Ika a Maui* and *Rakioura* respectively. Their total area is almost equal to that of the United Kingdom. The fertility of New Zealand soil has become proverbial and, as the climate approximates quite closely to that of England, the emigrant who leaves the mother country to make a new *home* overseas finds himself in a place where, once accustomed to the inversion of the round of the seasons, he has no need to change his old ways. In fact he has nothing new to learn about farming, for the climate favours the same cereals.

It seems that England has had the wisdom to choose the best places in the south seas to plant her flag, to settle her energetic people with their own customs and manners, and to found an empire in which the marvels of America are being re-produced daily. She found these lands scarcely a century ago, unknown and unused, inhabited by races who made nothing of any part of them. She came then to occupy this virgin soil, sending out first those of her subjects whom she refused to shelter any longer. Later, learning from experience, she opened the new lands to her excess population, too thickly crowded at home within the narrow limits of the Three Kingdoms. At last one fine day, the news suddenly spread abroad that this favoured land was rich in gold, and every adventurer in the world fixed his eyes on the country that had been unknown the day before.

When the great news was confirmed, there was a rush from all corners of the earth. Men from every nation, from the children of the Celestial Empire to the fair-haired descendants of the worshippers of Odin, came prepared to wrest from the soil its last *nugget*. They were followed in turn by emigrant farmers from England, Scotland, Ireland, Germany and elsewhere, who hoped to make a better life for themselves in the new lands. Gradually new states were established, each with a political life of its own and independent of the others: today they are striding, each along its own path, to a brilliant future under the guidance and powerful protection of the mother country, which leaves them free to govern themselves as they wish.

We come now to the most important part of this chapter, that in which we shall have to describe the political divisions of Australasia. Let us take first the great Australian continent.

New Holland was the name first bestowed on the country by the Dutch navigators, but in recent years the term has given way on our maps to that of Australia, which will be generally accepted in the future. Australia is divided into five great provinces, perfectly distinct from each other.

New South Wales, the first colony to be established by England in this part of the world, at one time comprised the whole eastern portion of Australia. It had been named by the illustrious Captain Cook,* the discoverer of all that part of the Australian coastline. The two colonies of Victoria and Queensland have been detached from New South Wales. From South Australia to the Pacific Ocean and from Cape York to Wilson's Promontory, these three colonies occupy thirty-six per cent, or a little more than one third, of the whole area of the continent.

South Australia, whose northern extension has been dubbed the Northern Territory, occupies the central southern part of the continent. It covers about thirty per cent of the total area, lying between the Indian Ocean on the north and the Great Southern Ocean on the south, and between Western Australia to the west and the colonies of Victoria, New South Wales and Queensland to the east.

In the west the colony of Western Australia occupies the last third (34 per cent) of the surface of the country. As its name

---

* Misprinted in the original, 'Captain Cock'.

indicates, it embraces the whole western part of the continent: it is bounded on the north and west by the Indian Ocean and on the south by the Great Southern Ocean. On the east it is separated from South Australia and the Northern Territory by the perfectly straight boundary formed by the one hundred and twenty-ninth meridian of east longitude.[1]

It was on the eastern coast of Australia at Botany Bay that the English made their first settlement. A few days later the establishment was moved to the more hospitable shores of Port Jackson where the city of Sydney, capital of the colony of New South Wales, stands to-day. In the beginning, as we have already noticed, this name applied to the whole of eastern Australia; but on 1 July 1851 the southern part of New South Wales was detached from the mother colony to form an independent colony which took the name of Victoria. Later on, in December 1859, the north imitated the example of the south and likewise set itself up as a separate province under the name of Queensland.

New South Wales, as it exists to-day and as it will in all probability remain, is thus defined on the map:

On the east its Pacific Ocean coastline extends from Cape Howe in the south to the mouth of the Tweed River in the north. The river mouth is protected on its southern side by a promontory marked on the map as Point Danger.

To the north the colony is bordered by Queensland.

Beginning at Point Danger the boundary runs along the crest of some mountains which, under the name of the Macpherson Range, are none other than a buttress of that great mountain chain which stretches from north to south along the eastern side of the Australian continent. This subsidiary range forms the watershed between the streams draining northward into the Brisbane River and those draining south into the Tweed, Brunswick, Richmond and Clarence. The Macpherson Range joins the main chain (the *Great Dividing Range*) at Mount Mitchell, and thence the crest of the main range marks the boundary between the two colonies up to a point a few miles north of the pretty little township of Tenterfield. From this place the border follows the course of the Dumaresq River from

---

[1] The meridians which serve as boundaries for the Australian colonies are numbered from the meridian of Greenwich (0°).

its source until it joins the Darling or Barwon,* and thence to the point where that river is intersected by the twenty-ninth parallel of south latitude. This parallel in its turn marks the border between the two colonies for nearly 650 kilometres until its intersection with the hundred and forty-first meridian of east longitude.

On the west this hundred and forty-first meridian, from its intersection with the twenty-ninth parallel southward to the point where it crosses the Murray, is the only border between New South Wales and South Australia.

Finally in the south the River Murray, the most important of Australian watercourses, serves as the boundary between New South Wales and Victoria, from the point indicated above right back to its source in the Australian Alps. A straight line between this point and Cape Howe separates the two provinces and terminates the southern boundary of the one that concerns us here.

To avoid costly quarrels with her two neighbours, Queensland and South Australia, it was necessary for New South Wales to determine her northern and western borders quite precisely. This need gave rise to one of the finest pieces of geodesic work to have been carried out in recent years.

A few years ago the New South Wales government sent one of its best officers from the Survey Department, Mr Cameron, to delineate the border, approximately 380 kilometres in length, between that colony and Queensland.

This work, under the direction of the colony's *Surveyor-general*, Mr P. F. Adams, was begun in September 1879 and completed towards the end of the year 1880. Mr Cameron's party had to contend with innumerable difficulties in an arid country, where lack of water caused them great hardship and well nigh forced them to abandon the whole attempt.

From a scientific standpoint, to fix the position of a parallel of latitude over a distance of nearly a hundred leagues is an unusual task, and one demanding a degree of care which men in the profession will appreciate.

A letter of 30 September 1880, from Mr Cameron to the undersecretary of the Department of Mines in Sydney, will give some idea of the material difficulties with which the expedition had to struggle:

* Printed in the original, 'Barwan'.

'Yesterday we finished fixing the position of the frontier line. Next December, when our horses have returned to camp, I shall put you in possession of the maps I have drawn up. I have sent the horses away to a place where there is a little water and grass, for there is none in the vicinity of Fort Grey. The lake is almost dry. This week Mr Crozier had the remaining animals sent to Cooper's Creek. We have had to undergo great hardships this last month and we have lost a horse. I sent one of our men to fetch the mail and provisions, but he lost his way and wandered towards Cooper's Creek for three days with nothing to eat or drink. He made his way towards the east and *struck a track* about twenty miles south of Fort Grey Station. There his horse died and he carried the mail bag and his saddle all the way into the homestead.

'It is impossible for us to survey blocks number 3 and 6 of Fort Grey Station without risking the death of all the government horses: there is neither grass nor water within a radius of a hundred and fifty miles (fifty leagues). We have learnt only too well the difficulty of getting them to the nearest waterhole (*gilgi hole*), sixty miles from Fort Grey, and it holds scarcely enough water to last a week.

J. Cameron.'

Really to appreciate the above letter, it must be remembered that drought and scarcity of water have been, and will always be, the great problem in the interior of this country which has been, up till now, so fatal to explorers. Cooper's Creek is the focus of sinister memories in the annals of Australian exploration, the grave of the first hardy explorers who set out to reveal to the world the secrets of this mysterious inland country. The bones of O'Hara Bourke* and his companions, Wills and Grey, are bleaching in the sands there.

Scarcely had these ill-fated men succumbed to the horrors of death from hunger and thirst in the midst of what seemed to them utterly desert country, when the *squatters*, already cramped for room nearer the coast, pushed inland even beyond this desert where their experienced eyes saw resources to which the explorers had been blind. After Alfred Howitt had discovered King, the last survivor of the unlucky expedition led by Bourke,*

---

* Misprinted in the original, 'Burke'.

in a state of indescribable misery in an aboriginal camp, it was only a few months at most before the first stations were formed on these endless plains and the bleating of sheep, breaking the silence of the desert, transformed it into a source of wealth.

Twenty years later the same sequence of events repeated itself, and almost on the same spot.

Scarcely had Mr Cameron returned to Wilcannia on the Darling, having completed his task of delineating the twenty-ninth parallel from its intersection with the Wango River to that with the hundred and fortieth* degree of east longitude, when gold was discovered at the foot of Mount Brown in the Grey Mountains and, a few days later, at Mount Poole. From all over New South Wales, Victoria, Queensland and South Australia there was a rush of *diggers*, ready to gouge the precious metal out of the desert quartz which served as its matrix. Canvas towns sprang up: the officers of the colony's survey department marked on their maps some more little black circles showing the position of the townships of Milparinka, Mount Poole and so on, and round these places a civilized establishment was formed. The patient Mongol, who is certain to make his appearance on every Australian goldfield, rigged his tent where he judged the ground to be rich in humus and, by hard work and perseverance, wrung from this apparently utterly barren soil enough vegetables to supply the needs of the new community.

At the time of writing there is a population of two or three thousand people in the district, and the townships are already connected by postal services with Wilcannia and Bourke on the Darling. Little by little shafts are being sunk, tanks being constructed to store rainwater and the resources of the district, which the explorers had depicted in such repellent colours, are becoming better and better understood. The area is repeating the history of Ballarat, Mount Alexander, Bathurst and all the other places which owe everything to the powerful lure of gold – their foundation, and the development of the resources of the surrounding countryside, whose pastoral and agricultural wealth sustains them to-day.

* A misprint or, possibly, the author's carelessness. The passage should read 'hundred and forty-*first* degree', as above.

Chapter Two

Administrative divisions of New South Wales – General appearance of the country – Pastoral districts – Land districts – Police districts – Electoral districts – Actual system of government – Administration and justice.

New South Wales is divided in many different ways – to serve the needs of the Survey department, to facilitate the sale of Crown lands and to provide for the administration of justice.

For survey purposes the colony is divided into *counties*, each one comprising a varying number of *parishes* or cantons. These divisions correspond roughly with our *départements* and *arrondissements*, with the difference that in France they are simply administrative units, while in the colony there are neither prefects, sub-prefects nor counsellors of one grade or another and the ponderous administrative machinery is reduced to the barest essentials.

In the early days before much settlement had taken place, New South Wales was divided into nineteen counties by the famous explorer, Sir Thomas Mitchell, who was then the *Surveyor-general*. These are still known to-day as the *nineteen old counties*, and there is still in existence a splendid map of them drawn up by that officer. In more recent years, as the interior was progressively opened up, this system of sub-division was extended to the rest of the colony.

The present Surveyor-general, Mr P. F. Adams, is a great administrator who has done everything possible to increase our geographical knowledge of the country. His far-seeing mind has understood better than anyone else's the pressure for the occupation of Crown lands, and he has long since realized the necessity for surveying accurately every scrap of colonial territory, so that the public may be furnished with the maximum amount of precise information. He directs the work of a great number of officers, whose employment by the department depends upon their possession of high theoretical, and especially practical, professional qualifications. These men are scattered throughout the country, where they work under the direction of *district surveyors* whose task is to map their areas as completely as possible. Other officers work at surveying the parcels of land which settlers are occupying daily, as well as delineating the boundaries of the great *blocks* that make up the inland stations.

Over and above these duties, Mr Adams has built up under his personal direction a team of officers picked from among those of the highest and best-attested capacity: these men are charged with the triangulation of the whole colony. It is an important task, and one whose immense difficulties will be appreciated by all who take any interest in the expansion of geographical knowledge. The whole country, unknown but yesterday, is traversed from north to south by a lofty mountain range which breaks up the terrain in a fantastic manner: further inland extend vast plains, scorched by a fiery sun which dries their surface and leaves to the traveller only an occasional drop of water – and what water! – to save him from dying of thirst.

For the past fifteen years or so squatters have been pushing farther out, beyond the western* and northern boundaries of New South Wales, hard on the heels of the explorers. Little by little their sheep, cattle and horses are occupying those endless solitudes which impose such severe trials on those who seek first to plumb their depths.

It should not be imagined, however, that Australian pastures resemble those of Europe where one may hear at every step the bleating of sheep, the lowing of cattle or the neighing of horses. Anyone who has not been initiated into the mysteries of station life, and who travels these vast territories without having first acquired a little colonial experience, would be completely lost.

Australia, as I remember it, is nothing like any other country in the world, least of all England or France. It is a land of contrasts, and it is not for nothing that it is situated in the antipodes. If men, women and animals do not stand on their heads, it is because the laws of physics forbid it: if that were not so, there would be no other compelling reason why they should not live thus. Nevertheless, a host of natural and other phenomena exhibit characteristics quite the opposite of those thought

* A misprint in the original, 'eastern'.

normal among us. Thus for example, the inexperienced traveller in the *back blocks* (the name given to the far western, inland parts of the colony beyond the Darling) would be tempted to believe like the first explorers, Sturt among others, that he has come to a veritable Sahara. A frightening solitude, its silence broken only at rare intervals by the cackle of the mocking bird (*laughing jackass*), or the harsh shrieking of a flock of *galahs*,* hems him in on every side. The land is empty, the vegetation almost everywhere the same, and the grass seems scanty. He would ask himself if it is really possible to get anything out of such fearfully monotonous and apparently arid country. If he were riding alone, he would soon find out that there are scarcely any indications of his route through the *bush* and that, to keep on the right path, one needs the experience of a *bushman*, which is not picked up in a day. If he should push a little further inland, all trace of roads will disappear and the compass must be his guide across those endless plains, covered with a stunted and sparsely scattered species of eucalyptus that offers no landmark or point of reference. He will find that he must travel thus day after day without meeting a living soul, without seeing a sheep or a single head of cattle. He will ask himself what on earth can have become of those millions of sheep, those hundreds of thousands of cattle he has heard about and which, as he would have satisfied himself in Sydney or Melbourne, furnish the staple exports of the country. Then perhaps he will fall in with a flock of two or three thousand woolly beasts grazing peacefully in the depths of the *bush*, without shepherds or even dogs, abandoned, so to speak, to their unhappy fate. After many days he will get a clear idea that, generally speaking, if the country is sometimes supremely fertile along the coast, on the tablelands, in the valleys and along the watercourses; in the backblocks, on the contrary, it takes five or six acres to feed a single sheep throughout the year and twelve or fifteen acres to support a bullock or a horse. The reason for the immense size of Australian stations will become clear, and when he is told that this or that squatter leases twelve or fifteen hundred acres from the government, he will not be unduly impressed. The wealth of inland Australia lies not in the value of the land, which though generally good is always liable to be depreciated by the uncertainty

* Misprinted in the original, 'gallahs'.

of the seasons and periodic droughts, but in the immensity of the areas available. If the climate should happen to change, if the rain should fall more regularly and the droughts become less frequent, there would be no limit to the productivity of every kind of crop. Such a change is improbable, but there will always be along the watercourses a considerable quantity of land easily adaptable to the needs of agriculture. As for the pastoral industry, for a long time to come it will be the only possible one that pays, apart from mining for gold and other metals which may be exploited in due course.

It must be understood that the above remarks apply only to the country that extends from beyond the Darling to the western coast of the continent. Ernest Giles, John Forrest and Warburton who, in their expeditions of 1873, 1874 and 1876, linked up the discoveries of the first explorers with the already known parts of Western Australia, traversed country identical in character with that which we have described. The sum of all the discoveries made in recent years is that the interior of the great Australian continent has all the appearance of being a desert. It does not necessarily follow, however, that it is uninhabitable or entirely lacking in resources: appearances are often deceptive. For example, nothing looks so profoundly desolate as those great plains covered with shrubs of a salty-tasting foliage (*salt bush plains*), if indeed one can apply the term 'foliage' to those long, thin, narrow, grey-drab leaves that cover the little bushes scattered over the reddish soil, where not a blade of grass is to be seen. Nevertheless it is precisely this kind of country that the squatters like best. Salt bush, which is not affected by the most terrible droughts, contains highly nutritive juices much sought after by sheep and cattle, which grow astonishingly fat in the midst of this apparent desolation.

Yet near these areas the traveller will come upon somewhat more broken country. The arid plains give way to rising ground and low hills which, although sandy, are clothed in green and smiling vegetation. A lusty shrub covers the rises and gives the whole landscape a more verdant air. In comparison with the stark country just traversed, one is tempted to believe it an oasis. That would be a great mistake: that bush is the *spinifex*, the enemy of the squatter and his sheep, and the country where it flourishes will not grow anything else.

10. The Zig-Zag on the Western line, New South Wales

11

12

11. Outside a bush tavern: 'penitential moments'
12. Brisbane in the 1880s

This is indeed the absolute desert!

Wherever this shrub makes its appearance, all trace of animal and vegetable life disappears. The very crows shun this country that produces nothing but stones, sand and the eternal spinifex.

But let us return to the way in which the administration is carried on. In its immense area of about 360,000 square miles New South Wales contains a very wide range of resources. Between the mountains and the sea there is some extremely fertile soil, suitable for both tropical and temperate-climate agriculture. On the tablelands and the great alluvial plains, especially along watercourses, wheat and other European grains may be grown successfully; and the time will come when the limits of farming land must be pushed back far beyond their present position. The rest of the country, that is to say the great inland plains, still holds out attractions only to the big graziers; but as the hills traversing these plains are rich in gold, copper, and doubtless other minerals, the miner in those distant parts is beginning gradually to compete with the squatter.

However, up to the present time the greater part of all the land in the colony is still occupied only by pastoralists. It has therefore been necessary to divide the country into pastoral districts, of which there are thirteen.

The Clarence and Macleay districts occupy the north-east coast; that of the Gwydir is in the north near the Queensland border. The Liverpool Plains and the New England pastoral districts adjoin the Clarence and the Macleay; the Warrego, Albert, Darling and Lachlan districts are to be found further inland, while in the central and southern parts of the colony are situated the districts of Wellington, Bligh, Murrumbidgee and Monaro.

In addition to these major divisions, the needs of settlers and the complexities of the different systems under which Crown lands may be occupied, have led to the creation of *Land Districts*, in each of which the government maintains an agent charged with the duty of making conditional or outright sales of the public domain.

During the last few years the number of these land districts has increased considerably. This expansion was brought about by the boom in land settlement since 1861, the year in which the parliament of the colony passed the laws which still regulate the alienation of Crown lands to-day. For the same reason it has been just as necessary to increase the number of *police districts*, another kind of territorial division, each of which is presided over by a *police magistrate* responsible for the administration of justice in his area.

Finally there exists yet another kind of territorial division of an essentially political character – the *electoral district*. Each of these, according to its importance and the size of its population, sends to the New South Wales parliament two or more representatives. The boundaries of these districts, like those of the judicial and territorial divisions mentioned above, are necessarily variable and change with the needs of settlement.

It may seem that the colony's administrative apparatus lacks cohesion; but actually these over-lapping territorial divisions tend day by day to unify it, in proportion as it is more closely settled by the colonists and the immigrants who arrive from the United Kingdom practically every month. It is easy to understand that the changes leading to population growth, and the formation of new farming, mining or other centres, ought naturally to bring about corresponding modifications in the country's administrative machinery. Such and such a district, which had a thousand inhabitants five years ago, may have twenty-five thousand to-day; and when its previously unrealized mineral and agricultural resources are developed suddenly, it becomes necessary to augment the judicial and other administrative personnel of the district, or perhaps even to divide it into two. Thus, then, the process of unification proceeds little by little. Already most of the judicial and land districts have exactly the same boundaries, and one day those of both will be assimilated to those of the counties.

In addition to these general divisions of the whole area of the colony, there exists a certain number of municipal districts or municipalities, which vary in size according to their location. As their name suggests, these districts comprise only the areas occupied by big cities and their suburbs, and by less important towns or townships. As the area of a municipality is more or less proportional to the density of its population, it follows that those with the largest areas are the least heavily populated. Under the direction of a *mayor* and several *aldermen* (municipal councillors), who are elected by the rate-payers, the municipalities administer their own affairs as they please.

When inland towns or villages are incorporated as municipalities with boundaries fixed by act of the colonial parliament, the central government reserves to itself only the administration of justice and the upkeep of main roads of general importance, which happen to pass through the district. Town affairs, the maintenance, lighting etc. of the streets, the construction of local roads, all such matters are the municipality's own responsibility. It is given the authority, moreover, to levy rates on land and real estate, and sometimes to add a few centimes for the building and maintenance of local services. In no case may these taxes exceed ten per cent of the income from the land or fixed property, the value of which for this purpose is estimated by a public official.

What has just been said about municipal self-government leads us quite naturally to speak about the colonial government itself, a subject on which we have to make some observations that, we hope, will not be without interest.

But we shall leave New South Wales for a moment to have a look at the British colonies in general throughout Australasia.

The convict system came to an end in Queensland in 1839, in New South Wales ten years later* and in Western Australia in 1868. Since that date there have been only two kinds of colonies in Australasia, *Crown colonies* and independent colonies.

Western Australia and, though they are outside the Australasian group, the Fiji Islands are the only Crown colonies. New South Wales, Victoria, Queensland, South Australia, Tasmania and New Zealand are all independent colonies: that is to say, they govern themselves as they wish, without either any kind of subsidy from the mother country or the payment of any tribute to it. Each is content to supply from its own budget the emoluments of a governor, sent out from the metropolitan country to the colony, as the representative of the sovereign who presides over the destinies of the British world. Consequently, each of the provinces we have just named has a

* This is rather misleading. In fact transportation to New South Wales ceased for all practical purposes in 1840. In 1849 two shiploads of felons were sent out, but Sydney people protested so strongly that later exiles were sent on to remote parts of the Moreton Bay district.

different system of government and pursues different internal and external policies. They negotiate with each other as sovereign powers, being independent not only of the mother country but of each other also.

As for the *Crown colonies*, they are governed directly by the *Colonial Office* in London, along lines quite similar to those we have adopted in France; but with the difference that the system is only temporary and is to be replaced by *self-government* as a colony becomes more important.

Now let us return to New South Wales.

It is well known that this colony began as a penal establishment to which, for many years, England used to transport the malefactors of the Three Kingdoms. Everyone has heard about Botany Bay and the *convicts* of New Holland: not only among foreigners but in England itself, there are still people who regard these lands as places of exile. There has been none of it for forty years past, God be praised!

In the beginning New South Wales was governed, as our penal colony of New Caledonia is to-day, by Marine Corps officers whose authority was more absolute than that of the King of England; and that state of affairs lasted as long as an exclusively penal system flourished. But following the arrival of free immigrants, it became necessary to introduce successive changes into the government of the colony. These people, whose numbers grew from day to day, had acquired considerable influence in the country, and the system of absolute and arbitrary rule could not satisfy them. The conduct of one of the officers who succeeded Captain Phillip, founder and first Governor of the Botany Bay establishment, hastened the course of events. The overbearing Captain Bligh had antagonized, not only the free colonists, but also the officers of the regiment stationed in Sydney. Discontent became general following an affair in which he had shown himself more imperious and arbitrary than ever, and which culminated in the imprisonment of a distinguished man to whom the colony owed the introduction of sheep and the development of its pastoral resources. To say this is to identify Captain Macarthur.* With the support of his officers and the principal free inhabitants, Major Johnston took it on himself to arrest the Governor. Bligh was in fact imprisoned but

* Misprinted in the original, 'Macarthen'.

later sent back to England by Lieutenant-Colonel Paterson, who had him released and sent to London aboard the *Porpoise*. The administrative system did not undergo real change, however, until 1821,* the year in which a legislative council, composed of members nominated by the Governor, was set up in the colony. It was during this same year that the two explorers, Hume and Hovell, discovered that part of Australia which to-day constitutes the colony of Victoria, and which they called Australia Felix.† The discovery of this rich country was bound to lead, before very long, to radical changes in the government of New South Wales. It was only in 1836, however, that Port Phillip, to-day's Melbourne, was definitely colonized. The more free immigration constantly increased the number of settlers and accelerated the development of the colony, the more obvious became the necessity of granting those wider liberties, which the colonists never wearied of demanding in the most vociferous manner. A legislative council, composed of creatures of the government, would satisfy them no longer. The country's budget had already reached a considerable sum, and they intended to obtain control of their own funds and to use them for something other than the maintenance of an administration, composed exclusively of *civil servants* from the mother country. Great numbers of these government employees drew enormous salaries and pensions from the colonial revenue, which was also charged with the upkeep of the convicts the home country sent to Sydney.

Tired of this situation, and wanting to try their wings at governing themselves in their own way, the colonists repeatedly laid their pleas at the foot of the Throne, petitioning at the same time the Queen and the English Parliament. These efforts deserved some success and at last, in 1843, a *'bill to provide for the government of New South Wales'* received the sanction of Parliament and the approval of Her Majesty, the Queen of the United Kingdom of Great Britain and Ireland.

This *bill* established a legislative council of fifty-four members, of whom thirty-six were elected by the colonists and the

---

* Actually 1823.

† In the original 'Hovell' is misprinted 'Howell'. Hume and Hovell's expedition was made in 1825, not 1821; and the district was named 'Australia Felix' still later, not by them but by Major Mitchell.

remainder nominated by the Crown.* The colony was then divided into electoral districts, and this first step towards self-government was followed almost at once by a movement for a purely elective government, responsible only to the people, of whom its members would be the elected representatives.

The separation of the province of Victoria from the mother colony, and the discovery of gold in both territories, led to considerable changes throughout Australia: the population suddenly increased to an astonishing degree, and the movement just mentioned became so powerful that England was fully persuaded she would do well to grant her antipodean subjects a constitution and charters of separation from each other.

This constitution was granted to New South Wales in 1854 and it has not been changed since. The same constitution, with minor modifications, was accorded a little later to each of the Australian colonies in turn. Tasmania received her charter in 1855, and in 1856 the two provinces of Victoria and South Australia were set up as self-governing communities, whilst Queensland received the benefit of a constitution from the time of her separation from New South Wales in 1859. Alone among the continental colonies, Western Australia still awaits the boon of representative self-government. In advance even of New South Wales, New Zealand had been set up as an independent colony from the year 1853.

The reader will pardon this digression in which we have tried to outline in a few words the whole political history of Australasia. We shall now return to the constitution of New South Wales to give the best idea we can of the liberality England has shown towards her great colonies, by putting them in a position completely independent of the mother country and granting them all their rights without claiming any duties in return.

At the head of the administration stands the Governor, nominated by the Crown for a term of seven years. As the Queen's representative, he fulfils the same function in the colony as that of the Crown in England. He acts, in a sense, as an intermediary between the imperial government and that of the colony over which he presides. Thus he gives or withholds his

---

* The bill was actually passed in 1842, and it provided in fact for a total of thirty-six members, of whom twenty-four were to be elected and twelve nominated.

assent to the acts of the colonial parliament, pending the approval of the imperial authorities. He also has the right of calling together and proroguing parliament and of nominating members of the legislative council; but in this latter business he must follow, more or less, the advice of his executive council. He receives a salary of two hundred thousand francs a year.

After the Governor whose powers, it should be understood, are extremely limited, comes the Executive Council we have just mentioned.

If, as is seemly for any monarch in a constitutional democracy, the Governor of New South Wales reigns but does not govern, the Executive Council governs but does not reign. It is made up of ministers chosen by the second chamber, which is known as the *Legislative Assembly*. Real power lies in the hands of this Council.

The ministers which compose it occupy in the colony a position exactly like that of cabinet ministers in France. They are responsible for their acts to the Assembly which, having chosen them, reserves the right to dismiss them. It is their task to draft the laws and present them for debate in the two houses which constitute Parliament: the Legislative Assembly and the Legislative Council.

The Legislative Assembly, which is nothing other than an exact model of the House of Commons in England, is composed of 108 members elected by the people on the basis of universal franchise. New elections must be held every three years.

The Legislative Council, which corresponds more or less to the English House of Lords or to our French Senate, comprises a limited number of members nominated by the Governor on the recommendation of the Executive Council. They bear the title 'honourable' and hold their seats for life.

Every bill brought forward by the Government must be passed by both Houses and approved by the Queen before becoming law. However, English laws remain valid in the colony unless they have been superseded by local acts of parliament.

Such is the system, with some slight modifications, under which all the independent colonies of Australasia are governed. As far as one can see, they enjoy the most complete liberty to manage their own affairs as they like. It is rarely, moreover, that the imperial government withholds assent to a bill, save in the most important cases.

In spite of the liberality of these arrangements there already exists, especially in New Zealand, a tendency towards even more complete independence of the mother country. In all the provinces the governors are still Crown appointees to a position which, though almost a sinecure, is sustained by the colonial budget. There is no reason why these officials, imposed by the Crown, should not be replaced by governors selected by the local parliaments. In New Zealand there has already been much talk of altering this last constitutional link that still binds the colony to the government of the mother country. This reform has many partisans and it is not impossible that, before long, the efforts of an influential section of the Legislative Assembly of that fine colony will be crowned with success. If this should happen in New Zealand, the other colonies in Australasia would, in all probability, hasten to follow their neighbour's example and the secession of the colonies from the mother country would then be complete. Australia would then be no more than a collection of republics which, having all sorts of interests in common, would end by forming a *federation* on the model of the United States of America: they would recognize by implication the primacy of England, while being in practice completely independent. Moreover the idea of an Australian federation and the creation of an *Australian Dominion* seems to be finding favour among the English themselves. The Duke of Manchester, on his return from a visit to Australia in 1881, speaking at a meeting of the Colonial Institute in London, announced his strong support for the federation of the great Australian colonies.

These speculations have distracted us somewhat from our subject, to which we shall now return without further digressions.

In the colony which concerns us at this point, the administration of the law is in the hands of a magistracy, which may be considered as irremovable, and whose functions are modelled exactly on those of the English bench. It is superfluous to say that no position in the state is more respected or more sought after, than that of a member of this branch of the judicial administration.

Instead of the complicated machinery of a system such as we have in France, with its courts of the first instance, its courts of appeal with their infinite number of presidents, lawyers, barristers and solicitors-general – receiving a salary which three-quarters of the time, in New South Wales, would not suffice to maintain the dignity of their position – the legal system is reduced to its simplest form.

The English consider that the magistracy, before all else, must be placed above any suspicion of being susceptible to political influence: hence, life appointment to the bench is considered an inviolable principle in the colony, as in Britain.

At the apex of this administrative structure, made up of men chosen from the most eminent members of the colonial bar, stands the Supreme Court, headed by a president who carries the title of Chief Justice, and comprising three other judges known as *Puisne Judges*. In criminal matters there can be no appeal from the decisions of this Supreme Court. Equally there is no appeal in civil cases, unless the Court itself authorizes the plaintiffs to appeal to the Court of *Queen's Bench* in England.

To ensure that the status of a Supreme Court Judge is the highest in the country, Parliament has written into the annual budget a sum of £2,600 (sixty-five thousand francs) for the salary of the Chief Justice and of £2,000 (fifty thousand francs) for each of the other judges.

These magistrates, nominated by the Governor in his Executive Council, are chosen, as we have already pointed out, from among the most distinguished members of the colonial bar.

The colony is divided into six great judicial districts whose courts correspond in some sort to our courts of appeal, except that with us each of these courts comprises a certain number of judges and counsellors, a solicitor and an advocate-general, whilst in the colony a single judge is considered quite sufficient to hear all ordinary cases: In a *Court of Quarter Sessions* this judge hears criminal cases which have been referred by *justices of the peace* or by *stipendiary magistrates,* who administer the law in each of the police districts we have already mentioned. Justices of the Peace are selected from among leading citizens: the title they bear is purely honorific – though much sought after – for they must needs be content with nothing more tangible than the honour of belonging thus to the colonial magistracy. Each of the six district judges we have mentioned draws a salary of £1,000 (twenty-five thousand francs) a year. A stipendiary magistrate, whose salary varies according to the importance of the place in which he is stationed, never receives less than £350, say 8,750 francs a year.

From what has been said it should be clear that, if the number of magistrates who draw their salaries from the colonial budget is very limited, their emoluments are, on the other hand, ample to enable them to maintain the dignity of their office. Although there is no law to this effect, the colonial magistracy and judiciary may be considered as irremovable: yet there have been cases in which the executive has had to act ruthlessly and deprive of their functions some magistrates, whose public and private conduct was tending to lower public respect for the office with which they had been entrusted. In no case, however, are politics allowed to serve as an excuse for any change whatever in the personnel of the colonial bench. The magistrate's duty is to apply the law, whatever political party has enacted it; and if his conscience will not permit him to discharge his duty faithfully, it is always open to him to hand in his resignation.

The same legal system with some minor qualifications, obtains generally in all the Australasian colonies, except Western Australia. As a Crown colony it is governed under English law, administered by judges appointed by the imperial government, and these are almost the only differences between its legal system and those of its neighbours.

The reader may be astonished at the handsome stipends paid annually to colonial magistrates, and judicial salaries are even higher in Victoria than in New South Wales: but the English hold that those called upon to dispense justice must be placed in a financial position which puts them beyond the reach of any suspicion of corruption.

In France we have always had the honour of possessing a judiciary that is a model of integrity, and its merit in this respect is all the greater, considering that it is so numerous, and also worse paid than in any other country on earth. However, when one remembers that we pay our comedians, under the pretext that they are artists, better than three-quarters of the members of our magistracy, one is inevitably driven to admire the honourable integrity of our judges even more, while at the same time feeling a certain shame at their treatment.

But let us return to the subject.

Chapter Three

By handing over to the colonists the direction of their own affairs, the mother country, in a sense, made to her Australian colonies a free gift of the territory they occupy. When she set free these off-shoots from the old parental stock, Great Britain set them up, so to speak, with a magnificent dowry in the shape of immense areas of freely saleable land.

New South Wales, after having two great colonies torn from her bosom to lead free and independent lives at her side, still had left a territory whose area was equal to that of France and Great Britain combined. She had at her disposal 199,139 square kilometres of land, of which about two-fifths were suitable for temperate-climate and tropical agriculture, while the other three-fifths consisted of grazing country, mountains and desert – the last more apparent than real. This was an inheritance that, wisely managed, should have become the source of incalculable wealth.

In addition to these agricultural and pastoral resources, the land held in its depths mineral treasures of inestimable value and extent, whilst its surface was covered in certain places with all kinds of timber, which some reports claimed would be another prolific source of wealth.

The need to provide for the wise administration of this huge estate made itself felt from the first years after the establishment of essentially popular government. Before that time the different governors, who had once enjoyed almost absolute power, had alienated Crown lands through a system of grants which was good in principle in the sense that, if it brought little money into the treasury, it at least tended to encourage the establishment of farms and landed property. It was also an excellent method of attracting free immigrants: it offered them the advantage of being placed, from the time of their arrival in the colony, in a position to earn their own living while, incidentally, they were enriching the country by developing its primary agricultural resources. But as the population increased, the value of the public domain became too great for it to be thus alienated without realizing in return what it was really worth.

The need to establish land laws, which would hold out worthwhile inducements to future settlers, then appeared to be the first duty of colonial statesmen. Thus in 1861 Sir John Robertson, the premier, presented for the approval of the two houses of parliament a bill embodying the principles we shall expound below.* These basic principles have still not been changed, though the land laws of 1861 were amended in 1875 and in 1880.

On the premise that the colony's future depended almost entirely on a system of Crown land alienation which would attract immigrants by offering them immediate advantages, Sir John Robertson devised a code of land laws from which he hoped great things. His aim was to create a class of small yeomen farmers, attached to their own plots of soil, and to inhibit the growth of great landed estates which had been favoured in the early days by the land-grant system. By that time the squatters had become the aristocrats of the Australian colonies, and had begun to carve for themselves veritable little kingdoms out of the public estate. It was against this class, then, that the main clauses of the laws passed by the New South parliament in 1861 were aimed. We shall see below to what extent the goal of Sir John Robertson and his supporters was realized.

The immense territory at the colony's disposal was far from being known as it is to-day. At most a fifth of the land was accessible to the immigrant farmer: the rest was too remote for him to settle, or still offered immediate inducements only to pastoral occupation. This state of affairs, which will continue for many years yet, gave rise to two different systems for dis-

* Robertson was secretary for lands at the time. Later he was knighted and became premier several times. The 'principles' were embodied in two bills.

176

posing of shares of the public estate. Under the first the government rents, for a limited period, immense blocks of land to squatters who wish to extend the area of their stations, or to found new ones: under the second the government makes conditional or outright sales of any land, not reserved by the Crown for public purposes, and of which the title has not already been transferred to any person or corporation whatever.

Although we have already dealt briefly with the subject in the first two parts of this book, it will not be pointless to give some description of squatting and station life here. We shall thus be able to discuss at the same time the first of the just-mentioned methods of disposing of Crown land.

In Australia a huge block of land, occupied by a big pastoralist and devoted exclusively to sheep and cattle raising, is known as a station. In New South Wales a station generally consists of one or more *runs* (from the English verb *to run*): this is a piece of land whose area is fixed by specially appointed officials, according to the fertility of the soil or its capacity to maintain 4,000 sheep or 800 head of cattle. In no case may a run be less than 25 square miles or more than a hundred square miles in area. That constitutes, it should be understood, a pretty little property. The government itself fixes the rent the *squatter* must pay for each of the *runs* that make up his station or stations. The term of occupation is fixed at five years; but if the squatter improves his *runs*, by digging dams or otherwise making them capable of carrying more stock than the number fixed by law, his lease may be extended for ten years. The rent is in a sense only nominal and amounts, on the average, to 15 centimes per acre, say about 40 centimes per hectare per year. The leasing of any land whatever to any squatter is no bar to the outright sale to another person of any or all of his station, even during the currency of his lease. This fact constitutes the greatest grievance, to which the squatters have been able to give some validity, against the system of alienating Crown lands in force in New South Wales since 1861.

Briefly, the system is based on the principle of *free selection before survey* of a block of land, not greater in area than one square mile or 640 acres, and not less than 40 acres.

That is to say that any person, of sixteen years of age or more, can go and choose wherever he likes, in any part of the colony where the land has not been reserved for public purposes nor previously alienated, a block of from 40 to 640 acres.

The *runs* are not considered as alienated lands, since they are still the property of the Crown which leases only the grazing rights to them. It follows that the squatter is constantly liable to see some intruder come and settle right in the middle of his *run*. When this happens again and again on the choicest parts of his station, his situation becomes desperate.

Lest this should seem too unfair, let us add that the land laws contain a clause permitting the squatter to buy *for cash*, at a fixed price of £1 per acre, any part of his run between 40 and 640 acres in extent, on which he has previously made improvements at least equal in value to the fixed purchasing price, that is to say improvements, worth at least £1 per acre.

The *free selection* system is extremely favourable to anyone wishing to become a small landed proprietor, for to this right of free choice of land it adds very easy terms for payment and for meeting other conditions of the purchase.

In fact the government asks of the *free selector* the immediate payment of only one quarter of the purchase price, which is invariably fixed at £1 sterling (25 francs) per acre. At the end of five years a further instalment of at least a shilling (1 franc 25) per acre must be handed over, and from that time onwards the *free selector* is bound to pay interest at the rate of only five per cent per annum on his remaining debt to the government, until its final liquidation. Thus he is free to discharge his indebtedness at a stroke, or to pay not less than a shilling per acre on account each year until the purchase is completed over a fourteen-year period.

But in addition to payment of the gross fixed price, the government stipulates that the purchaser should fulfil certain conditions. Failure to do so results not only in the loss of all rights to the land he has selected, but also in forfeiture of all moneys he has paid into the treasury to ensure its possession.

These conditions are as follows:

1st. Every *free selector* is bound to reside personally on the land of his choice for the first five years.

2nd. He is also bound, during this time, to make permanent improvements on his land to a value of at least ten shillings per acre, whether by the erection of substantial fences, by building a farmhouse, or by clearing and cultivating some of the ground.

The free selector thus enters with the government into a contract which is subject to cancellation, for he loses everything if he does not fulfil the above-mentioned conditions. Such, in a few words, is the system under which Sir John Robertson hoped to cover the colony with small farms, and to create a class of independent landholders in the country. But the results have often been quite the opposite of those he envisaged.

The squatters, who were the target of the system, quite naturally took thought in their own defence, and to avoid the invasion of their runs by their enemies, the *free selectors*, they made use of the provisions of the new laws themselves.

In the acts of 1861 there was a clause ordaining the sale by public auction of any selection that had been abandoned or resumed by the government because the selector had failed to fulfil the stipulated residence or improvement conditions. It was this clause which often served the squatters as a defensive, or even an offensive, weapon.

In essence, the most important thing for the squatter was to maintain the necessary access to all the main watercourses on his *runs*, and it was just there on the water-frontages that the *selector* would usually pitch his tent. To him water was, if possible, even more indispensable than to the pastoralist, and the land adjacent to watercourses was generally better for farming and richer in humus than anywhere else.

In such a badly-watered country, to deprive a squatter of his water was, so to speak, to pick the eyes out of his *run* and force him to use all possible means to protect his interests.

He therefore fell back on trickery to gain his ends and save his station from the threat of ruin. He had some of his dependents select the vital water-frontages on his *runs*, but since these bogus *free selectors* did not fulfil the conditions of purchase demanded by the law, the *selections* were declared forfeit and offered for sale at public auction. As the land had real value only for the squatter himself, he rarely found anyone bidding against him at the fixed price of £1 per acre. Once master of the water-frontages, he had no need to fear intruders and could sleep soundly in his bed: his enemy, the *free selector*, would not be worrying him again for a long time.

Moreover this system of alienating the Crown lands had other bad results, for it allowed the *selectors* to establish themselves in the best parts of the colony, engrossing the richest land and the most important water-frontages, so that only second-grade land was left for future farmers. Luckily the colony has immense stretches of country suitable for all kinds of agriculture, so that the evil, although already considerable, has not extended beyond areas having reasonable access to markets. But as railways extend into the interior, as new markets spring up, and as rich districts, once too remote to attract settlers, are placed in rapid communication with the new centres, the evil, if not arrested in time, will assume gigantic proportions.

Finally, this free selection system tends also to encourage a disorderly dispersion of the population. When, under its provisions they have settled at a great distance from towns, selectors often lead a miserable life. Their children grow up around them with no chance of being given any education whatever. The nearest school is perhaps fifty miles from their hut: how can they be sent to it? In our century, that is rightly waging an implacable war on ignorance, this is an unenviable situation.

Obviously the author of these laws, who certainly longed for the occupation of Crown lands, did not foresee all the consequences they would entail. But the English and their Australian cousins are above all men of common sense, and once they have recognized a mistake their first thought is to set about rectifying it. There is already a general conviction in New South Wales that the laws of 1861 were misconceived and that, although they have had some success in putting settlers on the land, they are far from having achieved what was expected of them.

At the present time the squatters, on the one hand, complain of their short-term tenure and would be willing to pay a somewhat higher rent for longer leases. On the other hand, the factors just mentioned are militating against the continuance of free selection before survey.

Besides, it is certain that a great part of the colony's land holds no attractions for the farmer and is still suitable only for pastoral occupation. In the other part, it is bad for the development of settlement that the best land should serve no other purpose but to feed sheep.

There is now a suggestion that the whole territory should be divided into two classes of land, the one exclusively pastoral and the other agricultural. In the first, which would comprise all the land difficult of access to the ordinary colonist and of little agricultural promise, the system of pastoral leaseholds would be maintained, but with amendments to provide for longer-term leases. By the same token, lessees would have to make certain improvements on their *runs* in return for the advantages thus granted them. The second class would comprise all lands suitable for agriculture and relatively easy of access. These areas would first be surveyed in blocks of from 40 to 640* acres, and the quality of the soil would be recorded by the survey department on the plans. These blocks would then be sold under the free selection system with its conditions of residence and improvement, to which would be added an obligation to bring under cultivation every year an area proportional to the size of the property.

In addition more land would be held in reserve for future town-sites, and suburban allotments, in which portions are sold for cash at public auction, would be extended. The existing fixed legal minimum price of £210† per acre in *suburban areas*, and £8 per acre in town-site reserves, would not be changed.

Besides making conditional sales, the *minister of lands* has the right to offer previously surveyed areas at public auction for cash sale at a price of not less than £1 per acre. This provision is aimed at helping to balance the colonial budget.

The government of New South Wales offers considerable inducements not only to the farmer but also to the miner.

Gold miners must pay the government a fixed sum of 10 shillings (12 fr. 50) per year for a *miner's right*. This document confers on its holder, without the payment of one farthing more, the right to dig for gold anywhere on Crown land.

To those interested in exploiting the other mineral resources of the country, the government leases the necessary land at a modest rate. It even transfers the land to them for £2 sterling per acre, subject to certain conditions of occupation and activity, which the lessee or purchaser must fulfil if the contract is not to be cancelled.

* Misprinted in the original, '64'.
† Misprinted in the original, '£2,105'.

The laws we have just outlined briefly for the reader are essentially local in character. The other Australasian colonies have each adopted a different system, generally speaking the more liberal in proportion to the extent of its territory. Thus the land legislation of Victoria, which is the smallest and most densely populated of them all, is far from offering the immigrant inducements as great as those we have just described.

We should willingly have spared our readers these rather arid details; but since the success of the English as colonizers is so often remarked upon, it is good to understand the reasons for it.

One hears every day in France people repeat the catch-cry: 'Oh! we don't know how to colonize. The English beat us hollow in this respect: and besides, we don't like to leave our own fireside or to lose sight of the steeple of the village church.'

It is true that our neighbours have a more practical genius, and are more willing than we are to try their fortunes overseas, in the lands towards which the very nature of things seems to have directed them. Indeed, some outlet for the surplus population, which Great Britain herself cannot feed, is very necessary. Having insufficient room at home, they are really compelled to go elsewhere. Our other neighbours, the Germans, are driven to emigration for exactly the same reason. But it is worthwhile to note a very significant aspect of this process: the emigrants always make for a free country like America or Australia, and rarely or never for colonies ruled directly by a metropolitan country, whatever inducements they may offer.

The reason is not far to seek.

In America and in the independent Australian colonies, emigrants enjoy freedom and have a say in the affairs of their adopted country. If they help to swell its revenues, at least they have the satisfaction of knowing that they can spend these same revenues as they think proper. The authority that governs them is of their own creation and they are not subject to the whim of some colonial service official who, as a rule, is only slightly acquainted with the country's needs, but issues arbitrary and arrogant orders which sometimes impinge upon the settler's vital interests. They make their own laws and they obey them. Governing themselves, they understand their needs and how to spend their revenues, better than officials sent from the metropolitan country to draw a fat salary, or qualify for a handsome retirement allowance, at the expense of the colonists. Again, it is a long time since the English stopped sending out inexperienced men as colonial governors. As the rulers of a great number of possessions of all sizes, scattered round the globe, it is easy for them to organize an efficient colonial service. The emigrant is repelled by too much administration: he does not leave his own country in order to go and look for a new kind of subjection in distant climes. His aim is to better himself while contributing to the development of his adopted country. In America and Australia he finds vast spaces, limitless resources and free institutions; and these satisfy his wants. If he succeeds, he will owe it to his own hard work and ability: every career in the country of his adoption is open to him.

If we consider English colonies still governed directly by the Crown, we shall see that they suffer from the same malady as ours – perhaps to a lesser degree it is true, but the root of the trouble is the same. Western Australia for example, although founded in 1829 before the colonies of South Australia, Victoria, Queensland and New Zealand, is to-day the most backward of all. Yet she is much more favourably situated than the eastern colonies: at the gateway to India and Africa and on the main route to Europe, she has much greater natural advantages than the other parts of Australia. In spite of all this, she has begun to develop a little only since 1868, the time when she ceased to be a penal colony and obtained a greater measure of free institutions. She will really take wing only when she enjoys the benefits of *self-government* which her sister colonies possess; and till then, whatever advantages she may offer the emigrant, he will prefer to head for the eastern provinces where he enjoys wide freedom of action and depends only on himself.

If the English colonist dislikes being governed by people who understand nothing of his needs, it is hardly surprising that colonists of every other nationality should have the same feeling. The German, for example, who emigrates to America to seek independence and fortune, would not care to sail for a colony where the institutions of his own country held sway: if there is nothing for it but to be a slave, better be one in one's own country than anywhere else.

Besides, the proof of the pudding is in the eating: one cannot do better than judge a system of colonization by its results.

Without looking beyond Australia we are presented with a striking contrast. On the one hand there is a colony governed under the arbitrary system, and on the other a group of self-governing provinces. As far as natural resources are concerned, the first is as well off as all the others put together. It is true that gold has not attracted by any means as many adventurers to Western Australia as it has to the eastern colonies, but by the same token these adventurers have not forced England to grant them freedom to manage things as they like.

When the colony of New South Wales was founded its first Governor, Captain Phillip, disembarked at Botany Bay with a party of penal officials and convicts whose numbers were as follows:

212 officers and soldiers with 28 women who had been given permission to accompany their husbands, and 778 *convicts* of whom 220 were women and children.

In addition the expedition had been furnished with the following livestock:

1 bull, 4 cows and a calf;

1 stallion, 3 mares and 3 foals,

as well as a few sheep, goats, and a dozen pigs.

Such were the humble beginnings of the colony which has given birth to such rich off-spring, and which bids fair to become the nucleus of a great nation.

Sixty-two years later, on the eve of the separation of Victoria from the mother colony, remarkable progress and prosperity were already apparent. The colony's revenues had long been sufficient, and more than sufficient, to meet the expenses of its administration, and the mother country had ceased to subsidize its government. Its annual budget had already reached the sum of £567,165 sterling, which was covered by a revenue of £575,794, say 14,394,850 francs, leaving a considerable surplus.

Sheep, introduced in the early days by Captain Macarthur, had become an immense source of wealth. The colony's pastures grazed 13,059,324 of them, plus 1,738,965 cattle and 132,437 horses.

Overseas trade and shipping was already very substantial. In 1850, 967 ships with a total burden of 234,212 tons imported merchandise to the value of 51,953,450 francs, while 1,014 ships exported to Europe 266,849 tons of local produce worth

59,989,500 francs. One can form some idea of the magnitude of public and private wealth, when one realizes that the total population had not reached 270,000 inhabitants: the actual figure was 265,503.

In 1862, that is to say after the separation of Victoria and Queensland, these figures were naturally diminished by the amount of all those elements which had formerly nourished these two branches of the colonial tree. As it was about then that the land laws we have been discussing were put into effect, it will be instructive to compare the statistics for 1862 with those for 1880, in order to get a clear idea of the impetus given by this liberal legislation to the whole progress of colonization. On this matter we shall leave the last word to the colonial treasurer, Mr Watson. In a long speech to the Legislative Assembly of New South Wales on 15 November 1881, that minister asked parliament for funds to balance the budget for 1882, and drew public attention to the following facts:

'The *free selection acts* came into operation on 1 January 1862.* At that date the colony had 6,145,000 sheep, 2,620,000 cattle and 273,000 horses.' (We may add that the colonial revenue had risen to 40,722,125 francs, imports to 233,366,125 francs and exports to 177,564,060 francs.)

'Now let us compare these figures with those given in the Statistical Register for 1880. There I find that last year we had 32,399,000 sheep, 2,580,000 cattle and 396,000 horses: so that in 19 years the tally of our sheep has increased by 26,254,000, a figure almost equal to that of the combined flocks of Victoria, South Australia, Queensland, Tasmania and Western Australia, for between them they graze no more than 26,700,000 sheep. If to this figure be added the New Zealand flock, which in 1880 stood at 13,069,000, we shall see that New South Wales pastures a little less than half of all the sheep in Australasia, a total of about 72,000,000. If however we take the report of the *Chief Inspector of Stock*, who has the means of determining these figures more accurately than the Registrar-General, we find that the number of sheep in the colony last year must be raised to 35,398,000: that is to say a trifle more than 49† per cent of the

* Misprinted in the original, '1882'.

† This figure is obviously incorrect. Probably it is a misprint for '47 per cent'.

total for the whole of Australasia which, on these figures, would reach 75,238,000.

'During this same period the cattle population has actually fallen by 40,000 head. This is due to the fact that there is much more profit in raising sheep than in raising cattle in this country. The number of horses has increased by 123,000, that is to say by 45 per cent in 19 years. In all the Australian colonies, including New Zealand, there were in 1880 1,206,000 horses, to which total we contributed one third.

'Facts like these show how our land laws have aided the progress of the pastoral industry, which has now attained gigantic proportions, in spite of the enormous losses inflicted by the terrible droughts that have ravaged the colony in the last two or three years.

'There is still another fact about the pastoral industry to which I want to draw the attention of the House, for it constitutes a telling proof of the immense progress made since the year 1862. I refer to our wool production. In 1862 we exported 13,428,000 lb. of wool valued at 32,095,450 francs. Last year these figures were raised to an export total of 154,871,832 lb. valued at 201,015,625 francs.

'What figures could possibly demonstrate more clearly and cogently the splendid advance made by our national industry in the course of the last nineteen years?'

Since we are making comparisons, we may note that further on in his speech the Colonial Treasurer budgets for the year 1881 a national revenue of about £6,400,000 sterling – a figure that confirms the contrast between wool-production statistics for 1862 and the current ones. In fact in 1862 revenue stood at 40,722,125 francs, while in 1881 it will attain the formidable figure of 160,000,000 francs. The Treasurer's speech is a veritable mine of statistical information and comparisons, and we cannot hope to do better than translate still more extracts from it.

Mr Watson set out to show that the progress in all branches of agriculture, industry and commerce sprang, in great measure, from the land laws; that, although on the one hand their prime purpose had not been achieved, on the other they had offered such advantages to colonists that the occupation, and consequently the productiveness, of the country had proceeded with extraordinary rapidity.

'Since that law was passed towns have become cities, hamlets have become towns, and villages of considerable importance
have grown up round previously isolated inns or settlers'
homesteads.

'I have referred already to the giant strides forward made by
industry and commerce in the colony since 1861. I shall now try
to demonstrate, with the help of some statistics, progress in all
manner of fields during the last twenty years. Let us first take
banking. We find that at the end of the year 1861, there were
still only eight of these credit-granting institutions in Sydney:
to-day there are thirteen, all of which have established branches
in every important town in the colony. In 1861 the total sum
deposited in them reached 125 million francs, while at the end
of the third quarter of this year, 1881, this figure had increased
to the enormous sum of *five hundred million* francs. Is not this
the most conclusive possible proof of the country's growing
prosperity?

'It would be easy to multiply comparisons of this sort:
suffice it to add that total savings-bank deposits on 31 December
1880 were 51,875,000 francs as against only 15,375,000 francs in
1861 – an increase in the twenty-year period of 36,500,000 francs.

'Our imports have risen from 366,000 tons of merchandise in
1861 to 1,242,000 tons in 1880, and our exports from 379,000 to
1,190,000 tons. Twenty years ago imports were valued at
139,875,000 francs and exports at 159,775,000 francs, making a
total figure for overseas trade of nearly 300 million francs. For
1880 these figures must be replaced by the following: value of
imports 350,000,000 francs, value of exports 378,125,000 francs,
making the enormous figure of 728,125,000 francs as the total
value of our overseas trade. This represents an increase, in
nineteen years, in the value of overseas trade of more than
400 millions in our money. It is noteworthy too that, if in 1861
the balance of overseas trade was against us since imports
exceeded exports, in 1880 the situation had been completely
reversed: during that year the value of exports exceeded that
of imports by the sum of 28,125,000 francs.'

No other country in the world could show such achievements,
and the rate of growth of the national income in the other
Australian colonies, and even in America, during this same
twenty-year period was slower than in New South Wales.

At the same time the population grew in an equally remarkable manner. Whilst the census of 7 April 1861 put it at 350,860, and that of 2 April 1871 at 503,981, the figure for the current year (1881) raised the number of colonists to 751,468. In the space of twenty years the population has, therefore, more than doubled, while in the last decade from 1871 to 1881 it has increased by 49·1 per cent. The population of the United States increased by only 30 per cent in the same period. But it is above all in the city of Sydney that growth has been fantastically rapid. Within the fixed boundaries of the city proper the number of inhabitants increased by 28,956, nearly 40 per cent of its population in 1871, thus raising the total population in 1881 to 103,202. The suburbs expanded even more rapidly, increasing their population during the decade by 100·13 per cent, from 60,588 to 121,096. These figures bring the total population of greater Sydney in 1881 to 224,298. There is nothing astonishing about this mushrooming of population in the suburbs of the great Australian city. In a few months whole towns spring up along a railway line tapping a new neighbourhood; and I myself, after an absence of seven weeks, have found an entire village built or in course of construction at a place where, before my departure, I had counted only a dozen houses. The tendency for huge agglomerations of population to form round certain centres exists, as these figures show, in the antipodes as much as in Europe and the United States.

If now we balance the total number of people in New South Wales against the national revenue, against the value of imports and exports, and against the total deposits in the hands of banks, savings-banks and other financial institutions, we get a very illuminating result which indicates the average income per head and gives an excellent idea of the general prosperity prevailing among all classes.

As far as national revenue is concerned, we must be clear that under this head is included a sum of nearly 50,000,000 francs derived from the sale of a certain amount of Crown lands: this reduced the colonial budget in 1881 to the still considerable sum of 110,000,000 francs. This figure would represent a little more than 145 francs per inhabitant. Comparing this result with the equivalent statistics we have before us, which relate to the financial situation of our own country in 1877 – a year which we have not been able to better since – we see the following picture. Receipts from direct taxation in France raised the sum of 1,068,768,508 francs, and from indirect taxation 1,314,497,000 francs. But there is no direct taxation in New South Wales: the revenue of that province is made up from customs duties, income from the railways which are all state-owned, revenue from posts and telegraphs and, it may be added, licence fees. In making comparisons between the budgets of the two countries we must, therefore, consider only figures relating to the same kind of receipts: hence we must set aside revenue derived from direct taxation in our own country and concern ourselves solely with that from indirect taxes. Basing our calculations on the returns for 1872, we find that the French people contributed to the national revenue at the average rate of 36 fr. 40 per head. Since we have already seen that the same rate, in the colony that concerns us, is 145 francs per head, it follows that the colonial citizen contributes *four times* as much to the national budget as the average Frenchman does to the revenues of his country. Moreover indirect taxes constitute a kind of voluntary contribution to national revenues that no-one is forced to pay, for no-one is compelled to indulge freely in alcoholic drinks, or to make frequent use of the transport system the state provides for travellers. These taxes therefore furnish, in a sense, the most accurate means of measuring national wealth, for each citizen contributes to them according to his means, and no-one is forced to pour into this section of the national coffer a farthing more than he wishes to. These figures lead inevitably to the following conclusions: if the average inhabitant of New South Wales has the means to pay out four times as much as the average Frenchman, under the same conditions, he must also have the means to become four times as rich.

This conclusion, valid as it seems, can only be absolutely true, however, as long as the people of the two countries are equally thrifty; for if the average Frenchman is also four times as economical as the average Australian, the latter will not be better off. But we have a ready means of clarifying this question – by comparison of the average sum per head deposited in the savings-banks of the two countries. Generally speaking the principal depositors belong to the working classes: people with private incomes are seldom clients of a savings-bank.

This fact guarantees the validity of our comparison, for it shows that we are considering the same classes of people in both Australia and France. A statistician, who has taken out the figures we need for France, finds that the total savings bank deposits represent an average of 18 fr. 29 per head. In the colony which concerns us, this average reaches the figure of 68 fr. 98.

The advantage still lies with the inhabitant of the antipodes. Not only does he spend four times as much as the average Frenchman, but he also saves three and a half times as much money. It may be objected that the Frenchman invests most of his savings in government bonds: we should reply that the Australian has plenty of facilities for investing his money in equally profitable ways, and that he makes just as much use of them.

We shall now leave to those readers, who have seen fit to follow us through this labyrinth of figures, the task of drawing their own conclusions. Let them then compare the results, if they have the inclination, with those furnished by the data in the statistical registers of our colonies, of Algeria or Indo-China for example. They will be able to devote themselves to some very interesting calculations which will teach them, perhaps, more than they would like to know.

It remains for us to say something here of the extension of the railway system in New South Wales. Again our astonishment could hardly be greater in the face of the immense achievements in this area since 1854, the year in which was laid down the first rail of the line that was to connect the metropolis with the city of Bathurst. This first line was extremely costly because of the difficulties of crossing the Blue Mountains: though not particularly lofty, these pose the greatest engineering problems by reason of their breadth and abruptness. A plan, therefore, was formed for the iron ribbon to climb the first ramparts by a series of zig-zags, then to follow along the ridge of the mountains and to descend again into the Lithgow valley on the other side by another series of zig-zags. The construction of this last section presented almost insurmountable difficulties for, to reach the lower level, the line had to skirt along the walls of a practically sheer precipice. However, owing to the skill of the engineer who still manages the New South Wales railways to-day,

Mr Whitton, the expensive and arduous job was carried out, and today the Lithgow Valley zigzag is one of the greatest engineering wonders in Australia. Problems of the same kind arose during the building of the Goulburn line, which now extends to the borders of the colony at Albury. From there a three-quarter hour omnibus ride takes the traveller across the River Murray to Wodonga, where he can catch a train on the Victorian railway system directly to Melbourne. Once clear of the great mountain chain that traverses the colony from north to south, there are no construction problems for the railway engineer.

In view of all the benefits to be expected from covering the colony with a network of railways linking the great up-country stations with the capital, the Parliament did not hesitate to sanction substantial borrowing on the English loan market to extend the network to the furthest inhabited confines of the country.

The first lines were naturally built to the most heavily populated inland centres: the two towns of Bathurst and Goulburn were placed within no more than a few hours of Sydney, whilst from the important port of Newcastle another line was built towards the north. This *Great Northern Railway* was to extend as far as Tenterfield near the Queensland border, and there to connect with the railways of that colony. Some time later Parliament voted the funds necessary to build a line linking the *Great Northern Railway* to the capital. This project would thus complete a route from Melbourne across Victoria to join the New South Wales line at Albury and, continuing thence through Sydney, to join the Queensland network at Tenterfield. Terminating in Brisbane, the capital of Queensland, such a line would provide speedy, direct and uninterrupted communication between that city and the capitals of the two principal Australian colonies. If, as is being seriously suggested, Brisbane should be linked by a transcontinental railway with Point Parker on the Gulf of Carpentaria, there would be an iron road spanning the whole Australian continent from the Gulf of Carpentaria to Port Phillip Bay.

But let us return to the railways of New South Wales. There was considerable debate about keeping in the colony the trade of its richest district, the Riverina. Since this commerce had been drifting towards Melbourne and Adelaide, Parliament felt the need to drive a railway line from Sydney right through to the town of Hay in the centre of the area. The line between Sydney and Hay is 650 kilometres long, and it is planned to extend it later to the township of Wentworth: there the line would connect with the South Australian system and put Adelaide and Sydney in direct communication with each other. The line to Hay branches off from the junction at Junee, while the *Great Southern* line continues on towards Albury. To complete the link between Sydney and Melbourne, there is now no more to be done than the building of a bridge across the Murray and about another four kilometres of line. As we write, hopes were being expressed that the New South Wales and Victorian governments would complete the job during the year 1882.

From Sydney the *Great Western*, a line directed towards the vast inland plains, terminates to-day at the flourishing town of Dubbo, 360 kilometres from the capital. Thence it will be extended to Bourke on the Darling, which it should reach in another four years, when it will attain a length of 812 kilometres. Hitherto the produce of the huge district, which this railway will link to the metropolis, has followed the River Darling down to the capital of the neighbouring colony of South Australia. But for this traffic the river needs to be constantly navigable right up to Bourke, a circumstance which makes communication with South Australia far from being as speedy and regular as the producers could wish. The Bourke–Sydney line will therefore have the effect of diverting to the capital the trade of these outlying districts. It will also allow the farmer to advance much farther inland to occupy the rich alluvial plains which extend along the courses of the big rivers in that part of the colony. Moreover the government plans to extend the railway to the Darling at three different points: at Bourke, at Wentworth, and between these two townships at Wilcannia, to which a branch of the Great Western line, setting out from Orange and passing through Forbes, will be built in the future. In this way four-fifths of the trade that has been handled by Adelaide will be taken over by Sydney, which will become, to a degree, the entrepôt for the whole commerce of the colony.

In fact during its last session Parliament voted the funds,

nearly two hundred million francs, needed to build and complete the railway system of the colony. The task, which should be finished in five years, includes, in addition to the routes already mentioned, one linking Murrumburrah to Blayney, one joining, that is to say, the great southern and the great western lines.

At the present moment the colony has 1,340 kilometres of railway in operation, and this figure will be raised to 2,700 kilometres in 1886 when the network sanctioned by Parliament will be completed.

Whilst the government thus covers the interior of this rich country with railways, private investors are continually improving sea communications and to-day the colony has a real merchant marine. In the year 1880, 41 vessels of all types, but principally coasters, were built in Sydney, while in the same year 94 others were registered as the property of colonial shipowners. During the last ten years no fewer than 481 sailing ships and steamers of all types were built in the colony, representing a total of 33,383 tons, and 900 ships of a total burden of 116,679 tons were registered there. From the two great ports of Sydney and Newcastle 1,937 ships, totalling 1,158,476 tons burden, sailed in 1880. Among these figured 19 French ships which alone carried 7,920 tons of mixed cargo, mainly coal for China, while 30 ships flying German colours bore away 15,089 tons.

The bulk of the colony's export and import trade is done with the mother country and the other Australian colonies: in fact, out of a total of 3,119,868,325 francs' worth of exports from 1871 to the end of 1880, foreign countries accounted for only 82,280,200 francs. Import figures for the same ten-year period are only a little more favourable to the foreign trader: the colony received goods to the value of 3,131,764,775 francs, of which foreign countries supplied only 172,292,350 francs' worth. It is true that the colony imports a certain amount of foreign merchandise in English ships, and likewise that a large part of the wool it exports is used in French, German and Belgian factories, which buy their supplies on the London market.

Here we shall close this long chapter of statistics, which practically concludes what we have to say about the mother colony of Australia, hoping to carry the reader along with us to glance at its off-spring and neighbours.

Chapter Four

The Colony of Victoria – Its rivalry with New South Wales – Protection and free-trade – The colony of Queensland – The sugar industry and the Chinese question – Project for a transcontinental railway – South Australia and the Northern Territory – From Adelaide to Port Darwin by rail – Western Australia – Tasmania – A few words on New Zealand.

Victoria has the largest population of all the Australian colonies: the Victorians claim their province is also the richest – a statement that I am not in a position to contradict.

It would seem that in the early days there were several half-hearted attempts to found a settlement on that part of the Australian coast which now belongs to Victoria. In a book that lies open before me, I read that in 1802 Governor King sent Lieutenant Charles Robbins, in a small colonial vessel, to make it clear to Captain Baudin that this southern part of the Australian coast was already under the protection of the British flag. It was believed that Baudin intended to raise the French colours there. It would seem too that in about 1826 we were again seized with the ambition of founding a colony in these parts, for in that year an expedition made up from two detachments of the regiments then garrisoning Sydney, was sent to Western Port to occupy a place now known as the *Old Establishment Point*, opposite Frenchman's Island. What is certain is that we were credited with intentions which in fact remained purely conjectural. There is nothing astonishing in that, for we are constantly making plans which we never carry out. The English talk less but make up for it by more action.

However the colonization of Victoria, then known as Port Phillip, scarcely began until 1836, although it proceeded rapidly thereafter; for we find that the population soared from only 224 persons in that year to 3,150 in 1839. But it was

THE COLONY OF VICTORIA

particularly after the discovery of gold in 1851* that the colony leapt ahead.

At first the inhabitants were afflicted with gold-fever, abandoning their ordinary affairs to rush off frenziedly in search of the precious metal. Ships, loaded with immigrants and adventurers from every nation, flooded the shores of Port Phillip with people and in a few years Melbourne, but yesterday a fishing village, became one of the greatest cities in the world.

In 1851 an act of the British parliament separated the Port Phillip district from New South Wales, and set it up under special charter as the new colony of Victoria.† At first it was only semi-independent of the mother country, but all power was handed over to the colonial parliament only five years later in 1856. The colony's independence dates from that time and, as in the other colonies, with the exception of Western Australia which still does not enjoy the benefit of self-government, there is no longer a single English soldier on Victorian territory. Australian governments pay only the governors sent out by the mother country. Their *aides-de-camp*, and sometimes their private secretaries, are the sole representatives of the British army. To police the South Seas, however, England maintains a naval squadron whose commodore flies his flag in Sydney: but neither the sailors nor the marines bear arms when ashore in any colonial port.

Situated to the south of New South Wales and to the east of South Australia, Victoria looks out onto two oceans, the Pacific and the Southern Ocean, which are separated by Bass Strait. In the east the country is very mountainous, watered by numerous rivers which, though of no great length or depth, are transformed into veritable torrents during the rainy season. In the west, on the other hand, are extensive plains occupied by big graziers' stations – like those already described in the neighbouring colony. Victoria's greatest ports are situated inside Port Phillip Bay, those of Melbourne (Hobson's Bay, Sandridge and Williamstown) and Geelong in Corio Bay. The others, like Portland and Port Albert, are scarcely more than open anchorages, whilst at a little distance from Port Phillip there is

---

* A mistake in the original – '1850'.

† Though Victorian separation was proclaimed in 1851, the act was passed in 1850.

another fine, almost landlocked harbour called Western Port. Unfortunately it is rather shallow.

Like its neighbour the colony is divided into districts and counties, and as local government is carried out in almost the same way on both sides of the Murray, we need not tarry over it here.

There are four great districts in the colony: the Wimmera, the Murray, the Loddon and Gippsland.

The first is essentially a pastoral district, hardly inhabited except by squatters and their sheep and cattle.

The second is blessed by a variety of resources: it is well watered, the soil is excellent, and in hilly areas many gold-bearing quartz reefs are being worked, whilst true agricultural localities are growing up round the mining-fields. In the north of the district there is a vine-growing region which yields heavy crops of grapes. Large-scale cultivation is beginning, and the colonial wine merchants in Melbourne do not give the impression of being worried about the future of their business.

It is in the district of Loddon that the richest gold mines in the whole colony are situated; and there is no-one who has not heard of Bendigo, to-day a city of 30,000 inhabitants called Sandhurst, of Mount Alexander, of Castlemaine, and finally of Ballarat, the second largest city in the colony with 50,000 inhabitants. Ballarat has some institutions of which much older cities would have reason to be proud, for example, a school-of-mines and public libraries which, between them, hold 30,000 volumes.

This part of the district is the centre of the mining industry: in the first days of the rush gold was gathered, literally, by the shovel-full, and even to-day millions of francs' worth are recovered from the bowels of the earth annually.

In the space of twenty-eight years, from the first discovery to the end of the year 1879, Victoria alone produced gold officially certified to have reached the value of £194,879,722 sterling – say 4,871,993,000 francs.

In one single year, 1856, production reached the figure of £11,943,964 sterling, say 298,599,100 francs.

To-day the yield of gold has fallen considerably, not because the supply is exhausted – far from it – for new fields are still being discovered; but because the population is attracted towards steadier occupations, less subject to sudden reversals of fortune.

Like that of New South Wales, the government of the colony is what we should call republican in form, with two chambers and an executive council of ministers under the chairmanship of the governor: but there is a great difference between the two colonies in the methods of recruitment for their respective houses.

In New South Wales only the Legislative Assembly is elective: the Legislative Council's members are nominated to their positions for life by the Governor-in-Council.

In the colony of Victoria both houses are elective. Members of the Legislative Assembly are elected by universal suffrage as in Sydney, but to the Legislative Council members are elected, for ten-year terms, under a restricted franchise, by those possessing a certain amount of landed property. Further, in Victoria Legislative Assembly members receive a salary of £300 a year, say 7,500 francs, while in New South Wales they receive not a penny.

The Victorian constitution is, obviously enough, thoroughly democratic. I should add that the benefits of *self-government* have been extended by the Victorian central authorities from the metropolis to the countryside, with its 115 *shires* or cantons and its 57 *municipalities* or communes. It amounts to practically the same system as the ultra-radicals would like to introduce in France, forgetting that, in the actual condition of the country, the realization of the principles of the Commune is impossible. In Australia, on the other hand, where conditions are very different, this system works very well. The *shires* and *municipalities* levy rates for the maintenance of their own streets, roads, water-works and, in general, all other essentially local services. Every pound raised by the canton or commune is subsidized by another pound from the central government.

As far as parliamentary elections are concerned, however, these local administrative divisions have no importance, and the boundaries of the different electorates are quite different from those of the *shires* and *municipalities*.

In New South Wales, Queensland and South Australia the principle of *local self-government*, that is to say of communal government, is equally accepted although not so extensively carried out. In all the colonies the numerous religious denominations are completely independent of the state, and they have all accepted the principle of compulsion in primary education, while retaining the right to found colleges completely under church control in the tertiary field. Thus in each of the three different universities of Sydney, Melbourne and Adelaide, courses are studied in three different colleges, Roman Catholic, Anglican and Scots Presbyterian.* Although primary education is compulsory, it is not in the least compulsorily secular. Nothing prevents this or that church from maintaining free schools of its own, though the national public schools are the only ones maintained by public money from the colonial education budget. Each denomination must underwrite the expense of maintaining its own schools.

A unique feature of Victoria is its fiscal policy, which differs markedly from those of all the other Australian colonies.

Victoria's policy is essentially protectionist, whilst all the other colonies lean more or less strongly towards free-trade. We are not called upon to eulogize either principle here, but it seems to us that in this matter the advocates of both policies in Australia are right. Which policy is the better depends on the different conditions which govern the present state and future prosperity of the different colonies.

Indeed, the reason why Victoria's neighbours follow free-trade policies is very simple and obvious. These other colonies each have at their disposal an enormous territory which must be settled first of all: their future prosperity depends upon the establishment in these vast domains of a productive class of miners, farmers and others. For many years ahead they will be well advised to exploit their immense natural resources and to strengthen the country's productive forces by a wise immigration policy. It is farmers, first of all, who must be protected and whose numbers must be increased, for in a country like New South Wales with limitless agricultural resources waiting to be developed, this ought to be the biggest class. For them it will be a great advantage if the English and foreign manufactured goods the country needs are not burdened with customs

---

* Marin La Meslée is wrong, or misleading, here. The University of Adelaide harboured no colleges in the nineteenth century, and the Sydney and Melbourne colleges were essentially residential, not teaching, institutions.

duties, which would raise their prices without bringing in sufficient revenue to make up for these additional costs, and which every inhabitant would very naturally resent. The larger colonies ought, then, to devise policies aimed at the rapid development of their natural resources. In them there is no case for inflating the numbers of the already numerous working class population in the big cities, nor for specially favouring that class at the expense of others. In addition, in Sydney particularly, the working class has no reason to complain of its lot. Wages are high, thanks to free-trade, and manufactured goods sell at a moderate price. The only dissatisfied people are loafers, who go about crying that they are dying of hunger because they cannot manage to find a job, whilst most of the time they are too drunk to work and devoutly pray that the Almighty will not send them any. In those colonies whose major asset is a vast supply of land, attention must be paid to the main point, and that is to bring about the settlement of this territory under the best possible conditions. In addition, colonial statesmen are too intelligent not to see the evils that would be entailed by changing the fiscal policies of the countries they govern.

In Victoria conditions are quite different.

First of all, the colony is confined to a small area, and most of its land is already occupied, following either conditional or outright alienation, or the leasing of vast tracts to the big graziers.

In the second place, the lure of gold attracted to this colony a population belonging mainly to the working classes. Accustomed to city life as they were, most of these people returned to their old ways once the height of the gold fever had passed: under these new skies they huddled together just as they had formerly done in the country they had quitted to seek their fortunes. They were not the kind of colonists that could be made into farmers. Hence, quite apart from the great city of Melbourne, they created for themselves in the country several other large centres of population which, necessarily, could live only by means of their respective industries. These people had to be taken into account, for universal suffrage had given them immense power. But free-trade and the importation, without any kind of tariff barrier, of British and foreign manufactured goods threatened to kill the infant colonial industries: labour was too dear, and manufacturers could not compete with the imported products. Hence it was necessary to lower wages – a step to which the workers would never have agreed – or to assist colonial industry by imposing almost prohibitive tariffs on imported goods.

The working class in Victoria was large, and it had to live. It was also the most powerful class: it wanted to impose its wishes, and it did so. From that time forward the colony of Victoria had a clearly defined future: it had to fulfil in Australia the role carried out by the Birmingham and Manchester districts in England. It is destined to become the great manufacturing centre of the southern hemisphere. Victorian goods, a little inferior at first, are going to improve year by year, and one day they will meet the whole Australian demand.

With a population at the same time more numerous and different in character from those of the neighbouring colonies, Victoria has necessarily embarked on the course that seemed most advantageous for her.

But no other Australian colony is interested in following a similar path: there are all the reasons in the world to direct them in a diametrically opposite direction.

Last year there was an attempt to establish a sort of *Australian Zollverein*, which failed because of Victoria's refusal to take any part in it. It ought neverthelesss to be pursued further, as it would do much to unify, along free-trade lines, the different customs duties of the Australian colonies.

New South Wales newspapers rightly deplored the break-down of the negotiations which had been begun largely under the influence of the premier of that colony, a very intelligent man called Sir Henry Parkes. Some even held that the collapse was simply the result of the jealous rivalry which has existed, ever since the time of separation, between the two colonies whose capitals are Melbourne and Sydney. No visiting stranger can help being struck by this rivalry. The Victorians declare that hanging is too good for their cousins on the other side of the Murray, and these in turn never miss a chance to heap abuse on the Melbourne people. This rivalry is particularly apparent in the tariff war, waged by the two colonies in an effort to attract the trade of the splendid Riverina district, of which we have already spoken, to their respective capitals.

Hitherto the Melbourne merchants have enjoyed a monopoly of the trade in wool and other products from all that part of New South Wales; but since the Sydney government has pushed railways out into the heart of the district, things have begun to change. There is even reason to believe that in the end Sydney will capture the commerce of the Riverina.

To-day the colony of Victoria is covered with a network of railways which radiate from Melbourne to all the main inland centres. The most important is the line from Melbourne to Albury, which is part of the link between the two great capital cities of Australia. Next comes the line to another point on the Murray, the important town of Echuca, from which a branch line constructed by a private railway company continues right on to Deniliquin, a town in the neighbouring colony. The Echuca line passes through Castlemaine and Sandhurst, from both of which places subsidiary lines branch off into the interior of the country. Another line runs south from Melbourne to the little manufacturing city of Geelong. Then it swings westward across country and through the gold-mining districts of Ballarat and Mount Ararat: to-day it terminates at Horsham, but it should soon be built on from there to reach the boundary of the neighbouring colony of South Australia, thus bringing Adelaide into communication with Melbourne and Sydney. When, in three or four years from now, the New South Wales railways have reached Tenterfield and connected with the Queensland system, and when the northern line, which now starts from Newcastle, has been linked with Sydney, it will be possible to travel by rail from Adelaide to Brisbane in a single journey of 600 leagues.

The last major Victorian line links the capital with the important eastern district of Gippsland, the most picturesque area in the whole of Australia, crossed by the lofty chain of the Australian Alps and furrowed with gorges in which grow the tallest trees in the world. At their feet flourish those graceful specimens of Australian *flora*, tree-ferns with their fretted, open-work foliage.

To-day Victoria has 1,600 kilometres of railways in operation and she has no intention of abandoning their further development. Every mile of permanent way belongs to the state, which had the whole system built with loans floated on the London money-market.

At the end of the year 1880 the Victorian population reached the total of about 850,000 inhabitants. The colony's revenue amounted to 115,532,050 francs, or an average contribution of 136 francs per head. At the same rate per head, France's revenue would be about 5 milliard francs instead of 3 milliards.

The total value of all exports and imports for the year reached the sum of 762,786,325 fr., or about 897 fr. 16 per head of population. It we take the population of France as 36,000,000 (certainly an under-estimate), quite a simple calculation shows that, at the same rate per head, the total value of our import and export trade would be 32,297,400,000 fr. in place of the 8 milliards it has scarcely yet reached. It is noteworthy that Victoria is by no means as prosperous as the neighbouring colony of New South Wales where, in 1881, the equivalent figure rose to 780 million francs. With a population, according to the census of the same year, of only 720,000 inhabitants, the average value per head of New South Wales' external trade was, say, 1,083 fr. 33. At that rate France's external trade should be able to reach the enormous sum of 39 milliards of francs.

These figures, taken from the statistical registers of the two colonies for the current year 1881, are extremely eloquent. They constitute a marvellous panegyric on the excellent colonizing policies of our cross-Channel neighbours, on their practical genius, and on the political sagacity of the *Colonial Office* in its relations with England's overseas subjects. By endowing the colonists with the free-hold title to their immense territories, England furnished them with the wherewithal to fashion a great future for themselves. It had been difficult to govern societies of this kind from a distance and to take in good time, and in the right way, the measures necessary for their development: it could be effectively done only on the spot, and by men well versed in the needs of their adopted country.

We have demonstrated above the results of this policy.

It would be futile to ask our readers to compare for themselves this state of affairs with what leaps to notice in our own colonies. That would be too distressing!

Frenchmen simply are not good colonizers, you would reply. That is not entirely true. Let us say that they are so no longer, for they once made excellent colonists – witness Canada. Since then they have become disgusted with colonization.

THE COLONY OF QUEENSLAND

But let us now return to the other Australian colonies.

The colony of Queensland, which lies between the northern border of New South Wales, South Australia and the Northern Territory, the Gulf of Carpentaria, Torres Strait and the Pacific, is, like Victoria, an offshoot of the mother colony.

In the beginning, when the northern parts of the continent were unexplored, it was simply a *convict* depot, known as the Moreton Bay penal establishment after the bay into which the Brisbane River flows. Transportation of prisoners to this point ceased in 1839, although the district was not officially opened to free immigration until 1842. Settlers flocked to its shores, where they found extremely fertile virgin lands and limitless resources, so that the district already had a population of 30,000 people in 1859, the year in which it was separated from New South Wales and established as a separate colony under the name of Queensland, in honour of the august and gracious sovereign of England. Since then, a considerable number of immigrants have been attracted by its rich soil, and by the discovery of prolific gold-fields in many parts of its territory.

Of all the Australian colonies Queensland is undoubtedly one of those most generously endowed by nature. Its soil, so rich in all kinds of natural resources, is divided into two regions by a chain of mountains, which separates the waters of its numerous streams and rivers. On one side the watercourses flow down through country where tropical vegetation mingles with that of temperate climates, and on the other side the range encloses a region of immense mineral resources. In the south on the Darling tableland, the Darling Downs, in the same latitude as Algeria, Tunis and Northern Egypt, wheat and all the other European grains grow prolifically, whilst along the watercourses, nearly all of them navigable, which dissect the Pacific littoral, tropical crops like sugar-cane, coffee and so on make the fortunes of planters. Every day sees great advances, especially in the sugar industry, and within a few years from now Queensland will be growing enough sugar to supply the whole Australian demand. Time, therefore, is running out for Mauritius, for the Australian market is almost the only one that supports the planters in that island.

What resources there are awaiting development in this splendid country, which is four times the size of France and possesses all kinds of climatic zones from the most temperate to the most torrid!

The province is divided into twelve huge districts: Darling Downs, Maranoa, Warrego, Gregory, Mitchell, Leichhardt, Wide Bay, Clermont, Kennedy, Port Curtis, Cook and Burke.

The Pacific coast is indented with harbours and watered by rivers, almost all navigable, like the Brisbane River on which the capital is built, the Mary River with its port of Maryborough, the third city of Queensland, and the magnificent Fitzroy River on the banks of which, ten leagues inland, stands the second city of the colony, Rockhampton, which aspires one day to become the capital of a new, independent colony. Indeed Rockhampton is within the tropics, in an area yielding quite different products from those in the Brisbane region. Europeans find the Rockhampton climate too hot for outdoor work, and if North Queensland is to be fully developed, it will be necessary forcibly to import labourers capable of standing the climate, be they Negroes, Hindus or Chinese. But in the south of the colony conditions are different: the European can work without having to complain of the climate, and he will naturally resist the introduction of a race that will bring about his downfall. There is therefore no community of ideas between the people of southern and northern Queensland, and there has already been talk on several occasions of dividing the colony into two separate provinces, North Queensland with Rockhampton for its capital and South Queensland with Brisbane.

Moving still towards the north, we find other important rivers like the Pioneer, the focus of the main sugar-growing district of which Port Mackay, which gives its name to the region, is the outlet. Still farther north the Burdekin and its tributaries, which drain a basin half the size of France, flows into the sea half way between the two important towns of Bowen and Townsville.

Finally in the far north, at the base of Cape York Peninsula, we come to the half-Chinese settlement of Cooktown, two-thirds of whose population of nearly six thousand people belong to that almond-eyed race, whose representatives look for all the world as though they are suffering from chronic jaundice. Cooktown is a corner of China transplanted to Australia: it is the great port of disembarkation for the subjects of the Son of

Heaven: it is the base from which the Mongol horde hurls itself on the rich gold-bearing districts of North Queensland, thence to spread like a dangerous yellow plague over the whole surface of Australia. To-day Chinese are to be met with everywhere in Australia and even in New Zealand. By the same token, this massive invasion that has overtaken the whole of Australasia is causing the politicians of this second New World to take thought. It is in Queensland particularly that the question is most serious and the problem of Chinese immigration most difficult to deal with dispassionately.

On the one hand the situation of this colony, bi-sected as it is by the Tropic of Capricorn, will sooner or later compel it to demand the services of coolies, whether Chinese, Negro or Hindu, to help develop its immense agricultural resources: there is no room for illusions on that subject. On the other hand the introduction of this cheap labour is becoming a menace to the working and farming classes in the southern part of Queensland, and a long-term threat to the same classes even in the neighbouring colonies. On top of that, retail traders are endangered, for the sober, patient, industrious Chinese, whose wants are minimal, can always under-sell the European and so necessarily bring about his downfall. The ruin awaiting the small tradesman in Australia, if something is not done about it, has already been visited by the Chinese on the Creole shopkeepers in Mauritius and in our other Indian Ocean possession of Bourbon Island.* There, about twenty years ago, grocers' shops and other such small businesses were all in the hands of Creoles: today, at most, there may be a handful of tradesmen who have been able to survive the competition of the Mongols. In Mauritius, when one needs some little household commodity, one no longer goes to 'the grocer's' for it, but to 'the Chinese at the corner'. It will be the same in Australia: it is already the same in North Queensland where the Mongols have monopolized everything.

But what defence can there be against people who have no respect for the law and who impose themselves on the country by their frugality, their patience, their eminently practical qualities and, in the final analysis . . . by the country's need of them?

* Known today, and for most of the time since 1793, as Reunion.

That is the problem! Let us glance briefly at the measures taken by Australian legislators to stem the threatening invasion.

Their first thought was completely to prohibit the landing at Australian ports of any member of the Chinese race. Bills to this effect were brought before the chambers of the different colonial parliaments and duly passed. But before becoming law, all resolutions of the colonial parliaments must receive the assent, which is very rarely withheld, of the Queen of England. This time, however, she was constrained to impose her *veto* on these bills.

By forcing China to open certain of her ports to British shipping and commerce, England was later bound by treaties with that power to grant the subjects of the Celestial Empire the right to move freely throughout her whole imperial domain. The colonies therefore found themselves bound by the mother country's treaties, and the Queen could not do otherwise than *veto* the bills we have just mentioned.

The Australians did not admit defeat. They imposed a poll tax of £10 sterling on all Chinese emigrants landing in Australia, forbade them to work on any goldfield, until it had already been exploited for three years by Europeans, and bound the captains of vessels coming from China to limit the number of Chinese passengers for Australia to *one per hundred tons of the ship's burden.*

Unfortunately the governments of all the Australian colonies did not act in concert on the Chinese question any more than they did on that of free-trade and protection. The less threatened provinces, Victoria for example, allowed the Chinese to enter the country on payment of a small tax amounting to a few pounds a head. Those who could, paid, and those who could not, had it paid for them by the Chinese emigration syndicates which were sending them out, and which always recovered these loans with interest. Thus they disembarked in Victoria and percolated thence into neighbouring colonies from which it was very difficult to remove them.* Besides they very easily evaded payment of the taxes, for Chinese all look so much alike that it is impossible to be sure which individual one is dealing with.

* Marin La Meslée seems here to have confused Victoria and South Australia. In fact many Chinese gold-seekers were landed in South Australia to march overland to the Victorian goldfields.

Not only then are all these measures said to have been abortive, but none of them strikes at the root of the evil.

Above all the Chinese invasion threatens retail trade and certain industries such as cabinet-making, which is already completely in their hands, as is market-gardening. Gold-miners claim that the Chinese, who, let it be whispered, are more sober, hard-working and frugal than the diggers, are a source of ruinous competition on the fields. Day labourers, navvies and other unskilled workers have more reason than the miners to fear this competition, especially in Queensland. On the other hand, such people cannot work in the tropics, and it is certainly necessary that the work should be done.

The need to uphold the sanctity of treaties was the reason given by the Queen of England for refusing her assent to the prohibition of Chinese immigration to Australia. By forcing China to open certain of her ports to English commerce, Her Majesty's government had incurred the obligation to accord the same rights to Chinese subjects in England, as had perforce been granted to Queen Victoria's subjects in China.

This reasoning seemed to the Australian colonies to suggest, in some sort, the policy they might pursue with regard to the Chinese. It was quite simply a question of taking the treaty literally, and granting to the Chinese solely those rights which were accorded by them to Europeans.

The Son of Heaven had opened *only certain* of his ports to the English: the Australians need only do as much and designate a certain number of places as the *only* ones where the yellow men might establish themselves.

In the Chinese treaty ports English merchants were permitted to do business only within a particular quarter of the town, to which they were more or less confined. Why not have the same regulations for Chinese in Australia?

Foreigners in China, save within their respective concessions, are not allowed to own land, either personally or collectively. This was the third clause to be added to the rough draft of a law on the question, which would hoist the detested race with its own petard.

The Chinese legislation contains no clause which helps, or even permits, the naturalization of foreigners.

So *Article 4* might read; – A Chinese may not, under any

circumstances whatsoever, become a naturalized British subject in any Australian colony.

Finally, under one pretext or another, foreigners are prevented from moving freely on Chinese territory, without obtaining prior permission through the intercession of their respective consuls.

Hence a proposed *Article 5*; – The same restriction to apply to the pig-tailed men on Australian territory.

All these conditions would seem to be prohibitive in their effect, and they could easily be added to those already in force in the different colonies, where the presence of the subjects of the Son of Heaven is considered a present evil and a future threat of chronic racial jaundice.

But a sixth provision should be added for invocation in regions such as the north of Queensland, the Northern Territory of South Australia and the north-western portions of Western Australia.

There would be nothing easier than to pass a law along these lines:

1st. Designation of the territories within which the following law would be applicable.

2nd. Within the above-mentioned areas, any person needing a certain number of Chinese, solely to perform necessary labour in some tropical agricultural enterprise, must make application for them in writing to the commissioner in charge of this branch of immigration.

3rd. Special residence permits will then be issued to the men selected by the applicant, or his agent. On each permit will have to be recorded the name, age etc. of the coolie, the domicile of his employer, the type of work for which the coolie is employed the term of his indenture and the conditions of his employment.

4th. At the end of his term of indenture, the coolie will automatically come again under the jurisdiction of the special laws concerning individuals of the Chinese race and will be returned, at his employer's expense, unless he enters into a new contract of service, to one of the ports where he and his countrymen have the right to live.

5th. Throughout the territories designated in article 1, Chinese are forbidden to engage in any occupation, trade or employment other than that of indentured coolie.

The Queen would be unable to refuse assent to such regulations, since they would bestow upon the Chinese in the colonies the same privileges granted to foreigners in China, and they do it without formally prohibiting the admission of Chinese to British territory. This last was a right that could not be denied them, once they had been forced to open their harbours to British commerce.

Hitherto, all the treaties between England and China have been to the latter's advantage. In a nutshell, the Son of Heaven has conceded very little to the Children of Earth who, in return, give to his pig-tailed subjects the same privileges as they themselves enjoy in their own country.

In our opinion the best way of thwarting the Chinese invasion and halting the advance of the yellow peril would be, quite simply, to grant these people in Australia only that which is granted to foreigners in China.

This digression has made us forget that we have not yet left the beautiful colony of Queensland, on whose government and institutions we shall say nothing, since they parallel very closely those of her southern neighbour, New South Wales.

But we cannot pass over in silence the rapidity with which railways are being built into the interior. Lines leave from several points on the Queensland coast to service, perhaps agricultural and pastoral districts, perhaps gold, copper or tin-mining fields which are scattered over her territory.

The line inland from Brisbane divides at Toowoomba, one branch going off to join the New South Wales network at present under construction, whilst the other extends far out into the station country. It has already reached Roma, a town of more than 2,000 inhabitants, more than a hundred leagues from the capital and the centre of an important farming and pastoral district.

From Maryborough a line runs to the rich Gympie mining-field, which in recent years has produced considerable quantities of gold. The population of each of these towns is about 6,000 people.

From Rockhampton the Central Railway pushes inland as far as Withersfield, with a branch line being built to the copper-mining centre of Peak Downs.

Finally another railway inland from Townsville puts that

town in rapid communication with the gold-mines at Charters Towers.

But that does not exhaust the ambitions of the Queenslanders. They now want to construct a transcontinental line which would connect Roma, the present rail-head from Brisbane, with a recently discovered harbour on the Gulf of Carpentaria, easy of access and capable of berthing the largest ships in the world. This harbour, known as Port Parker, is situated at the head of the Gulf, opposite the Wellesley Islands.

The other railways in the colony, whose extension would be speeded up, would be connected with this transcontinental line as would the New South Wales and South Australian systems in due course. Eastern Australia would then be covered with a vast network of speedy lines of communication, and it is to be hoped that settlement would extend further inland in these rich areas so that, in a few years, their prospects would be completely transformed.

South Australia was the first colony to raise the question of spanning the continent with a railway. This route would have to follow the telegraph line which connects Adelaide with Port Darwin, and which thence connects Australia with the entire world. Darwin is the terminal of the overseas submarine cable, or rather cables, for there are two of them to-day. The project has been mooted for some time now, but the Adelaide government still has nothing like sufficient resources to undertake it. As for the Queenslanders, it must be admitted that they are much more enterprising, for between 1878 and 1881 they sent out three successive expeditions to make preliminary studies of the country to be traversed. The first, led by Monsieur Favenc, was sponsored by a Queensland weekly journal, the *Queenslander*, which has a good and well-merited reputation throughout Australia. At that time the recently discovered harbour on the Gulf of Carpentaria, Port Parker, was still unknown, and the aim of this first expedition was to probe the prospects of establishing rail communication between Brisbane and Port Darwin in the Northern Territory of the neighbouring colony of South Australia. The expedition had to undergo great privations, but Monsieur Favenc's reconnaissance of the terrain showed not only that the project was feasible, but also that it presented no difficulties at all from the railway engineering point of view.

Monsieur Favenc carried out a real journey of exploration, for he had to traverse unknown regions, and he found in central Queensland country like that beyond the Darling, which we have already described. It was only near the northern coastline and along the river-banks that tropical vegetation really flourished. Elsewhere the flora was characteristically Australian, and in his account Favenc publishes an admirable description of the delusive appearance of the sand-hills, covered with *spinifex* that disguises under its apparent verdure the most utter desolation.

The second expedition, led by Mr Watson in 1881, set out for the new harbour that had just been discovered. It traversed country that was, for the most part, known and already occupied by squatters, gold-seekers and prospectors of all kinds. Mr Watson's preliminary survey established the feasibility of constructing a railway along the route followed by his expedition, and he concluded his report with a glowing picture of all the benefits to be gained by the colony from implementation of the project. This route would have the great advantages of not crossing the boundaries of Queensland and of encouraging the growth of an important port at the head of the Gulf of Carpentaria. Not only would the scheme foster settlement in central Queensland, which has immense natural resources, but it would also facilitate occupation of the Gulf coast which, with its many rivers navigable for some distance inland, holds out considerable promise for tropical agriculture.

As for the third expedition, it was, in effect, little more than a later division of the second.

Mr Watson's report so strongly recommended the prompt execution of the project that the colonial government, not feeling in a position to carry out the work itself, offered to grant the right of building and running the line to a private company. The government would guarantee the shareholders an annual revenue of so much per cent, and grant the company vast areas of land adjacent to the line.

Encouraged by these inducements, a syndicate for floating a company was formed in London. This group commissioned General Fielding, an English officer of the Engineering Corps, to re-trace Mr Watson's tracks and make a careful study of the land to be traversed by the railway. In the light of reports from the leader of the expedition, action was to follow in London. General Fielding completed his journey towards the end of 1881, but his report has not yet come through to us.

The colony of Queensland, like her sister provinces, has a brilliant future before her. Set up as a self-governing state scarcely twenty-one years ago, she already has a population of 221,964 inhabitants. Her annual revenue amounts to the sum of 40,307,850 francs, and the total value of her imports and exports is 163,386,400 francs.

As with her neighbours, Queensland's main product is fine wool: she also supplies commerce with a great quantity of hides and tallow, and industry with a considerable amount of minerals – gold, copper, tin, coal etc.

One senses already an approaching separation between the north and the south of the colony. In the religious sphere separation is already a fact: the Anglican and the Catholic churches have each established two dioceses, one in northern and the other in southern Queensland, both owing allegiance to the metropolitans in Sydney.

In Queensland, as in South Australia with which we shall deal in a moment, there is a large German element in the population. As is usually the case wherever they are found, the Germans devote their energies especially to farming, and they have a considerable stake in this part of the colony's productive processes. They are a sober people, careful of their own interests, who prefer this steady life to the more unpredictable, somewhat nomadic, pastoral existence so beloved of the English and Scots. There are also a great many Irish people who have considerable political influence. Irish members are as numerous, and quite as disruptive, in the colonial parliaments, as they are in the House of Commons. It is lucky that in the antipodes they have not the same grievances as they have in Europe.

Unlike Victoria and Queensland, which were originally integral parts of New South Wales that later achieved political separation, South Australia was founded and settled by an English company under a charter granted it by the British government.

On this matter we shall quote briefly from a work published by Messrs. Gordon and Gotch, *The Australian Handbook*, to which we have been indebted for other interesting information.

In a short historical résumé of the history of the colony, the authors write thus:

'South Australia was colonized in 1836 by parties of emigrants, sent from Great Britain under the auspices of the *South Australian Colonization Company** which, in the previous year, had obtained from the government title to the colony's land under the following conditions:

'Land was not to be sold at less than 12 shillings per acre (this minimum price was later raised to one pound sterling), and the money from land sales was to be used to form an *emigration fund* with a view to assisting needy emigrants to reach the colony.

'Control of the colony's affairs was to be entrusted to a commission, nomination of whose members would have to be approved by the Minister for the Colonies. The Governor was to be nominated by the Crown.'

This state of affairs lasted until 1856, at which time a constitution similar to those obtaining in some neighbouring colonies was granted to South Australia, thus putting a legal end to the existence of the Colonization Society* we have just mentioned.

Some years earlier, at the time of the discovery of the famous Burra Burra copper mines, the colony's development had received a considerable impetus. The finding of gold in the neighbouring province of Victoria hurt South Australia by luring away many of her people. But once the gold fever had abated, things returned to normal and South Australia's steady progress became more and more noticeable.

This colony, founded with the basic aim of developing the country's agricultural resources, has witnessed the creation of a numerous and powerful class of small landed proprietors; and this great *desideratum* of all Australian governments has not been achieved as quickly or as successfully anywhere else.

In fact the cultivation of wheat and other cereals is the main occupation of the settlers in this province: there are also many big squatters, but wheat is the great South Australian product. Adelaide feeds the rest of the continent and exports

* Marin La Meslée seems to have confused the National Colonization Society (1830–1) with the South Australian Association, founded a few years later.

wheat also to the markets of Mauritius, the Cape of Good Hope, China and even Europe.

South Australia is a country of plains, of great salt lakes like Lake Torrens, Lake Eyre, Lake Gairdner and Lake Amadeus, and of numerous lagoons, likewise salt, all of which dry up during the fiery heat of summer. The inland watercourses are, for most of the time, equally dry, and the interior of the country suffers from a kind of chronic drought. But proceeding farther north one comes to the Northern Territory, which was annexed to the colony in 1862, and which South Australia undertook, a few years ago, to develop. There tropical vegetation flourishes in all its profusion and the country is watered by many splendid rivers, of which some are navigable for thirty or forty leagues inland from their mouths. Gold discoveries have attracted a great number of Chinese to this part of the Territory, and several centres, round which civilization is spreading gradually, have been established. But things move slowly, more slowly than in the south, for the heat is excessive and the white man is hardly able to work in such latitudes. Moreover, this part of the country will make real progress only from the day when the question of the immigration of Chinese, or any other race of coolie labourers, has been resolved.

What a wealth of resources lies hidden, nonetheless, under the leafy arches of these virgin forests!

Railways are advancing gradually towards the interior of South Australia, for the Murray brings to Adelaide scarcely much more than the products of the neighbouring colonies across which it and its many tributaries flow.

The first section of the great projected railway from Adelaide to Darwin has already been built, to a place nearly four hundred miles distant, called *Government Gums*,* near Lake Eyre. Will the decision be made to extend it towards Darwin? That is a question which will certainly be answered in the near future.

But if the South Australians are slow to carry out this gigantic project, they have been by no means slow in constructing, across the whole extent of their territory, the telegraph line between their capital and Port Darwin. Last year, in addition, they completed an equally difficult task: at Eucla the telegraph wires following the coast of the Great Australian

* Now known as Maree.

Bight were joined to the line which puts the far western part of the continent in instantaneous communication with the great eastern colonies. This line, terminating at King George's Sound, enables the news to be flashed to the great eastern cities, when steamers from Europe reach Albany.

South Australia's immediate neighbour, Western Australia, is at the same time the most extensive, the most favourably placed, the least known and the most backward of all the English colonies on the Australian continent.

This springs from the fact that this province remained essentially a penal depot for *convicts* right up till 1868*. In spite of its handy situation with regard to India and Africa, and of its many natural resources, the presence of the *convict* element has been enough to keep immigrants far away. Although established in 1829, it still has hardly more than 30,000 inhabitants and ranks lowest, even among those colonies founded much more recently. The manner of its government encouraged free immigration hardly any more than the stigma of convictism: free men felt ill at ease, surrounded as they were by the human refuse of the Three Kingdoms.

It should be recognized, however, that the English have known how to make the best of the elements they cast out of their own society. Roads, docks and public works of all kinds have been built by the convicts, who are compelled to carry out quotas of labour in proportion to their strength.

There is no lack of philanthropists in England who deplore the system, but the authorities in Perth do not set much store by their complaints. The convicts are there to work, and work they do.

Since transportation came to an end, however, the country has taken on a livelier tempo and its natural resources are beginning to be developed. Cereals grow splendidly and sheep do well, but unfortunately the occurrence of poisonous grasses in the province's pastoral areas has had a good deal to do with retarding progress in the grazing industry.

During the last few years the interior of Western Australia, previously almost unknown, has been a well-known field of exploration. Ernest Giles, Warburton and the Forrest brothers

---

* A misleading statement. Convicts were sent to Western Australia only from 1850 till 1868.

have crossed and re-crossed this still incompletely explored territory.

Previously the *Swan River* district and adjoining areas was the only part of the country to have been explored and, to some extent, occupied: since the journeys of these explorers, settlement has been rapidly extending into newly discovered areas.

Railways are already pushing out into the great *jarrah* forests, which are being exploited at Northampton and in the neighbourhood of Geraldton to the north of the capital.* The fisheries along the north-west coast produce first quality pearls to a very considerable annual value, and the recently explored Kimberley district, with splendid pastures and several great watercourses, was to have been thrown open to settlement last year. The whole north-western part of the colony is said to be very rich, and before long its immense solitudes should be covered with the squatters' flocks.

As the province is still in its infancy, we need not tarry longer over a description that can be only comparatively accurate, for the settled country extends scarcely beyond the valley of the Swan River, and the few inland stations are known only sketchily, even to their owners.

Tasmania, formerly known as Van Diemen's Land, is situated due south of Victoria from which it is separated by Bass Strait. At first it was a dependency of New South Wales, and the island served as a place to which those incorrigible *convicts*, whom a sojourn at Botany Bay had failed to reform, were re-transported. More recently its history has been substantially that of the other colonies. Transportation came to an end, free colonists came to establish homes on its soil, and gold and tin-mining fields, the latter especially of fabulous richness, were discovered and exploited. Gradually the colony became a political entity, to which England granted independence, within the limits already determined for the neighbouring provinces.

Richly endowed with grasslands and fertile valleys, as mountainous as Switzerland, dissected by deep gorges and with an ample rainfall, Tasmania also enjoys a matchless climate. The proximity of Victoria has helped not a little to retard

* In fact the best jarrah was (and is) found to the south of Perth, not to the north.

Tasmania's progress. The island is small, or at least it is thought to be so, though its area is about the same as Ireland's; and Australian squatters feel cramped for room there. So its population is only about 114,000. Pastoralists claim that they cannot make money quickly enough there: on the other hand those without much capital, who content themselves with a small farm instead of a big-scale property, perhaps achieve a comfortable living more surely, without having to fear the sudden reversals of fortune which often affect their great neighbours.

Its very cool climate and natural beauty spots have made Tasmania a *sanitarium* for the rich Australian squatters. From all over the northern colonies they come to spend the summer in Hobart Town, the capital, delightfully situated on the River Derwent in the midst of greenery reminiscent of France or England. Hobart Town is linked by rail with Launceston, some distance up the River Tamar and a few hours' sail from Melbourne. Launceston is really the great commercial centre of the colony, about equi-distant from the gold and tin-mining fields scattered over northern Tasmania.

Moreover, Tasmania is a byword throughout the southern hemisphere for the beauty of its female inhabitants. Tasmanian ladies are indeed charming, but their beauty has perhaps been exaggerated. Their principal charm lies in the freshness of their complexions, which does make a striking contrast with the natural pallor of their Australian sisters.

A superb climate, marvellous beauty-spots and beautiful women: these three features suffice to characterize this verdant island which lacks only a poet to sing its praises.

The settlement of the islands comprising New Zealand began in 1840, and the rapidity of the development of all the natural resources of that archipelago is probably unparalleled in the history of colonization. In 40 years the population of European origin has risen to a total of 500,000 inhabitants; the islands have been criss-crossed by nearly 1,800 kilometres of railway; bridges have been built, and all kinds of public works have necessitated the borrowing of enormous sums which the British public, confident of this fine colony's future, has hastened to subscribe.

In 1860 New Zealand's revenue rose to the sum of 81,084,900 francs, and the total value of her imports and exports to

312,867,575 francs. These figures make comment superfluous and obviate the need to say any more about the opulent self-governing colony in Britain's antipodes, whose politicians still seek to divest themselves of the last formal link attaching them to the British Crown – the governor imposed on them by the mother country, whom they would like to replace by one of their own choice. If they succeed, the Australian colonies will be certain to follow their lead and the foundation day of an Australasian Federation, analogous to that of the United States, will not be far off.

To-day the colonies which sprang from the Botany Bay penal establishment have a combined merchant marine of 578 steamers and 1,745 sailing ships, with a total burden of 270,023 tons.

Australasia still stands only on the threshold of her prosperity: her natural resources are being developed more intensively every day, and it cannot be doubted that a great future awaits her.

France carries on a very large 'indirect' trade with Australia: that is to say, she imports 'through the London market' very substantial quantities of wool, just as she exports to these countries, through the same channel, all kinds of merchandise – novelties, silks, Parisian goods etc. whose value is just as great.

Last year, however, the French parliament voted subsidies to the *Compagnie Messageries Maritimes de France* for the establishment of a mail service to New Caledonia, by way of Australia.

It is to be hoped that this development will lead to direct trading between the two countries, and that the manufacturers of woollen goods in the north of France will buy their raw material on the Sydney and Melbourne markets, entrusting its transport to the French company.

For this to come about, the freight charges from Australia to Marseilles, plus those on the Paris–Lyon–Mediterranean and the northern railways, must be low enough for the wool to reach the north of France for less than the manufacturers would have to pay for its shipment by way of London. It is true that the new route would obviate brokerage and warehousing charges in London and customs duties, and that the wool could be bought on the best markets in Sydney and Melbourne. It seems to us, however, that it should have been possible to arrange for the French line's ships, while leaving from Marseilles, to return via

Mauritius, the Cape of Good Hope, Le Havre or Dunkirk. The Company's interests would have been best served by letting it inaugurate a direct service between the Cape of Good Hope and Australia by way of Mauritius, and it would certainly have succeeded in monopolizing the considerable trade between this island and the other two places.

Some Bordeaux merchants tried to start a second line, but they had insufficient capital. To meet British competition, it is absolutely essential for our steamers to be as fast, as perfectly equipped and as *well found* as those of our neighbours. It would also be essential to provide a regular service, and that entails the provision of a real fleet of first class steamers of three or four thousand tons apiece. To try to establish a service with ships of an inferior type, charging higher fares and of dubious cleanliness, would be a complete waste of time, trouble and money.

To succeed we must do as well, and even better than, the English; and to do that, we must create a powerful company with a capital of twenty or twenty-five million francs. Anything less will end in failure.

THE END

Appendix

Transactions of the Royal Geographical Society of Australia, Vol. xi, June 1894

BIOGRAPHICAL NOTICE

EDMOND MARIN LA MESLÉE, F.R.G.S. AND M.C.G.S., PARIS,

Who, with Madame La Meslée and five others, met an untimely death through the foundering of a pleasure yacht in Sydney Harbor, on the 17th December, 1893, was one of the founders and the first Honorary Secretary of the Royal Geographical Society of Australasia. As a young man he served in the French navy, and fought in the French ranks at the disastrous battle of Sedan, during the Franco-German war of 1870–71. At the close of the war he retired from the navy and went to Mauritius, where he became French tutor in the Jesuit College. Some years later he came to New South Wales and obtained an appointment in the Lands Office, but was subsequently transferred to the Statistical Department, which position he filled up to the time of his death.

Mr La Meslée was a scholar and an indefatigable worker. In the year 1883 he published and dedicated to the Surveyor-General of New South Wales (P. F. Adams, Esq.) a book entitled 'L'Australie Nouvelle.' He was also a regular contributor to the columns of the *Revue deux Mondes, Nouvelle Revue, Le Temps, Courier Australien* and other journals.

The influential part Mr La Meslée took in the founding of the Geographical Society may be gathered from the following extract from a paper read by him at the preliminary meeting to establish a Geographical Society, held in Sydney on the 2nd April, 1883: –

The idea of forming in Australia a Geographical Society occurred to me for the first time when about to take my leave of the Secretary-General of the Geographical Society of France. M. Mannoir had several times mentioned the fact that the want of such an institution was probably the reason why very little information about our part of the world reached the continent of Europe, and that that which the sister society of London possessed was comparatively small. Should such a society be established at Sydney or Melbourne, kindred societies at home and on the Continent would be glad to enter into correspondence and exchange information which would tend to develop commercial and other relations between the old world and Australasia. . . . . . Situated as we are here, in the centre of that part of the earth's surface which is the least known, surrounded by mighty islands, such as New Guinea, and the numerous archipelagos which stud the surface of the Pacific Ocean, and by the almost unexplored wastes of the Austral and Antarctic Ocean, extending to the South Pole, there lies before an Australian Geographical Society enough useful and interesting work to undertake. . . . The formation of a society with such a programme might be called a national work, as it is intended that it should be to all that is Australian what the Royal Geographical Society of London is to all that is English, and that of Paris to all that is French. Such is the project which is introduced for discussion to-night. It might have remained in the state of an unborn idea had other gentlemen less obscure than I am not taken it up and presented it to the public. Dr. Belgrave and Messieurs Du Faur and Gerard have taken the project in hand, and it is to be hoped that it will meet with general approbation.

At the conclusion of the reading Mr La Meslée was greeted with evident marks of warm appreciation.

Public feeling was much stirred by the sad catastrophe through which Mr and Madame La Meslée lost their lives. Their remains were interred at the Necropolis on the 9th January, 1894,* in the presence of a large number of spectators. The funeral cortège consisted of two hearses and a number of coaches and other vehicles containing friends of the deceased lady and gentleman, including Dr. Marano (Italian Consul), M. Schaumard (*Courier Australien*), M. Ulmo, M. Desjardins, Mr. J. J. Lachaume, Mr. T. A. Coghlan (Government Statistician), and a number of Government officials. The coffins were covered with handsome floral tributes of respect.

* An error. The bodies of husband and wife were buried on 19 December 1893, two days after the fatal boating accident.